Current Issues in Criminal Justice
Vol. 11

ACADEMIC PROFESSIONALISM IN LAW ENFORCEMENT

Garland Reference Library
of Social Science
(Vol. 998)

Current Issues in Criminal Justice

General Editors: Frank P. Williams III and Marilyn D. McShane

STRANGER VIOLENCE
A Theoretical Inquiry
by Marc Riedel

CRIMES OF STYLE
Urban Graffiti and the Politics of Criminality
by Jeff Ferrell

UNDERSTANDING CORPORATE CRIMINALITY
edited by Michael B. Blankenship

POLITICAL CRIME IN CONTEMPORARY AMERICA
A Critical Approach
edited by Kenneth D. Tunnell

THE MANAGEMENT OF CORRECTIONAL INSTITUTIONS
by Marilyn D. McShane and Frank P. Williams III

INNOVATIVE TRENDS AND SPECIALIZED STRATEGIES IN COMMUNITY BASED CORRECTIONS
edited by Charles B. Fields

THE WINDS OF INJUSTICE
American Indians and the U.S. Government
by Laurence French

ALTERED STATES OF MIND
Critical Observations of the Drug War
edited by Peter Kraska

CONTROLLING STATE CRIME
An Introduction
edited by Jeffrey Ian Ross

MEDIA, PROCESS, AND THE SOCIAL CONSTRUCTION OF CRIME
Studies in Newsmaking Criminology
edited by Gregg Barak

ACADEMIC PROFESSIONALISM IN LAW ENFORCEMENT
by Bernadette Jones Palombo

ACADEMIC PROFESSIONALISM IN LAW ENFORCEMENT

Bernadette Jones Palombo

GARLAND PUBLISHING, INC.
New York & London / 1995

Library of Congress Cataloging-in-Publication Data

Palombo, Bernadette Jones.
Academic professionalism in law enforcement / Bernadette Jones Palombo.
p. cm. — (Garland reference library of social science ; vol. 998. Current issues in criminal justice ; 11)
Includes bibliographical references.
ISBN 0–8153–1863–4 (hc. : alk. paper)
1. Police professionalization—United States. 2. Police training—United States. 3. Law enforcement—United States. I. Title. II. Series: Garland reference library of social science ; vol. 998. III. Series: Garland reference library of social science. Current issues in criminal justice ; vol. 11.
HV8142.P35 1995 94–47477
363.2'071'5—dc20 CIP

Printed on acid-free, 250-year-life paper
Manufactured in the United States of America

The paramount obligation of a college is to develop in its students the ability to think clearly and independently and the ability to live confidently, courageously, and hopefully.

Ellen Browning Scripps

Contents

Appendixes

Foreword

Increased emphasis on education for police officers since the 1960s has been one of the salient hallmarks of police professionalism. Historically, the formal education of police practitioners, as distinguished from their training, has never been one of the priorities of police administrators or governments. Rather, money and resources needed for such education were always placed on the back burner when it came time for government to balance its budget. Incentives for individual officers to seek higher education, such as time off or schedule changes, were virtually nonexistent in police organizations. In fact, formal education was treated as unnecessary for successful police performance.

The growth of police education was by no means voluntarily initiated by the police. The impetus came from vast amounts of federal money pouring into criminal justice programs. For instance, the Law Enforcement Education Program (L.E.E.P.) was established to provide funds for student enrollment in higher education. This sudden attention to police education was welcomed by police administrators who at least recognized their need for better-educated officers. A large number of colleges, upon being apprised of the federal largesse, set up departments and programs. The number of these programs grew from a few in the 1960s to well over a thousand by the mid-1970s.

When federal support ended, a large outcry occurred, and many criminal justice educational programs continued anyway with increased numbers of preservice police officers. However, the number of in-service officers trying to obtain more education decreased, making it very clear that police and governments wanted the advantages of an educated police force but at the same time were unwilling to make sacrifices necessary to achieve this goal. Even today, relatively few police departments offer pay incentives for higher education or assistance in meeting school expenses; neither are they willing at times to make simple administrative adjustments, such as shift or job changes, to facilitate class attendance.

What is at stake is the professionalization of police service. Studies of police and professionalism confirm that educational achievement is an integral component. Education significantly contributes to competent job performance and personal contentment.

At the beginning of chapter 1, Dr. Palombo quotes August Vollmer in his 1930s prediction that a new police era was about to begin. The importance of an officer's education was becoming recognized. Vollmer's dream is not yet a reality, however. The application of a baton or gun is still favored by many if not most police administrators as the preferred method of controlling crime. As pointed out in this excellent book by Dr. Palombo, police professionalism still has a long way to go. In examining the history of education in police agencies, growth of educational achievement, methods of policing affected by education, difficulties of attaining high police education standards, and presentation of the results of in-depth research into the education/professionalism paradigm in the Los Angeles Police Department, she has produced a book that addresses the issues of today.

George T. Felkenes
Claremont, California
May 1994

Series Editors' Preface

Bernadette Jones Palombo follows the tradition of the *Current Issues in Criminal Justice* series in this volume on police professionalism. Reporting on a study of a large metropolitan police department, she merges scholarly analysis with a readable discussion of the issues.

In *Academic Professionalism in Law Enforcement* Palombo explores the link between education and professionalism in modern policing. Through litigation, scandal, and the influence of private sector practices, education has become an integral though still controversial part of law enforcement entry criteria. Ironically, the introduction of education to police departments seems to have faced much the same struggle as did the integration of women and minorities. This is particularly the case when we view the goal as not just to tolerate education but to appreciate it as instrumental to a quality police force. Although education, diversity, and professionalism may appear as three separate topics, they are, as this work demonstrates, especially linked together when it comes to public perceptions and assessments.

Reports like the Christopher Commission, the Webster Commission, the Amnesty International Investigation, and the Kolts Report have clearly pointed out many common problems in law enforcement. However, they lack the depth of analysis that can come only with careful consideration of the findings of the many related research studies. Palombo has assembled and interpreted that information and carefully considers the overall implications. Everything one needs to know about police professionalism and education is here.

Frank P. Williams III
Marilyn D. McShane

Preface

Research testing the relationships between college education and police officer performance and attitudes has grown steadily over the past two decades, primarily in response to the 1967 President's Commission on Law Enforcement and the Administration of Justice's *Task Force Report: The Police.*

The primary method for testing such relationships has been through empirical "criterion" validation, one of the three validation methods described in the *Uniform Guidelines on Employee Selection Procedures.* Subsequent to a landmark 1971 Supreme Court ruling that endorsed the criterion validation approach for a manual-laborer position, federal court decisions have endorsed the Equal Employment Opportunity Commission guidelines' "construct" validation approach, recognizing that more complex professional positions, which include police officers, require characteristics that are extremely difficult to measure empirically using a criterion validation method. This work, therefore, applies the construct validation approach in determining whether college-educated patrol officers in the Los Angeles Police Department (L.A.P.D.) possess attitudinal characteristics different from non-college-educated officers.

Second, method multivariate analyses of the relationships between educational level, probationary performance indicators, academic status, and "professionalism" scales administered to a sample of patrol officers have shown that qualities necessary for effective performance differ significantly between college-educated and non-college-educated officers.

Additionally, a "general functional elaboration" model has been developed through the testing and confirmation of six hypotheses, which assists in explaining the complex but statistically significant relationships between higher levels of education, academic status of officers, effective probationary performance, and officer professionalism.

In a pragmatic sense, college-educated minority and Caucasian officers possessing such characteristics may be more cost effective in the long run, considering the economic expense of police misconduct and awards against police agencies due to constitutional violation challenges against individual officers. The policy implications for the L.A.P.D., as well as other urban law enforcement agencies, would be (1) a serious consideration of upgrading their minimal educational requirements to include at least some college education for entry-level recruits, and (2) a more aggressive recruitment strategy in order to attract both minority and nonminority college-educated applicants.

Introduction

> In the U. S. and elsewhere education continues to be regarded as the key to excellence. Considered by many to be the father of modern policing in America, August Vollmer believed that training and education, comparable to that of the publicly recognized professions, was the means by which the police could be recognized as professionals. (Tafoya, 1990:206)

Demands for reform in governmental agencies in general and law enforcement agencies in particular during the twentieth century have resulted in the rise of the professional, administrative state of public administration in American society (Redford, 1969). This transition from what "progressive" critics have portrayed as a localized, corrupt, special interest–oriented, and inefficient form of public service has given rise to a more efficient, bureaucratic, equitable, and rational administration of governmental services overall. Such "professionalization" of public administrative services has been cited as a necessary condition for the "professionalism" of role occupants within these agencies, particularly in law enforcement (Price, 1977); however, this process in itself is not considered to be a sufficient condition to ensure the professional attitudes, values, and service of individual public service employees.

The unique problem for law enforcement personnel (particularly for officers on patrol) is that whereas the citizenry demands various forms of services (which often are not adequately provided for by other governmental agencies), it also demands that law enforcement agencies function in the role of the antagonist or adversary vis-à-vis portions of the populace in order to suppress, control, manage, and deter criminal and deviant activities. Generally, law enforcement officers are expected to enforce the law, as established by national and state legislatures and defined by the courts, and to provide a variety of other services to those communities over which law enforcement agencies have jurisdiction.

A leading proponent and reformer in the early twentieth century for the professionalization of law enforcement agencies and professionalism of the officers was August Vollmer, police chief of suburban (Berkeley) and urban (Los Angeles) police departments. Influenced by the national and local progressive movements at that time, he campaigned internally within law enforcement for more centralized, administratively efficient agencies as well as for more intelligent, well-educated officers in order to eliminate the prevalent problems of corruption and lawlessness within law enforcement (National Commission on Law Observance and Enforcement, 1931). Vollmer believed that more disciplined, well-trained, and highly educated officers functioning within a professional administrative agency would provide not only better quality, but also more equitable police services overall. Both the International Association of Chiefs of Police and the International Association of Police Professors have been in agreement with Vollmer as well as those academic scholars who have argued for more than fifty years that police officers require a college education in order to acquire "knowledge and habits of mind that are important in sustaining a commitment to public service" (Saunders, 1970:4).

Reports from the President's Commission on Law Enforcement and Administration of Justice (1967), the National Advisory Commission on Criminal Justice Standards and Goals (1973), and the McCone Commission (California Governor's Commission on the Los Angeles Riots, 1965) have followed this professionalization theme by urging the improvement of the quality of police personnel through higher educational requirements for its recruits. As Ward and Webb point out, although these commissions acknowledged training as one important goal necessary to improve policing, a "professional system" requires higher educational standards for all its members (Ward, Webb and Joint Commission on Criminology and Criminal Justice Education and Standards, 1984:28).

Subsequent to the time that this present project was conceived to determine whether higher educational attainment resulted in more "professional" police officers, the Los Angeles Police Department became the focus of the international community. The now infamous Rodney King brutality incident not only raised the ire of law enforcement's most vociferous critics[1] and the concerns of citizens as to whether the average police officer is either a "friend or foe" (Neithercutt and Carmichael, 1991:17), it also resulted in the comprehensive investigation of America's "most professionalized" police department.

This investigation, by what is commonly known as the Christopher Commission (Independent Commission on the Los Angeles Police Department, 1991), was primarily concerned with the problem of the use of excessive force by officers within the L.A.P.D., concentrating on the problem's "causes and cures." In addition to finding that approximately 20 percent of all officers had at least one complaint of the use of excessive force or improper tactics filed against them, the commission also found that the department's complaint system itself was "skewed" against complainants. Among its other findings, the commission also asserted that the problems of negative attitudes and racial bias by officers aggravated the problem of excessive force and that such attitudes were transferred into other forms of unacceptable performance in officers' encounters with citizens (Independent Commission, 1991:ix–xxi).

Although the Christopher Commission investigated the organizational structure, the administrative, training, and supervisory policies, as well as psychological attributes of individual officers, it failed to examine the possibility that a college education may play a critical role in shaping officers' attitudes in positive ways, which may then be translated into more professional behavior. This present study, while not critical of the commission's findings, attempts to pick up where the commission left off. There is no doubt that many of the commission's recommendations need to be implemented in order to improve the L.A.P.D. as an organization.[2] The primary task of this present study then essentially complements the commission's findings with a focus on the critical variable of higher education, a selection criterion recommended by Vollmer and his progressive reformer followers to improve the quality of police service that was overlooked in the commission's investigation.

Vollmer pointed out more than a half-century ago that the "poor quality of personnel is perhaps the greatest weakness of police departments in the United States" (Vollmer, 1936:3) Now, in an era when police officers have a new visibility, the public needs to know that effective law enforcement requires more than a "strong back" in present-day officers; a high level of skill, as well as a high level of intelligence, is a fundamental prerequisite for sworn police personnel.

A great number of publications on law enforcement generally and police officers specifically have been produced in the past several decades since the release of the 1967 President's Commission Task Force Report on the Police. This present study incorporates and reviews only a small portion of the total literature. It is expected, however, that a review of the research reflected here which is directly related to the present topic and the results of the present study will leave readers with the idea that implementation of college education requirements for law enforcement personnel will not only provide the benefit of a "professionalizing" influence on police agencies and their officers, but will also have positive long-term effects on the quality of performance of law enforcement in America.

NOTES

1. For example, a former L.A.P.D. sergeant and practicing attorney specializing in police brutality cases against police officers is quoted as saying, "It's not just in the LAPD; it's everywhere. . . . It's all a part of the mentality, that in our war against crime, the ends justify the means" (Katz, 1991).

2. The present controversial issue of absolute autonomy for police departments apart from the wider social arena and community at large (labeled the "macropolitical arena") was not the intent of the original progressive reformers. Those reformers wanted to remove localized

agencies from capture by individual and oftentimes illegal special-interest groups, i.e., "micropolitical" arenas. The commission recommended the strengthening of the Police Commission to essentially represent the larger "macropolitical" arena and to provide citizen oversight of the L.A.P.D. (Independent Commission on the Los Angeles Police Department, 1991:183–224).

CHAPTER 1

The Problem of Academic Professionalism for Police Officers

> Within a comparatively short time the old policeman, who believed that there is more law in the end of a night stick than there is in all the books in all the libraries, will disappear and in his place there will be found a man especially trained to service the people more intelligently. (August Vollmer and the National Commission on Law Observance and Enforcement, 1931:7–8)

College education is based upon the principle of vicarious learning, a principle that contrasts the anti-intellectual belief that one must personally experience a role in order to understand that role. In fact, a joint study conducted in the 1930s by the California Department of Education and the Los Angeles Police Department (L.A.P.D.) determined that capable and effective patrol officers needed to possess academic knowledge of a multidisciplinary nature which could not be acquired in a single field of study (Saunders, 1970:17).

Until recently, the L.A.P.D. had achieved a reputation, at least among police administrators and large segments of the public, as being one of the most corruption-free law enforcement agencies in America (Sherman, 1979:48; Shaw, 1992c:27). The L.A.P.D. has prided itself on the absence of financial corruption, primarily the result of efforts and success by internal affairs investigations. As the Rodney King incident has shown, however, other forms of corruption and police wrongdoing beyond the financial undermine a police agency in the eyes of the public "more than taking bribes or free meals" (Shaw, 1992c:27).

Extensive international media coverage of the Rodney King incident has disclosed that the "old policeman" who believes there is more law in the end of a night stick than in all the books in all the libraries has not disappeared entirely within the L.A.P.D.[1] Although many officers are more highly educated and trained today to professionally service the citizens more intelligently, those officers who do engage in unethical behavior against the citizenry tarnish not only their personal reputations but also the reputation of law enforcement generally in the minds of the public (Lynch, 1976b:288).

The tarnished reputation of law enforcement agencies was one of Vollmer's primary concerns at the turn of the twentieth century. Vollmer pointed out that if the legal, engineering, and medical professions recruited their members as randomly as policing did, the results would be disastrous; the modern police officer required professional training comparable to that required by the most skilled professions (Vollmer, 1936:231). In addition to professionalizing law enforcement administratively, Vollmer also pursued the goal of upgrading the quality of all police personnel through advanced higher education. He and his fellow reformers, Sherman points out, had no concrete evidence that higher education would solve the problems of policing; their belief was primarily a matter of "faith" in the value of college education generally (Sherman, 1978:31–32).

For the past half century, higher education for all police officers has been a central element in police reformers' strategies for positive change. Despite the recommendations of various commissions, however, this higher education criterion has not been implemented with regard to police personnel as in other socially recognized professions. The recommendations of these commissions were also based primarily upon faith in the value of college education rather than upon any studies confirming the value of higher education with improved officer performance.

Resistance to the implementation of higher educational requirements for police officers is based upon several unsubstantiated beliefs: (1) a tenuous relationship between higher educational levels and officer performance;[2] (2) the higher economic costs of hiring "overqualified" employees;[3] and (3) the possible discriminatory aspects against minorities if such a requirement were widely instituted throughout policing.[4]

Significance of Earlier Studies

In an effort to show that the need for higher educational requirements is one important component in the professionalism of officers within professionalized agencies, some academic researchers, using a strict empirical or **criterion validation approach,**[5] have attempted to show that increasing levels of college education improve the specific performance tasks of officers. Some of these studies have shown small but significant differences for particular criteria; others have shown no differences. However, in only two of the more than forty studies reviewed for this project has educational level been positively correlated with a lower performance level using this criterion validation approach.[6]

Additional researchers have either expanded the criteria of "successful performance" beyond officially recorded data, thereby continuing to use the criterion validation approach, or they have applied the **content validation**[7] approach between level of education and tasks to be performed successfully on the job. Results of studies using this approach have also been mixed. A third method has been a combination of criterion, content, and **construct validation**[8] approaches. One example utilizing this approach is an examination of the relationship between higher education and overall performance during academy training, which is then considered a valid construct for on-the-job performance. The three methods of criterion, content, and construct validation have been established by the Equal Employment Opportunity Commission in its *Uniform Guidelines on Employee Selection Procedures*[9] and noted or applied in various federal cases in which hiring standards were at issue.

In only one study (Shernock, 1992) have academic researchers used the strict construct validation approach in determining whether a relationship exists between college education and traits deemed important to successful officer performance. The limited use of the construct validation approach may be due to (1) the decision of the U.S. Supreme Court in *Griggs* v. *Duke Power Co.* (1971), which held that a high school education requirement for a manual, blue-collar job was unconstitutional since it discriminated against minorities in effect even if not in intent; (2) the belief that challenges against higher educational standards for police officers would be struck down by the courts since the courts might apply the same standard as that applied in *Griggs* (which required a criterion validation approach for selection criteria); (3) the concern that higher educational standards would in effect be discriminatory against minorities and could not be established as a bona fide occupational qualification;[10] and (4) the general view that police officer positions are comparable to manual, blue-collar positions rather than professional positions which require "skills or abilities which are extremely difficult to define with precision and even harder to test for or measure."[11]

Overview of the Problem of Officer Professionalism

Despite the professionalization of law enforcement agencies over the past seventy years, the social disruptions of the 1960s have caused contemporary reformers, academicians, and local and national governmental commissions to study and critique what has been perceived as problematic, unevenhanded, and brutal law enforcement responses, especially within minority communities (California Governor's Commission, 1965; National Advisory Commission, 1973; President's Commission on Law Enforcement, 1967).[12] Professionalization of the agencies, in and of itself, has not resulted in the anticipated professionalism of law enforcement officers in regard to their services to the general public.

Ideally, basic principles of constitutionalism and the rule of law mandate that the provision of police services within a free, democratic society be impartial, equitable, and just in enforcement of the law through the legitimate, coercive use of force. At the same time, however, democratic principles demand that police acknowledge the dignity of the individual while engaging in the full range of service functions.[13] The problem may be that the "professionalized" agencies do not inculcate these basic constitutional and human values in their personnel (for example, see Felkenes, 1984; Muir, 1977). Such values, which are manifested in officers' attitudes and behavior (e.g., Rokeach, 1973), must be discussed, learned, debated, and internalized in order for individual officers to fulfill their mandate of democratic policing within a democratic society. This is just one of the many tasks of higher education.

Although the general value of higher or college education recently has been critically questioned (e.g., Smith, 1990), present-day proponents of college education for changing law enforcement officers' attitudes, values, and behavior (to accord with that of professional public service agents) believe that the higher education of officers is a necessary component of the professionalization movement.[14] Critics, however, contend that the luxury of more costly, college-educated officers does not result in the more efficient overall performance of officers and that the professionalization of agencies has resulted in cynicism, that is, nonprofessionalism, among the more highly educated lower-ranking officers (e.g., see Niederhoffer, 1967).

Results of empirical research within the past several decades concerning the value of college-educated police officers have been inconclusive, although the majority of studies lean in the direction of the positive impact of a college education. In the present conservative economic climate, some police agencies within California, doubting the general and overall performance value of a college-educated officer, are recruiting future officers with a high school or general education diploma (GED).[15] Since the State of California's formal education requirement for police officers is currently a minimum of a high school education or a general education diploma,[16] it is anticipated that more agencies, due to economic and political reasons, may begin to follow this trend. Whereas Vollmer's dream of professionalizing law enforcement administrative agencies is in the process of being realized, his dream of professionalizing police officers through college education and advanced training in order to distance the officers from the vagaries of local, special-interest politics and various forms of corruption may be facing a severe challenge with unintended consequences.

In light of the previous discussion, it is important to determine whether higher educational requirements (i.e., at least some level of college education) for law enforcement personnel professionalize the practitioners in particular and the occupation in general, thereby improving overall police services to the general public. Due to the complexities and conflicting views of what represents professionalism for law enforcement, this question is addressed both theoretically and empirically through the extensive literature and empirical studies relevant to the current controversy over the need for college-educated officers for professional law enforcement. Whereas analysis of the literature addresses and discusses law enforcement in general, empirical research from the present study focuses on one large, urban, highly professionalized law enforcement agency in particular—the Los Angeles Police Department.[17]

Prior studies of the L.A.P.D. on the relationship between performance and higher education using official agency indicators (i.e., agency performance data such as arrests, field probation evaluations, and sick days) have provided mixed results. Although use of formal, officially recorded performance data may be closer to the actual performance of officers, the value of higher education in these prior studies has been determined within (1) the narrower view of the crime control function as the primary determinant of the role of policing, and (2) the short-term efficiency needs of the employee and the administrative agency. Such a model does not take into account those service-related and discretionary functions that comprise the majority of an officer's time and attention and that have been shown to contribute qualitatively to the department in the form of a truly professional style of performance overall.[18]

The results of a self-administered police officer attitudinal and performance survey, developed and analyzed by a Claremont Graduate School research team (including the present author) and funded by the John Randolph Haynes and Doris Haynes Foundation, are explored here. The purpose of the initial research had been to determine whether self-reported performance and professional attitudes differed among Caucasian, minority, and female officers (Felkenes et al., 1990). Results of that study revealed that in the majority of instances, between-group differences were not statistically significant; there were very few attitudinal or performance differences between the groups. At the same time, a cursory review showed that within-group differences on several performance indicators and attitudinal responses were apparent. Because of the purpose of that initial study, however, these within-group differences were not explored further.

Main Issues Addressed in This Work

The main issues to be addressed here are whether a relationship exists between the preservice educational level of patrol officers in the L.A.P.D. and (1) early career self-reported performance indicators, i.e., citizen complaints and agency commendations during the field training probationary period; (2) continuing educational advancement; and (3) professional attitudes toward the public, the organization, and the individual officer's societal role, taking into account officer ethnicity, gender, rank and experience, age, and prior occupational experiences.

More specifically, the main questions to be examined here concerning Los Angeles patrol officers are as follows: 1. Does a relationship exist between levels of higher education and self-reported probationary performance indicators, controlling for gender, ethnicity, age, and prior occupation? 2. Does a relationship exist between level of higher education and professional attitudes (as measured by previously validated professionalism scales), controlling for gender, ethnicity, age, rank, years of experience, and prior occupation? 3. Does a relationship exist between self-reported probationary performance indicators and professional attitudes, controlling for gender, ethnicity, age, rank, years of experience, and prior occupation? 4. Does a relationship exist between probationary performance indicators and academic status, controlling for gender, ethnicity, age, rank, years of experience, and prior occupation? 5. Does a relationship exist between academic status and professional attitudes, controlling for gender, ethnicity, age, rank, years of experience, and prior occupation? 6. Does a relationship exist between educational level and academic status, controlling for demographic variables of gender, ethnicity, age, rank, and prior occupation?

The importance of ethnicity, gender, rank, years of experience, age, and prior occupation as control variables lies in their possibility to function as intervening variables and to influence the results of the hypothesized relationships. Theories linking these hypotheses are explored and discussed in subsequent chapters.

Problems of Prior Methodological Research

The majority of prior empirical studies have attempted to test the relationship between levels of college education and effective performance of police officers as well as the differences between the performance of high school/GED–educated officers and college-educated officers. Measuring performance as a criterion or output variable in quantitative terms, however, does not take into account the quality of those interactions (which also may influence the total number of citizen complaints) during officers' responses to critical (i.e., reactive, crime-control) incidents. Nor does it take into account the myriad of complex, discretionary administrative, managerial, and service-related duties, both reactive and proactive.[19]

What some of the performance-related empirical studies have shown is that little or no difference exists between the educational groups, resulting in findings that would support arguments in favor of hiring non-college-educated officers in response to the short-term, economic, and efficiency needs of the administrative agency. However, studies of this type tend to overlook or slight important factors or dimensions in officer role performance that enhance or improve the overall organizational mission in regard to the security and welfare of its clients, the citizenry.[20] This approach ignores the long-term effectiveness needs of the administrative agency and its concomitant efforts to establish legitimacy within all social classes and cultural groups in society.

In addition to determining empirically what constitutes effective performance and dealing with problems of statistical methodology used to determine relationships between the predictor (selection or hiring standard) and criterion (performance) variables, the federal courts have acknowledged the inadequacy of applying the strict empirical validation approach. For those professional positions requiring a complex set of tasks that are not adequately measured by the criterion-related approach, federal courts have moved away from requiring proof of job relatedness through criterion validation. In *Davis* v. *City of Dallas* (1985), the Fifth Circuit Court of Appeals, following this trend, has accepted the construct validation approach, an approach that is supported by one criterion or empirically validated study. And, although the U.S. Supreme Court has not directly decided this issue, it subsequently has cited with approval the Fifth Circuit's findings (*Watson* v. *Fort Worth Bank and Trust,* 1988:2795).

It is argued that it could be beneficial to move away from the criterion or empirical validation approach and adopt a construct validation approach approved by the various federal courts.[21] It would then be possible to examine the relationships between levels of college education and the constructs or values of professionalism required to perform effectively in a professional law enforcement agency. The model developed for these relationships also takes into account the relationship between levels of education, early performance indicators, academic status of the officers, and previously developed professionalism indexes.

Prior Definitions of the Problem

August Vollmer believed that intelligent, well-trained law enforcement officers with exposure to a college experience would result in a police force comprised of the "best and the brightest" officers, in contrast to the cadre of brutal, lawless, corrupt, and inefficient officers that comprised a large number of police agencies during the 1920s. Vollmer's belief was supported by the fact that he had recruited and trained college students while he was police chief at the Berkeley Police Department. While at the L.A.P.D., he had administered the Otis Army

Intelligence Test and found that the L.A.P.D. officers' scores fell below an acceptable I.Q. range and also fell below those of a sample of college students. His efforts to upgrade the quality of police officers at that time included improved technical training and exposure to academic classes taught by faculty from the surrounding colleges. He did not take into account at that time, however, that such I.Q. tests might be culturally biased nor that upgrading educational requirements may discriminate against minority groups (primarily found within the lower social classes) to a greater extent than the present system already had.[22]

Affirmative action legislation of the 1960s and subsequent federal court cases have contributed to the growing numbers of minority students entering the academic college arena and the dominant middle-class social structure. A problem of discrimination, however, may continue to exist in regard to the lower socioeconomic classes (both Caucasians and minorities) in an effort to upgrade educational requirements for law enforcement work.[23]

College education in general and criminal justice education in particular (a newly emerging discipline to prepare students for a professional career in the larger criminal justice arena) have been criticized recently for not adequately preparing students for their new roles in the larger social arena (e.g, Smith, 1990; Sherman and National Advisory Commission, 1978; Ward, Webb, and Joint Commission, 1984). Despite such criticisms, an underpinning value of higher education institutions is that they are dynamic, continually in the process of improving. This dynamic institutional process suggests that Vollmer's "best and the brightest" ideal officers are positively influenced by a college experience and that college-educated individuals are generally different from, and academically superior to, their high school–educated counterparts.

It would seem that the technical training of officers would prepare them primarily for the technical aspects of their jobs. Advanced college education, conversely, would prepare them for the more abstract, cognitive, and problem-oriented dimensions of their social role, including addressing the physical, psychological, and legal needs and rights of their clients.

To conceive of officer performance in terms of the narrower view of the police function (i.e., as officially recorded quantitative outputs) ignores the quality of interaction while officers are engaging in crime-control or critical incidents (i.e., the quality of response to criminal incidents). Such a conception also ignores the quality of their performance while engaging in the various noncriminal, order-maintenance or service-related activities that various studies have shown comprise the majority of the police officer's time.

The issue as to the overall impact and effectiveness of college education on officer performance in both discretionary and nondiscretionary role tasks, as well as on organizational performance generally, has not yet been resolved. The present study, through the application of a theoretical as well as a construct validation empirical approach, examines such relationships and hopes to assist in clarifying a century-long debate on the merits of college education for police.

Looking at Patrol Officers in the L.A.P.D.

In determining whether the "good" or professional police officer[24] is the more highly educated officer (i.e., exposure to at least some college experience), what must be explored is whether a large, urban administrative law enforcement agency, such as the L.A.P.D., values the contributions of intelligent, college-educated officers in the continuing professionalization of the agency.[25] Rather than contributing to increased cynicism, this modern, complex, hierarchical bureaucracy has been praised as being among the vanguards of professional agencies. Although the agency has not been without its institutional problems, critics, and detractors, at present the L.A.P.D. is known as being relatively free from corruption and intrusive local political interference, which was Vollmer's original intent.[26]

The L.A.P.D. has not mandated college education requirements for its individual officers; however, prior research has shown that they have aggressively recruited intelligent, highly educated Caucasian and minority officers (Felkenes et al., 1990). In addition to "hiring the educated," this agency has also provided incentives for officers to continue their college educations, resulting in educating the noneducated officer and further educating the educated officer. This practice intuitively supports the view that the L.A.P.D. places a high value on intelligent, highly educated officers. This premise seems to be supported by the prior study on the L.A.P.D. in which survey respondents generally were highly satisfied with their jobs, felt a sense of independence and autonomy in performing their jobs, and exhibited highly professional (as opposed to cynical) attitudes toward the population they were hired to serve (Felkenes et al., 1990). However, the study also discovered a small number of low scorers in these areas; and the question subsequently arose as to whether these "abnormal" responses were attributable to lower levels of education. Perhaps the absence of a college education as a socializing mechanism results in officers that have an unprofessional, cynical view toward their jobs, their agency, and the public.

In examining the questions discussed earlier, it is necessary to explore the problems and promises of what is considered to be a modern, professionalized law enforcement agency operating within the confines of constitutional principles and the rule of law as well as a shrinking agency budget. Theoretically and empirically, similar types of modern urban police agencies have been shown to exhibit both professional and nonprofessional styles of policing (see Muir, 1977; Niederhoffer, 1967; Slovak, 1986; Wilson, 1968).[27] To suggest, however, that the professionalization of law enforcement agencies themselves has *caused* the nonprofessionalism of officers (including the more highly educated ones) or has resulted in the suppression of civil liberties[28] is to engage in a form of unsubstantiated mythmaking in the absence of systematic data covering the period prior to the twentieth-century professionalization movement.[29]

In the course of untangling some of the problems of prior academic research, it is necessary to link theoretical studies with an examination of the relationships between preservice education as a predictor variable and several criterion variables. These include (1) probationary performance such as citizen complaints (a highly questionable measure of performance but theoretically relevant) and agency commendations (also an extremely rough and biased measure of performance); (2) further educational advancement (commonly known in the literature as either in-service or continuing education); and (3) professional attitudes (indexed into several dimensions through factor analysis).

Since the results of prior studies testing the relationship between educational level and actual performance of the officers have been mixed in addition to being criticized on methodological grounds, the current approach to examining this relationship with professional attitudinal variables[30] may reveal that the provincial, narrower view of officially recorded officer performance is inadequate in determining overall professional performance qualitatively. In fact, this is what the Fifth Circuit Court of Appeals in *Davis* v. *City of Dallas* (1985) suggested when upholding college education requirements for entry-level police officers.

Both nonparametric and parametric statistical analytical methods, which are described and explained in chapter 5 and appendix A, will ultimately show that a statistically significant relationship has been found to exist in the present study between these criterion variables, and that each of them are significantly related to the variables of higher education at the time of the officer's initial employment. Additionally, these relationships are also examined for their differences with respect to ethnicity, sex, age, rank, and experience of officers, and occupation of officers prior to their appointment to the L.A.P.D.

Second, advanced statistical methods have been employed to determine the strengths of the relationship between the theoretically independent or predictor variable of higher education and the theoretically dependent or criterion performance variables to assist in supporting the view that higher educational standards (rather than lower educational standards) should be implemented in the current era of social turmoil and fiscal constraint. Finally, a profile of the differences in characteristics of non-college-educated and college-educated officers has been developed from the survey data to show that distinctions in professionalism and styles of policing do exist between these groups of officers.

In addition to the theoretical discussion and empirical analysis, a legal analysis of federal court decisions as to the constitutionality of higher education requirements for police as public service officers has been conducted. The resulting findings and analyses are discussed in chapter 3. Although the U.S. Supreme Court has not ruled on this issue, the analysis in chapter 3 discusses the issue as to how the Supreme Court would rule if it chose to do so. Analysis of the various decisions will provide insight and guidance to law enforcement agencies, which, while cognizant of affirmative action mandates concerning the hiring of minorities and women, have anticipated revising their educational standards above the mandated minimum set by the California Commission on Peace Officer Standards and Training and the California Government Code.[31]

NOTES

1. This problem, of course, is not unique to the Los Angeles Police Department. A recent fatal shooting of an unarmed African-American young male by African-American police officers in Pittsburgh, Pennsylvania, has been the center of discussion and concern, especially among white residents. The major fear is not police abuse and violence, per se, but incidents of abuse involving Caucasian officers against African-American residents, a situation that could lead to rioting and polarization of Afro-Americans and Caucasians within the city. (This incident could not be documented through the press, since Pittsburgh newspapers had been on strike for three months at the time of the shooting.)

2. As Saunders (1970:6–7) has pointed out, level of schooling can be considered as a rough measure of intelligence, which must be weighed with other factors of character, personality, and background. Also, the federal courts have acknowledged that the value of higher education for law enforcement cannot be measured precisely, any more than for any other profession. See discussion in chapter 3.

3. Hooper states that many extra dollars are being paid nationally to officers with college experience to perform basic patrol duties "that might be performed just as efficiently by less educated personnel for a

reduced cost" (Hooper, 1988:29). However, Sherman points out that this view fails to acknowledge that "a transformation of aggregate educational levels in an occupation can lead to transformation of the nature of the job, rather than merely rendering people overqualified for an unchanging job" (Sherman, 1978:178).

4. This issue is addressed in the section entitled "Affirmative Action, the Law, and College Requirements" in chapter 3.

5. This method demonstrates that particular criteria such as official performance data indicating successful job performance (e.g., number of arrests, average response time to critical incidents, etc.) correlate with test scores (or in the present case, educational level) with the criteria identified.

6. See chapter 2, table 1.

7. This approach demonstrates that tests or hiring criteria/standards closely represent on-the-job tasks to be performed by the officer (e.g., scaling a six-foot wall, etc.).

8. The construct validation approach demonstrates the extent to which recruits possess certain characteristics or traits that are deemed important to successful overall job performance (e.g., maturity and judgment in situations of conflict.)

9. *Uniform Guidelines on Employee Selection Procedures* 29 CFR Part 1607 (1978).

10. Carter, Sapp, and Stephens (1988:1–27) argue that despite a discriminatory impact, college requirements for law enforcement personnel are a "bona fide occupational qualification" (b.f.o.q.) exception based upon their studies and legal analysis of court rulings.

11. *Davis* v. *City of Dallas,* 777 F. 2d 205 (5th Cir. 1985) at 215–218, acknowledging the sworn police officer position as a professional one.

12. A recent article in a local newspaper has revealed that the problem currently is not only with minorities. An off-duty, Caucasian Riverside police officer recently lost a testicle when Fontana police officers engaged in extreme physical abuse against the officer during a minor incident. This incident cost the city of Fontana $2.5 million in a civil suit verdict awarded in favor of the abused off-duty officer (Anderson, 1992).

13. Redford's discussion of administrative agencies indicates that the problem of acknowledging the dignity of individuals within a bureaucratic environment is not unique or exclusive to law enforcement agencies (Redford, 1969).

14. For example, Gerald Lynch's testimony in *Davis* v. *City of Dallas,* 777 F. 2d 205 (5th Cir. 1985) at 218–223; Also, President's Commission on Law Enforcement and Administration of Justice, (1967b:36, 126–128).

15. Informal discussion among educators at the annual conference of the Western and Pacific Association of Criminal Justice Educators, November, 1990. Also see, Sherman and the National Advisor Commission (1978:167).

16. State of California, Commission on Peace Officer Standards and Training, California Code of Regulations, Title II: Peace Officer Standards and Training, art. 1, sec. 1002. This regulation is rather flexible in that a police agency may choose to implement requirements ranging from a minimum of a high school degree to a maximum of a four-year college degree.

17. Despite the current controversy surrounding the L.A.P.D. and its diminished reputation in the eyes of the public, this researcher's opinion, is that the L.A.P.D. continues to be one of the highest-caliber, most professional, large urban departments in the U. S. The *Los Angeles Times* agreed with this opinion, at least prior to the King incident. For example, see "The LAPD: How Good Is It? A Special Report," *Los Angeles Times,* December 18, 1977, sec. 8, p. 1, which states: "The Excalibur of police departments, the cutting edge for modern law enforcement in the United States, perhaps even the world. That's the reputation of the Los Angeles Police Department. And maybe the reality, too." Also see Woods (1973).

18. Although Hooper's study on the relationship between levels of education of L.A.P.D. officers and "official" performance indicators concludes that a statistically significant relationship overall does not exist between the two, he also acknowledges the importance and contributions of advanced education to such nonmeasurable areas of performance as planning and research, positive community interaction skills, and the use of non-incarcerative sanctions (Hooper, 1988:117).

19. This problem of the validity of official department indicators as to their effectiveness in officer performance is discussed in the American Bar Association Project on Standards for Criminal Justice report (1972). For example, the American Bar points out that to measure the quality of police performance based upon the number of arrests made is analogous to measuring the performance of a physician based on the number of operations performed, "without any regard for the need for the operation or for its success" (American Bar Association, 1972:114).

20. Vogel and Adams point out that the nature and extent of the impact of education on law enforcement professionalism remains an empirical question, with research results confounded by variations in the operational definition of professionalism itself (Vogel and Adams, 1983:476).

21. Discussed in the legal analysis section, chapter 3.

22. Chief Parker had implemented a mandatory I.Q. requirement of 110 during his tenure at the L.A.P.D. during the 1950s and 60s. This new requirement, according to Hooper, led to the "transformation of the agency into the most professional law enforcement organization in the nation" (Hooper, 1988:118). The L.A.P.D. no longer uses I.Q. as a selection criterion. Criticism of the use of the I.Q. as being culturally biased against ethnic minorities can be found in Gould (1981:146–234).

23. In addition to minorities and Caucasians in lower socio-economic groups, Lynch also suggests that educational requirements unfairly discriminate against present law enforcement personnel "no matter what safeguards, timetables or grandfathering is suggested" (Lynch, 1976a:64).

24. Muir uses these terms interchangeably in his investigation of various styles of policing within a highly professionalized agency (Muir, 1977).

25. This discussion is explored in chapter 2 in the section entitled "History of Professionalization."

26. Nonetheless, Freed (1990) shows that the L.A.P.D. in particular and the criminal justice system within Los Angeles are not without their problems in their service-related and crime-control functions.

27. For styles of policing in the L.A.P.D. that are specifically discussed in chapter 4, see Brown (1981) and Brown (1985).

28. See Niederhoffer (1967:17) on the effects of the drive for professionalization increasing cynicism for individual officers. For Woods' view on the suppression of civil liberties, see Woods (1973). Later in his study, Niederhoffer points out that "[e]ven without professionalization, cynicism is a common phenomenon in the police occupation" (Niederhoffer, 1967:175).

29. In fact, the first national study conducted when the professionalization movement was in its infancy clearly showed that what would legally be considered civil rights violations today were systematic and endemic throughout law enforcement in the early part of the twentieth century (National Commission on Law Observance and Enforcement, 1931).

30. This approach uses attitudinal variables that have been empirically translated into larger dimensions or values and are perceived as being closer to actual behavior than individual attitudes. For this approach see Rokeach (1973:7–19).

31. California Government Code, Title 1, art. 2, sec. 1031(e).

CHAPTER 2

History of the Professionalization of Law Enforcement

> The patrolman of today may be the sergeant, lieutenant, captain, or chief of tomorrow, and for this reason, if for no other, the highest degree of intelligence available is not too good for the police service. The organizational chain is no stronger than its weakest link, and the stupid, blundering idiot, who by his acts can disgrace an entire organization, becomes the public's measuring stick for the whole department. One inferior man in an emergency can ruin the reputation of an otherwise excellent police force.
> (August Vollmer, 1936:227)

A review of the history of the professionalization of administrative public agencies generally (see Redford, 1969; Gormley, 1989), as well as law enforcement agencies (see Price, 1977) and the L.A.P.D. in particular (Woods, 1973), has shown that a reform movement within law enforcement has coincided with the impetus for overall reform by a larger national progressive political movement in the twentieth century. According to Gormley, the progressive reformers of the early twentieth century promoted bureaucratic autonomy for agencies within the federal government in order to minimize political control of administrative agencies by the chief executive and political parties (Gormley, 1989:7). Bureaucratic specialists, the progressive reformers believed, would be free to engage in their duties without the burden of political allegiances. Agencies independent of such allegiances would then promote "efficiency, good government, and the common good" (Gormley, 1989:7–8).

This early progressive political movement has been characterized by Gormley as a "quest for direct democracy and expert management" (Gormley, 1989:37). The reformers in this era were perceived as architects building an efficient bureaucracy that would be a solution to the problem of government inefficiency, ineffectiveness, and corruption. The reformers themselves, however, were upper-middle-class, well-educated protestants directly opposed to the influence of political machines especially at the municipal levels of government. They essentially believed that by eliminating machine politics from controlling the government, all aspects of public services, including that of local, municipal policing would improve (Urchida, 1989).

The first American police departments developed along the model of the London Metropolitan Police, but as Urchida points out, the police agencies borrowed selectively rather than following the model exactly (Urchida, 1989:17). As a professional civil service agency and an extension of the national government, the London Metropolitan Police had been removed from direct political influence of special interest groups. London "bobbies" were disciplined and trained according to strict guidelines suited for the crime prevention function, and their legitimacy was based on institutional authority; i.e., grounded in the unwritten English Constitution—rules of law determined by constitutional principles embodied in tradition, common law, and more recently, parliamentary statutes (Urchida, 1989:19).

As Price points out, nineteenth-century American police agencies reflected the ideology of social Darwinism, which dominated American culture at that time; an ideology incorporated into policing emphasizing "police strength, bravery, courage, and hand-to-hand combat ability in keeping order by controlling crime-prone, disorderly immigrants" (Price, 1977:40). In contrast to the London Metropolitan Police, nineteenth-century American police systems, following the style of local and municipal governments, were an extension of local, competing political factions. In many American cities, the city mayor and the local political machinery capitalized on the local police departments in order to expand their involvements in graft and corruption as well to fulfill political obligations to their "patrons" (American Bar Association, 1972:82).[1] As a result, patrol officers were basically brutal political functionaries rather than the London-style professional bobby dedicated to the impartial application of public service ideals. Whereas the American police officer may have formally sworn his allegiance to the Constitution, on a more personal level he gave his physical and political loyalties to both the ward boss and the police captain who appointed him to the force.

The earliest formally recognized professionalization movement of the police, according to Price, occurred in the 1870s. In 1871 police executives from around the nation met in St. Louis to discuss concerns about rising crime and violence in American cities. A major outcome of this meeting was success in obtaining federal government support for technical improvements such as improved criminal identification systems (Price, 1977:39). This form of professionalization, however, fit in with the prevailing philosophy of that era and was concerned with the intrinsic interests of policing generally, and its rhetoric did not go beyond expressing those interests.

In Los Angeles at the turn of the century, a strong faction of the national progressive movement, consisting of the white American middle class, contested control of municipal government and services by political factions of the immigrant groups (Price, 1977:39). According to accounts by Woods and Walker, police departments were a major political football and a major prize in local political factions' struggles for power. Winning factions attempted to take advantage of their temporary political control of police agencies by altering the local police department's administrative structure to achieve permanent political control (Woods, 1973; Walker, 1977:26).

The middle-class reformers determined that the police were not only captured by special political interest groups, but also that they were undisciplined, lacked strong leadership, and most of all lacked qualified personnel. To improve conditions within police departments, these reformers recommended three major changes: centralizing the administration of police agencies; upgrading sworn officer personnel; and narrowing the police function from that of a "service orientation" to that of concentrating on fighting the rising tide of crime. The progressive reformers' view was that by eliminating the type of service provided by the police to their communities, the police department's ties to ward bosses and political factions would be severed, and the police departments could focus on fighting crime (Urchida, 1989:23).

For reforms by the progressives to take root within policing, a movement advocating that the police adopt a "professional model" needed to be championed by law enforcement leaders themselves. According to Woods, the police professionalization movement was generated mainly within police departments (Woods, 1973:viii). By the 1920s the major innovator of police reform and recognized dean of police chiefs, August Vollmer, had achieved a national reputation in law enforcement circles for his pioneering work in professionalizing the Berkeley, California, police department.

Vollmer had been extremely critical of the quality of police officers at that time and believed that the idea of a "professional officer" was synonymous with a high-quality police officer; for an officer to become an "expert" in policing, he must have the requisite credentials provided by a college education. Essentially, Vollmer believed that college-educated persons had more favorable attributes to do the work required in policing than those with less formal education. In addition to proposing the recruitment of college-educated officers, he initiated college-level police education programs that included classes in the social sciences as well as in the natural sciences (Walker, 1977:130; Urchida, 1989:25). Being an expert police officer, according to Vollmer, meant being able to handle both criminal and noncriminal problems requiring a vast amount of knowledge primarily acquired through a college education:

> In the discharge of general service functions, many of which deal with non-criminal problems, special qualities—of intelligence, tact, and sympathy—are required; knowledge is needed of the laws, federal, state, and local, or medicolegal evidence, and even of general and medical psychological principles; special techniques, such as first aid, scientific investigation, and mob control, must be employed. (Vollmer, 1936:222)

As both president of the International Association of Chiefs of Police and police chief of the Los Angeles Police Department in the 1920s, August Vollmer's professional reputation resulted from his firm belief in the application of scientific methods to both the administration of the police as well as to the apprehension of criminal offenders. Although Vollmer was no liberal in the common notion of the term, he believed that the civil rights of offenders must be closely observed; according to Woods, his allegiance to civil liberties and "his devotion to constitutional law was genuine" (Woods, 1973:167).

In addition to recruiting and employing highly qualified police officers as experts who applied their knowledge gained in college in performing their tasks, professional departments were to embody several other important characteristics. For the police department to be unconstrained from external political party influences, the department needed to establish its own rules and regulate its own personnel. Additionally, the department was to be an efficiently run department, and, as any other business engaging in successful practices, it needed to establish its own mandate to carry out its crime control function and enforce the law through the use of modern technology (Urchida, 1989:24). Vollmer's classical view of professionalism consisted of three core components: professional knowledge, professional autonomy with a commitment to the service ideal, and the efficient management of the police department.[2]

Vollmer's campaign to professionalize law enforcement gained both momentum and some fortuitous support on the national scene in the 1930s. The ignoble history of early American municipal police departments and the concomitant efforts of early police progressive reformers, such as Vollmer, prompted formation of the National Commission on Law Observance and Enforcement in 1931. This commission, commonly known as the Wickersham Commission, recommended not only the removal of political involvement from within police departments nationwide but also that departments be run by professional police administrators serving a fixed term of office. As for its evaluation of the status of current rank and file officers, the commission announced its findings that the majority of police officers were not suited by either temperament, education, or training for police work. It also found that at least 75 percent of police officers in the United States were mentally unqualified to engage in police work

(American Bar Association, 1972:81; National Commission, 1931:58). At this same time, a large number of college graduates lacking other employment opportunities were being recruited into the policing occupation. What was seen as a progressive trend toward the employment of highly educated officers, however, lasted only a short period of time until after the Depression (Goldstein, 1977:184).

The first phase of the police professionalization movement lasted from approximately 1910 to 1960 (Urchida, 1989:24). In addition to civil service provisions, around mid-century the application of scientific principles to the management and administration of police agencies became the cornerstone of modern-day policing. The utilization of highly educated management and technical experts from academic institutions provided the rationale for the principle of academic professionalism within policing (Woods, 1973:39). Severed from the politics and political scandals of an earlier era, modern-day police agencies participated in the progressive professional ideology emphasizing administrative and managerial efficiency as well as political neutrality (Greene, 1989:349).

By the 1960s, the Los Angeles Police Department, after numerous scandals, became the professional model for police agencies across the nation. Much like Vollmer, Chief William Parker had reorganized the police bureaucracy, simplifying the command structure. Having established a reputation for changing the L.A.P.D. from a corrupt, traditional-type agency into an innovative, professional one, Parker is best remembered for careful planning and management, administrative efficiency, and rigorous officer selection and training procedures. Additionally, his public relations skills enabled him to gain the respect of both the media and the community (Woods, 1973:425–429; Urchida, 1989:25).[3] The L.A.P.D. was perceived as having achieved its professional goals to a greater extent than any other urban police department in America. Many large departments were found to be rapidly following its example.

During this period of time, however, the central tenets of Vollmer's classical professionalism began to change, and the dominant focus within law enforcement included managerial efficiency, technological sophistication, and an emphasis on crime control. The idea of the social service aspects of policing lost ground, and the professionalization movement itself was being critically questioned. Corruption scandals within large urban departments continued to perplex police administrators; and the impersonal and often brutal forms of service received by segments of minority populations exacerbated police–community tensions, creating severe racial tensions between the police and the policed (Urchida, 1989:28).

By the end of the 1960s, results of the earlier legacy of police professionalization specifically, and state and federal reform generally, were considered to be ambiguous. Critics have argued that the professionalism movement within policing has essentially placed a primary emphasis on efficiency and effectiveness, with an improvement on the organizational structure, at the expense of the substantive, service-related goals of a professional police officer (e.g., Walker, 1977; Goldstein, 1979). Not only were citizens angry with the form of policing they were receiving, police officers themselves felt disenfranchised and alienated from both their work and their organizations (Greene, 1989:357).

Police departments, and agencies at all levels of government, were being perceived as not only "arrogant and intrusive" but also as inefficient and ineffective (Gormley, 1989:10). Whereas the early progressives aggressively promoted a reform of governmental bureaucratic autonomy as a solution to the corruption and inefficiency that pervaded government in the late nineteenth and early twentieth century, in the 1960s and 1970s modern reformers viewed out-of-control, self-serving bureaucracies as the present-day problem against true democracy. Whereas early reformers were considered "architects," modern-day reformers were considered "fixers," reformers trying to improve on a dilapidated and insensitive system. Modern-day reformers devised changes within government generally and law enforcement specifically that simultaneously promoted efficiency with accountability, effectiveness with responsiveness, and promoted fairness, equal treatment, due process, and integrity. Modern-day reformers also recognized that the progressive's quest for direct democracy and expert management needed to be replaced by a philosophy of representative democracy and the management of experts (Gormley, 1989:35–38).

The decade of the 1960s, with its social and political turmoil and rising tensions between minority groups and law enforcement, produced additional reforms within policing. The President's Commission on Law Enforcement and the Administration of Justice in 1967 believed that improved police performance could be achieved by a series of reforms within law enforcement, including both the employment of increasing numbers of minorities to serve minority communities and increased educational requirements for all officers entering policing.[4] This reform in the quality of officers has only been implemented in a small number of agencies, and it has been suggested that political demands for a greater number of minorities within law enforcement has displaced the necessity of hiring more highly qualified and highly educated police officers (Weirman, 1978).[5]

One major reform in this recent period was the structuring of police discretion through administrative policy-making. Another was the initiation of team policing programs, a community relations innovation introduced into police services as an alternative to the classical bureaucratic administrative style that had dominated police management practices (Angell, 1971). Since the classical management style—promoting the detachment of police from the communities they served—had been diagnosed as part of the reason for the social disorders and riots in the 1960s, the new patrolling concept emphasized officer familiarity with the community and its residents. However, the life of team policing was short-lived and "died at the hands of middle managers, police sergeants and lieutenants who resisted the loss of organizational power" (Greene, 1989:358).

The modern campaign for police professionalism since the period of social disorders of the 1960s has primarily been seen as an organizational reform effort. Central focus has been placed on the centralization of executive authority of police chiefs and the enhancement of centralized control over the exercise of street-level discretion by patrol officers (Slovak, 1986:9). By the 1970s, police agencies nationwide, rather than attempting to achieve Vollmer's goals of classical professionalism, have experienced an anti-professional reaction in which police agencies once again glorified the simplistic use of force. During this era, the L.A.P.D., previously recognized as the "most professional police force" in America, once again was perceived as having little regard for democratic values or constitutional principles (Woods, 1973:507–511). According to Woods, the early progressive reformers would not have approved of these results as outcomes for their labors (Woods, 1973:511).

Professionalization v. Bureaucratization

The previous section has shown that August Vollmer had encouraged and endorsed a view of policing that has been termed the classical model of academic professionalization of law enforcement. This view was not only concerned with administrative efficiency, centralization of planning, and the technical competence of employees, but also with the quality of services provided by individual officers to the populations they serviced. This view of professionalization was also adopted by Vollmer's student, O. W. Wilson, who, seeking the inculcation and internalization of a code of ethics by the officers, believed that such values would be learned by the officers through a preprofessional classical college education (Sykes, 1989:287).

During the 1930s, however, as Walker documents, the dominant model of the police mission was that of law and order as well as crime fighting; the minority model that incorporated service delivery and due process concerns was suppressed (Walker, 1977:166). This view, which is known as the academic, managerial, bureaucratic, and technical efficiency model of professionalization, coincides with Price's view of the development of hierarchical, bureaucratic, militaristic police organizations initiated in the early 1920s. This model coincided with the dominant social and political ideology of "Americanism": a striving for the assimilation of diverse cultural and minority groups into the mainstream, middle-class white culture.[6]

During the 1950s the L.A.P.D. was cited as the model of efficient managerial professionalism, which stressed not only centralized administration and control but also the application of stringent selection procedures and strict discipline for officers. This emphasis on efficiency of the department over the effectiveness of the officers' role tasks not only stripped officers of their discretion but also resulted in officers becoming faceless to the communities (Staufenberger, 1977:679).

The dominant political ideology in America changed in the 1960s and 1970s to that of social liberalism, with an emphasis on individual rights and the rights of minorities. Entrenched, administratively oriented, militaristic police bureaucracies were slow or resistant to recognize their obligation to acknowledge the importance of civil liberties and due process concerns. According to Price, departmental response has been the adoption of community relations or agency rhetoric espousing Vollmer's original view of professionalization absent the necessary component of action or police effectiveness required to meet consumer demands for improved service. At the same time, however, this focus on community relations also led agencies to recognize the need for officer skills in interpersonal relationships with members of the community, a "speciality" previously unrecognized by the occupation (Price, 1977:65).

This traditional model of academic managerial professionalization or bureaucratization has been criticized as viewing police officers at the lower levels of the administrative hierarchy as skilled, blue-collar public employees to be strictly controlled through stringent regulations rather than as professional officers (Carter and Sapp, 1990).[7] Such an approach stifles the judgment and innovative abilities of the more analytical, college-educated officers who recognize the importance of discretionary judgments in carrying out their complex tasks.

At the current time, community pressure exists to moderate and reform this strictly managerial, bureaucratic philosophy of professionalization. The efficiency of the police organization may be seen as less important than its responsiveness to the community it is required to service (Petersen, 1979:9–16). Vollmer, however, had placed primary emphasis on both the efficiency and effectiveness of law enforcement, acknowledging due process concerns of citizens.

These two concerns are not considered incompatible by critics of professionalization reform (Walker, 1977:54). A broader model of professionalization, as Skolnick points out, also needs to be concerned with those values conveying the message that the "police are as much an institution dedicated to the achievement of legality in society as they are an official organization designed to control misconduct through the invocation of punitive sanctions" (Skolnick, 1966:238–39). Professionalization in this view not only incorporates but is also determined by the values of a democratic legal order rather than exclusively by technological efficiency.

The quality and legality of professional law enforcement is not only influenced by the level of education of its officers, the services it provides, and the respect it gives its citizens. It is also influenced by the type or model of bureaucracy under which it functions, the body of systematic knowledge available for appropriation by the policing profession, as well as the nature of the leadership within law enforcement. These three key areas are perceived as primary barriers inhibiting the development of policing as a profession (Price, 1977:8–11).

Models of Bureaucracy within Law Enforcement

It is not the bureaucracy, per se, that is perceived as the antithesis of professionalism within government generally or of police organizations specifically. It is the bureaucratic model adopted by agencies to enable them to become more efficient administrators. Four types of bureaucracies identified in government generally are the formalist model, the expertise model, the judicial-review model, and the market-pluralist model (Gormley, 1989:19).

A bureaucracy that is a highly centralized, efficient, and disciplined mechanism for implementing the wishes of its creators is considered the formalist model. One that recognizes bureaucratic discretion, enabling its experts as professionals to be creative, flexible, and effective in its decision making is considered the expertise model. That which is subject to the rule of law through careful judicial scrutiny is acknowledged as the judicial-review model. One in which legitimacy flows from the operation of either political interests or market forces within the bureaucratic structure is considered the market-pluralist model. An ideal type of bureaucracy characterized by administrative efficiency combined with a pluralistic, legalistic, democratic orientation is considered the "golden mean approach." This approach acknowledges the adaptability of bureaucracies, generally, in reconciling the needs of administrative efficiency and pluralistic democratic effectiveness (Gormley, 1989:19).[8]

An examination of bureaucracies developed by law enforcement agencies in response to a drive for professionalism has distinguished and classified four types of bureaucracies influencing the dominant styles used by the agencies in handling responses for services (Brooks, 1989:128). This typology of bureaucratic organizations within policing characterized by the two dimensions of professionalism (measured by educational level of officers) and extent of bureaucratization includes the fraternal type, the militaristic type, the service type, and the legalistic type of bureaucracy (Brooks, 1989:128).

Departments with a low level of professionalism of their officers as well as a low level of bureaucratization have been typed as "fraternal" agencies. Those with a low level of professionalism but a high level of bureaucratization have been typed as "militaristic." In contrast, agencies with a high level of professionalism but a low level of bureaucratization have been typed as "service," whereas those with both high levels of professionalism and bureaucratization have been typed as "legalistic."

According to this model, departments emphasizing professionalism of officers but also an increasing degree of bureaucracy are found to shift from a conciliatory response to a punitive response in settling disputes.[9] Departments with a low level of professionalism but a high level of bureaucracy (militaristic departments) would lead to the most punitive type of response by officers. This latter type of bureaucratic organization has been identified as one of several conditions impeding the advancement of law enforcement as a profession.[10]

Shortcomings to Professionalization

Chief William Parker's style of professionalism in the L.A.P.D. in the 1960s has been acknowledged as resulting in the most efficient and most militaristic department in the nation, a department which stifled the ambitions and talents of the few of its more highly educated officers (Walker, 1977:171–72). Parker's militaristic-style bureaucracy had developed only one dimension of Vollmer's broader vision of reform for law enforcement.[11] Parker's emphasis on authority and power not only alienated the department's officers from the communities they were to protect, but also reinforced many of the minority residents' belief that the police "acted as an army of occupation" (Woods, 1973:499). Adherents to Parker's style of bureaucratization of law enforcement believed in the primacy of efficiency: more men, riot control training, powerful weapons, and massive retaliation.

Adherents to Vollmer's progressive view of reform, however, believed in maintaining the force as an efficient "peacekeeping" tool, but urged the introduction of a greater number of more highly educated police officers who could seek more intellectual solutions to human problems that confronted police officers in the daily performance of their tasks (Woods, 1973:499). This approach to reform is akin to the "moderation approach," an approach in which a highly centralized bureaucracy must introduce a strong "dose of pluralistic politics" (Gormley, 1989:19). This reformist approach in law enforcement has been labeled the "new professionalism" approach, which emphasizes a reduced militaristic structure, educated and trained specialists for particular problems, increased contacts between citizen and patrol officer, and improved quality of services to the community (Price, 1977:65).[12]

The second reason the policing occupation has fallen short of a profession is the lack of a systematic body of knowledge, which is seen as necessary to improving the quality of service to police clientele.[13] Police professionalism, which incorporates this knowledge or occupational expertise, is perceived as providing a set of ethical principles or values affording recognition by the public of law enforcement's professional status. The traditional professions, however, require an extended period of preprofessional education in addition to accredited professional training, and critics acknowledge that law enforcement falls short of this goal of classical academic professionalism (e.g., see Price, 1977; Steinman, 1986).[14] What seems to be needed is a transformed organization that will facilitate the growth of individual professionals through requiring at a minimum a preprofessional college education prior to accreditation as a police officer.[15]

Although there has been scholarly debate as to what information and emphasis this preprofessional training for law enforcement should include, a study of the effects of education generally show that "students' intellectual aptitudes, including the ability to think critically and independently, increase as they progress through college" (Sherman and the National Advisory Commission, 1978:44).[16] Vocationally oriented students, however, seem to be less amenable to attitudinal change in regard to political views, civil rights, and authoritarianism than those engaging in general education studies.[17]

What constitutes effective knowledge and important values for educated police officers working in a generalist or patrol capacity has been identified by police educators and police officers themselves (Tannehill and Janeksela, 1984). Knowledge in areas such as criminal, civil, administrative, and juvenile law, scientific and technical skills required for on-the-job performance, and familiarity with departmental operations were identified as important for professional performance. However, cognitive and attitudinal skills incorporated into an educational curriculum were identified as more important than substantive knowledge of the law and technical and scientific skills.

To improve officer and departmental relations with the community, both police officers and educators have expressed the view that verbal and nonverbal communication abilities as well as enhanced analytical abilities in handling conflict situations are extremely important for professional policing. Additionally, they have identified "positive attitudes" toward the general public, their own police role, and criminal justice institutions as critical in developing effective human relations skills and as necessary components to professional police officer performance (Tannehill and Janeksela, 1984:22–23). This view of student police officers and police educators themselves supports Vollmer's view of classical academic professionalism.

The third reason identified as a barrier to "true" professionalization of policing is that of supervisors and leaders within law enforcement who continue to view the preprofessional education of officers as unimportant to their police role. As with any organization, a leadership with special interests and concerns does not always further the professionalization of the occupation. However, many professionally oriented police administration leaders have publicly espoused the critical relationship between the quality of service by their departments and the advanced education of their police personnel (Cascio and Real, 1976:55). Many police administrators have urged a college degree for entry-level police officers as well as advanced degrees for ranking officers as a mandatory professional requirement (Woods, 1973:2). Others, however, continue to view college education as irrelevant to police work and harass and restrain those officers who attempt to apply human relations skills to their handling of the public (American Bar Association, 1972:212).

The critical beginning point in establishing a professional police department as well as a professional police culture is the development of a set of professional values, that is, a professional philosophy of policing. Such values are not only transmitted through the formal educational arena and infused within the police culture, but are also transmitted through the police chief's own personality (U.S. Department of Justice, 1989:165–66). The extent to which a chief's personality has influenced the professional or anti-professional attitudes and philosophy of a department's officers has not been ascertained.

What has been ascertained, however, is that the L.A.P.D. has included a minority percentage of idealistic, college-educated officers who embody the highest professional concepts, which not only include respect for legal decisions influencing the judgments police officers make and the behaviors police officers engage in daily, but also respect for those decisions protecting the constitutional rights of citizens. These highly educated L.A.P.D. officers, together with their counterparts in other departments, represent what Wood characterizes as the innovators or vanguard of academic professionalism (Woods, 1973:54). These officers, however, conflict with the more militaristic, bureaucratically oriented supervisors and their rank-and-file following who continue to espouse anti-professional values and beliefs and engage in anti-professional behavior in fulfilling their law enforcement duties.[18]

Advancement of law enforcement toward what is known traditionally as a profession will not only require changes within policing itself, but will also require a continuing dialogue between the academic community, professors, and police leaders to judge the advancement of police professionalization toward the classical model of academic professionalism. It will also require law enforcement's acknowledgment and acceptance of professional associations such as the American Academy for Professional Law Enforcement and the Academy of Criminal Justice Science as representative of and setting the standards, ethical considerations, and educational requirements for a professional sworn officer force. According to Lynch, this process of acceptance will to a large degree only take place through a process of higher education of all law enforcement personnel (Lynch, 1976b:286).

Professionalism of Officers

The previous discussion supports the belief that the actual development of "professionalism" within law enforcement has been concerned primarily with the administrative, managerial, and technical efficiency of its officers. However, the changing social, political, and legal climate beginning in the 1960s, which includes the due process revolution focusing on individual rights and the civil rights of minorities, has mandated the revision of this model of police professionalism. Nonetheless, police professionalism continues to have different meanings within law enforcement itself, meanings not only dependent upon the nature of the organizations in which officers are employed, but also upon the various positions held by officers within those organizations (Brown and Vogel, 1983:27).

Police officer professionalism has been acknowledged by various federal courts as well as by many police executives themselves as being broader than the narrow efficiency view of professionalism.[19] As will be discussed in chapter 3, police officer professionalism incorporates values and behavior that are essentially concerned with the unique responsibility police officers possess in their public safety role, which includes the provision of critical services to the public.

At the present time, the police role is considered one of the most critical and difficult of public service roles to perform, and every available device to improve the quality of this role should be encouraged (e.g., Jagiello, 1971:121). In the invocation of police powers, a college education may not be indicative of the "exact" knowledge required to perform a particular position. However, the judgment, flexibility, maturity, and positive service-oriented attitudes toward the public provided by an advanced education are important, perhaps even critical, components of police officer performance within the broader view of professionalism.

August Vollmer's classical view of academic professionalism acknowledges that police officers with higher levels of education are aware of and value the dignity and civil liberties of individuals within the communities they service. Additionally, professional officers become knowledgeable of and adapt to the changing social, political, and legal climates within a democratic social order. To accomplish this, professional officers, as chief interpreters of the law for the community members with whom they interact (Skolnick, 1966:4), must be motivated to learn the dynamics of changes within society and be sophisticated in the application of this knowledge, especially with portions of the communities which themselves are neither tolerant, flexible, nor knowledgeable of the changing social and legal climates.

The American Bar Association has stressed that police departments need sworn personnel who have acquired characteristics that a college education seeks to foster: intellectual curiosity, analytical ability, articulateness, and "a capacity to relate the events of the day to the social, political, and historical context in which they occur" (American Bar Association, 1972:212). Additionally, because of the impact of a police officer's actions, the power legitimized in the officer role and the discretionary situations in which officers must make the best judgments and decisions, professional police officers should be required to possess professional qualifications similar to those of other professionals within the criminal justice system (Jagiello, 1971:117). As Hoover has pointed out, since improvement in the operation of the system is "intrinsically related to the quality of the staff," the improvement of the quality of the staff is achieved through higher educational standards. In this view, "genuine professionalism" is based upon a service ideal that is "intrinsically related to higher educational standards" (Hoover, 1975:2).

A portrait of ideal professional police officers with higher education is that they exhibit a greater sense of self-esteem, are more adaptive and flexible in their approach to the environment, and possess a heightened sense of human worth, enabling them to better handle social problems more expeditiously (Guller, 1972; Smith, Locke, and Walker, 1967). Such officers, while pragmatic in their learning and questioning of the relevance of theory to the outside world, thrive on excellence in their performance of duties, perceiving themselves as goal-oriented problem solvers (Knowles, 1972).[20] Such characteristics are considered as important as, if not more important than, the skills that written examinations are intended to measure (Goldstein, 1977:264). More important, not only does the individual police officer benefit from this enhanced level of professionalism, but also police management benefits as a result of improved social service skills and overall improvement of the quality of police work (Reed, 1988).

The importance of preprofessional education for police officers prior to their certification and professional training, as is required in other professions, has been demonstrated by Vogel and Adams. The impact of educational socialization prior to employment as a police officer is found to be an important element in the professionalizing process. Officers who acquire college education prior to entering law enforcement are considered to be sufficiently critical and innovative in their adaptation to many of the norms of the police culture that have historically created problems between the police and the community. In contrast, officers who attend college after employment within law enforcement, motivated by their prior police culture socialization experience as well as by their "credentialist" view toward the importance of a college education for promotion, oftentimes insulate themselves from the total student experience and do not acquire the full range of benefits that the college education experience provides (Vogel and Adams, 1983:482).

In a more recent study, Worden points out that police officers who earn their degrees as in-service students develop a set of occupational attitudes and operational styles that inhibit attitudinal or behavioral changes normally experienced by preservice degree recipients (Worden, 1990:568). The findings of his study partially support this observation in that his sample of patrol officers receiving their degrees as in-service students defined their "professional" police role more narrowly than those patrol officers who received their degrees as preservice students (Worden, 1990:582).

Arthur Niederhoffer, a pioneer in the study of the impact of the process of police professionalization on the attitudes of more highly educated officers, has remarked that the advocates of "true" professionalism stress the qualities of police integrity rather than that of mere performance (Niederhoffer, 1967:71).[21] He also has pointed out that professionalism within the training academy for the large urban police department he studied was oriented more toward that of the social sciences than the "lock-em-up philosophy" (Niederhoffer, 1967:52).[22] However, his results showed that this training academy experience was not an adequate socialization experience in itself to prevent new patrol officers from acquiring cynical attitudes or hostility toward the members of the communities they serviced.[23]

Niederhoffer also specified those elements that are necessary for an occupation to achieve professional status. These elements entail both organizational practices and individual capacities of the officers. The first element is a high standard of admission for all police officers. Second, a special body of knowledge and theory is essential in order for an officer to perform his or her role as a professional rather than an amateur. A lengthy period of training is required together with certification or licensing of members and a code of ethics to be internalized by the officers. It is this internalized code of ethics with its associated attitudes and ideology that denotes the extent or degree of professionalism characteristic of the occupation. Finally, officers must have pride in their profession and be altruistically dedicated to the service ideal.

These criteria would lead to a public recognition and acceptance of policing as a profession accompanied by status and prestige; policing thereby being granted legitimacy by the public (Niederhoffer, 1967:18–19).[24] As a profession, policing would then gain autonomy and regulatory control over its members.[25] Niederhoffer also expressed the view that police organizations were making an effort to improve the quality of personnel as well as the quality of their performance in order to meet the professional standards established by a consensus of experts.

In the present era, modern professional agencies have been faced with budgetary constraints as a result of the conservative economic climate of the 1980s. Agencies are beginning to lower their educational standards rather than raise them. This decision, of course, is strictly a political one rather than a reasoned approach to the problem. Nonetheless, improved professionalism through advanced educational requirements for patrol officers, who relate directly with and provide services to their clients, and for supervisory-management personnel, concerned with the needs and rights of their employees, could be deemed more cost effective in both the short and long terms. Such a requirement could mitigate the rising trend of civil rights violations suits filed and won against law enforcement agencies over the past decade.[26]

Further study in this area, however, would be needed in order to determine whether or not college-educated law enforcement officers are more cost effective in this area than their less professional, non-college-educated counterparts. At any rate, a review of the previous studies on professionalism and officer performance as well as the present study seem to suggest that they would be. The following section discusses some of the findings from earlier studies.

Summary of Previous Studies

The first comprehensive study evaluating the impact of college on students generally was published in 1969 as *The Impact of College On Students: An Analysis of Four Decades of Research.* This study, which evaluated approximately 1,500 empirical studies, had examined the effects of college on students and demonstrated that, in addition to college education increasing students' intellectual aptitudes and critical-thinking abilities, students were shown to become more open-minded during their college careers. As a result, students' authoritarian and prejudicial attitudes declined during this period and they became less dogmatic (see Sherman and the National Advisory Commission, 1978:44). A follow-up comprehensive study by Pascarella and Terenzini (1991), entitled *How College Affects Students,* essentially supported these initial results.

In a major study by Milton Rokeach, educational level of participants was found to be positively correlated with constructed values. The importance of *values* as constructs and as intervening variables between attitudes and performance was tested by Rokeach on a general sample of the population of more than 1,400 respondents. He found statistically significant differences between educational level and such terminal and instrumental values as self-respect, independent judgment, logical reasoning skills, and personal responsibility in that as educational level increased, the value of these *values* also increased (Rokeach, 1973).[27] These values' relation to higher education for officers or to officer performance in a law enforcement environment was not examined by Rokeach.

The 1967 President's Commission on Law Enforcement and Administration of Justice recommended college education requirements for police officers based on the subjective belief that the benefits derived from higher education generally would positively affect the attitudes and performance of law enforcement personnel. The commission's *Task Force Report,* however, offered no empirical research evidence establishing that higher education did, in fact, have a positive measurable impact on officer attitudes or performance. Subsequent to these recommendations, academic scholars have used various methods to measure officer attitudes (including the construct of professionalism) as well as various types of performance indicators in order to determine what, if any, impact higher education has on officers' views of their police role and performance.

A series of studies, beginning in 1967, concerning the relationship between college education and various indicators of officer attitudes and performance are decidedly mixed in their findings. Seven of those studies reviewed for the present research disclose that higher education may have a negative influence on attitudes, attrition rates, and field performance evaluations of officers. Sixteen studies indicate that college education has no impact on attitudes (including professionalism) nor on the performance and effectiveness of police officers in the eyes of the public. Thirty-one studies reveal that education has at least some level of positive effect on the attitudes, training success, and performance measures of law enforcement personnel. A composite summary of these studies is shown in table 1.

TABLE 1

PERFORMANCE / ATTITUDINAL DIFFERENCES OF LAW ENFORCEMENT OFFICERS AS A RESULT OF EDUCATION

College Education as a Negative Influence

Niederhoffer, 1967	Patrol officers more cynical
Regoli, 1976b, 1977	Patrol officers more cynical in small agencies
Trojanowicz and Nicholson, 1976	Attrition higher
Milton et al., 1977	More involvement in violent incidents
Weirman, 1978	Higher attrition
Hooper, 1988 (L.A.P.D.)	Lower field performance evaluations
Shernock, 1992	Less respect for citizens

No Difference

Kelly and O'Rourke, 1973	Attitudes toward police–community relations
Smith and Ostrom, 1974	Attitudes re: civil liberties
	Effectiveness of police in eyes of public
Rafky, 1975	Cynicism scores
Regoli, 1976b, 1977	Cynicism scores for patrol officers in large agencies
Wilt and Bannon 1976	Cynicism scores
Miller and Fry, 1976–78	Endorsement of the professional model
Cascio and Real, 1976	Supervisory ratings
Maddell and Washburn, 1978	Overall performance
Wycoff and Susmilch, 1979	Four attitude scales
Sherman and Blumberg, 1981	Discharge of firearms
Murrell, 1982	Discharge of firearms
	Suspensions
Burwell, 1983	Authoritarianism
Jones, 1984	Authoritarianism
Dorsey & Giacopassi, 1986	Cynicism for males
	Cynicism for females
Hooper, 1988 (L.A.P.D.)	Overall performance
Worden, 1990	Citizen evaluations
Shernock, 1992	Commitment to service ideal
	Self-regulation
	Suspicion of outside world
	Exercise of discretion
	Effectiveness and efficiency
	Obedience to superior officer

College Education as a Positive Influence

Niederhoffer, 1967	Lower cynicism scores for superior officers
Smith et al., 1967, 1970	Less authoritarian
Geary, 1970	Lower attrition
	Fewer disciplinary problems

	Less derision by youths More pride by local citizens
Saunders, 1970	Higher performance ratings
Cohen and Chaiken, 1972	Fewer total complaints Fewer citizen complaints Fewer sustained complaints Fewer disciplinary actions Fewer sick days Fewer disapprovals for injury time Fewer allegations of harassment More promotions
Guller, 1972	Lower dogmatism Higher self-esteem Greater flexibility/adaptivity to environment
Bozza, 1973 (cited in Sherman and Blumberg, 1981)	More arrests
Gross, 1973	Higher academy training success
Dalley, 1975	Less authoritarian Less conservative Less rigid attitudes Less inclined to resolve incidents by arrests
Finkenauer, 1975	Fewer incidents of arrests in discretionary situations
Finnegan, 1976	Higher supervisory performance ratings More promotions
Parker et al., 1976	More open-minded
Weiner, 1976	More likely to accept minorities/approve of black protest
Cascio and Real, 1976	Higher intelligence and motivation scores
Cascio, 1977	Higher performance ratings Fewer injuries by assault/battery

	Fewer disciplinary actions Fewer preventable accidents Fewer absences Fewer complaints re: excessive force Fewer physical force violations Fewer verbal discourtesy violations
Sanderson, 1977 (L.A.P.D.)	Higher training academy success Lower absenteeism Lower attrition Fewer disciplinary problems Fewer sustained complaints
Barry, 1978	Greater perception to perform law enforcement duties well
Roberg, 1978	Lower dogmatism Higher overall performance
Smith, 1978	More favorably disposed to the U. S. Supreme Court
Weirman, 1978	Higher on overall academic ability Higher overall performance (ADI) Lower number of dept. dismissals
Geary, 1979	Patrol performance—higher
Plummer, 1979	Higher training academy success
Wycoff and Susmilch, 1979	Higher administrative measures
Ledoux, 1980	More open-minded
Murrell, 1982	Less sick leave More awards/commendations Fewer reprimands Higher promotional test scores Higher felony arrests Higher felony arrest filing rate Higher performance evaluations
Lester, 1983	Higher training academy success
Copley, 1987	Higher training academy success Higher supervisor evaluations

Hooper, 1988 (L.A.P.D.)	Higher report completion proficiency
	Higher training academy success
	Fewer complaints
	Less sick leave
Carter and Sapp, 1990	Better decision makers
	Flexibility in problem solving
	Greater empathy toward minorities
	Less authoritarian
	Less cynical
Worden, 1990	Less negative attitudes toward legal restrictions
	More discretion-control-oriented
	Less inclined toward rigid enforcement of the law
Shernock, 1992	Less support for insularity
	Higher value for ethical conduct

Negative Relationship between Education and Indicators

Arthur Niederhoffer's comprehensive study of cynicism within one urban law enforcement agency is considered the ground-breaking study examining the relationship between higher education and other independent factors and the problem of police officer cynicism. The problem of cynicism, Niederhoffer believed, was pervasive in the policing occupation.[28]

In order to examine the relationship between education and cynicism, measured by a twenty-item cumulative cynicism index, Niederhoffer dichotomized the higher education variable into two categories: officers with less than two years of college education and officers with two years of college or greater. Comparing the mean score of 69.3 of the more highly educated group of patrol officers with an overall mean score of 62.2, Niederhoffer found through a bivariate analysis that the educated officers' scores were significantly higher. Another notable difference on scores in his study was that both foot patrolmen and Jewish patrolmen scored significantly higher than the overall mean score, with scores of 66.4 and 71.9, respectively (Niederhoffer, 1967:234). Additionally, he found that for superior officers, as opposed to patrol officers, the higher the educational level of the officer the lower the mean cynicism score.

Niederhoffer's examination of the relationships between certain types of independent variables and his dependent variable of cynicism did not simultaneously control for any interactive effects. In fact, the relationship between his dichotomized variable of education and cynicism may be spurious since Jewish ethnicity was determined to be significantly related to a higher cynicism score. Since being Jewish as well as being on foot patrol were variables that significantly affected the mean cynicism scores, these variables would need to be controlled for when determining the absolute effects of education on cynicism.[29]

Rafky (1975), Wilt and Bannon (1976), and Regoli (1976b, 1977) attempted to replicate Niederhoffer's findings on cynicism but did not arrive at the same results. Findings from Rafky's 1975 study refute Niederhoffer's results on the relationship between educational level and cynicism. Using a smallest space analysis (which is analogous to factor analysis) for a sample of respondents from a different Northeastern city, Rafky found a mean cynicism score of 2.51 in contrast to Niederhoffer's grand mean of 3.23. He concluded that, contrary to Niederhoffer's findings, cynicism was not endemic among police officers within the lower ranks (Rafky, 1975). The results of his study also contradict other of Niederhoffer's findings, such as Rafky's finding that officers scoring highest on the cynicism scale were high school graduates.

Wilt and Bannon's study of a sample of police officers within the Detroit Police Department also contradicted Niederhoffer's original findings. Rather than dichotomizing the educational variable into two levels as Niederhoffer had, Wilt and Bannon separated the level of education into a five-level ordinal variable. Their results, in contrast to Niederhoffer's New York findings, showed no pattern of relationship between education and cynicism. The overall mean cynicism score for the department was 60.94 (compared to 62.2 for Niederhoffer) and these researchers concluded that, at least within the Detroit

Police Department, "rampant cynicism" was not characteristic of the department (Wilt and Bannon, 1976).

Regoli's study on cynicism scores for officers in various large and small law enforcement agencies was also unable to confirm some of Niederhoffer's initial findings. Regoli also dichotomized the level of education variable into officers with less than two years and those with two or more years of college education and found that level of education was not related to scores on the composite cynicism scale. However, when controlling for size of the agency, he found that for his small agency sample the relationship between level of education and overall cynicism score was a positive one. For his large agency sample, there was no statistically significant relationship between level of education and the overall cynicism score. Regoli concluded that the relationship between level of education and cynicism score, at least for his sample of large departments, was inconclusive (Regoli, 1977:96).[30]

A more recent study by Dorsey and Giacopassi (1986) utilizes Niederhoffer's original unidimensional scale in order to test for differences between male and female officers, controlling for factors such as length of service, rank, and level of education. Employing one-way and two-way analyses of variance on the total scores as well as *t*-tests of differences between sample means of male and female respondents, they found significant differences in scores when testing for rank as well as for gender. Although this study found no differences in the relationship between level of education and cynicism, a two-way analysis of variance revealed significant interaction effects between both sex and education. Male officers with a higher level of education achieved a mean cynicism score of 58.4, and those without higher education achieved a score of 60.3. Female officers with a higher level of education, in contrast, attained a mean cynicism score of 62.7, whereas those with no higher education received a mean score of 60.1.

Studies by both Trojanowicz and Nicholson (1976) and Weirman (1978) show that the attrition rate for the more highly educated officers is significantly higher than for their less-educated counterparts. Trojanowicz and Nicholson attribute this difference to the lack of promotional rewards within the department as well as the failure of the police organization to recognize the talents of the college-educated officer (Trojanowicz and Nicholson, 1976). Although Weirman found that college-educated officers were more likely to voluntarily leave the department more frequently than non-college-educated officers, these officers were less likely to be dismissed by the department for cause than the less-educated officer (Weirman, 1978:36).

The results of these three studies contrast with the results of two studies of police departments in California by Geary (1970) and Sanderson (1977). Geary, while reshaping the Ventura Police Department in the 1960s to require a bachelor's degree, found that the attrition rate for officers with a degree was lower than for those without a degree. Sanderson's study of 150 L.A.P.D. officers who had graduated from the training academy in 1965 found that 95 percent of those officers who had resigned from the department by 1975 had received no college education (Sanderson, 1977:62–63).

In a 1977 study for the Police Commission on the use of deadly force, Milton et al. found that police officers with a higher level of education were likely to have been involved in more violent incidents than the department as a whole.[31] However, more recent studies conducted at the beginning of the 1980s by Sherman and Blumberg (1981) and Murrell (1982) indicate that the use of deadly force or the use of firearms was not related to an officer's level of education; that is, no differences were found based on the police officer's level of education. Although level of education was not related to discharge of firearms in Murrell's study of officers working in Southeastern police departments, college education was found to be a significant factor in superior work performance on eight independent measures.

Hooper's (1988) study on the relationship between level of education and police officer performance for L.A.P.D. officers found that college-educated officers received significantly lower field performance evaluations during their probationary period than the high school–educated officers. They also received fewer departmental commendations. A multiple regression analysis revealed, however, that I.Q. rather than educational level emerged as a statistically significant predictor variable in those areas in which performance differences were found. Multiple regression analysis also disclosed that level of education had no impact on commendations and explained only 3.2 percent of the variance of field performance evaluations.[32]

Finally, a recent study by Shernock tested for differences in relationships between higher levels of education and attitudinal attributes of professionalism identified in the literature on police professionalism. Shernock found a significant difference on only one of five dimensions: more highly educated officers scored lower than their less-educated counterparts on "respect for citizens" (Shernock, 1992). However, a partial correlational analysis revealed that when both age and work experience were controlled for, the original relationship between level of education and the mean level of professionalism on this dimension was no longer significant. Essentially, Shernock found that younger, less-experienced officers were more educated but less respectful of the public (Shernock, 1992:84–85).

Educational Levels Resulting in No Differences

A study by Kelly and O'Rourke (1973) assessed the attitudes and beliefs of 200 nonvoluntary participants at a police training institute. Using analysis of variance, they found that there were no differences in the mean scores regardless of the educational level of the officers. Overall, however, they found an extremely high degree of positive attitudes toward police–community relations among all the officers.

Smith and Ostrom's 1974 attitudinal study of both officers and citizen attitudes toward those officers found a weak but statistically significant relationship between level of education and officer attitudes toward civil liberties. They found that more highly educated officers were less critical of Supreme Court decisions and more tolerant of public protest and dissent. More highly educated officers were also found to be less willing to accept innovation in the structure of their departments as well as to have a lower estimation of the need for the use of force in solving crime problems. An examination of citizen perceptions regarding officer performance in departments whose officers had achieved higher levels of education showed that, overall, citizen beliefs in more professional services by officers were negligible (Smith and Ostrom, 1974:58–67).

One law enforcement study, using the original Hall/Snizek revised professionalism scale (Snizek, 1972)[33] identified five subscales or dimensions concerning work-related issues through a factor analysis of the Likert-type items of this scale. Overall, Miller and Fry found no differences when examining the relationship between an officer's educational level and whether or not he or she expressed endorsement for the professional model (Miller and Fry, 1976, 1978). They did find, however, a relationship between the number of law enforcement–related college units the officer respondents had completed and their orientation toward and dedication to public service. These researchers suggested that although results from the five subscales may portray what the collective self-image of law enforcement may be like, it provided little indication as to what professionalized law enforcement actually is like on the behavioral level. Their suggestions support Price's view that professional rhetoric and professional action are not synonymous but are discrete yet necessary components to law enforcement professionalization (Price, 1977).

A study of 940 Dade County, Florida, police officers sponsored by the Police Foundation (Cascio and Real, 1976; Cascio, 1977) reveals that more highly educated officers were not evaluated any higher by their supervisors than their less-educated counterparts on a behaviorally anchored rating scale. This scale includes dimensions of job knowledge, judgment, initiative, dependability, attitudes, relations with others, and communication abilities.[34] However, overall rated performance was found to be related to level of education. This study found weak yet statistically significant inverse correlations between officers' level of education and injuries by assault and battery, disciplinary actions from accidents, preventable accidents, sick time used per year, and physical force violations (Cascio and Real, 1976: 55; Cascio, 1977:90). The reason for fewer injuries due to assaults was explained as being related to an individual's superior ability to analyze and diagnose situations, resulting in an officer not having to resort to the use of force. Fewer verbal discourtesy allegations were attributed to the officer's ability to speak clearly and articulately. As a result of the study, the authors concluded that

> With the complexity of our social setting placing an increasing demand on the police officer, he is expected to assume many roles. The broad intellectual base, along with the diagnostic and logical skills that an individual tends to develop through college course work, could be decisive in his ability to handle the dynamics and complexities inherent in the job of a contemporary professional law enforcement officer. (Cascio and Real, 1976:55)

Cascio and Real's study also showed that among college graduates, the area or discipline of college study had no discernible overall effect on the individual's rated performance or the individual's objective performance. Maddell and Washburn's (1978) study addressed this same issue as to whether the type of degree had an effect on performance. Their study also found that the type of degree received by an officer had no effect on overall officer performance (Maddell and Washburn, 1978:40–42). This same finding was also made by Hooper (1988) in a more recent study of L.A.P.D. officers.[35] Although an earlier study of Baltimore police officers by Finnegan (1976) also arrived at the same findings, Finnegan had determined that when criminal justice degree holders were excluded from the analysis, officers schooled in the social sciences tended to perform better in ratings than the other disciplines.

Evaluation of a 1973–76 Police Foundation project survey for the Dallas police department by Wycoff and Susmilch (1979) found no differences in attitudinal measures regardless of the officer's level of educational attainment. These attitude scales consisted of four dimensions: proper officer demeanor, community service orientation, administrative tolerance, and crime fighting orientation. However, these researchers did find differences in several administrative measures in that supervisory ratings were higher for more highly educated officers, and the number of sick days was lower for the more highly educated group. They also found no difference in the administrative measures of auto accidents and total number of complaints (Wycoff and Susmilch, 1979:19–22).

A 1984 study of 481 Alabama State Troopers found no differences in authoritarian attitudes between college-educated troopers and non-college-educated troopers. This study essentially determined that the higher level of education of officers did not significantly alter their scores on Rokeach's scale instruments for authoritarianism (Jones, 1984). Earlier studies on the relationship between level of education and authoritarian attitudes had opposite findings. For example, a 1967 study by Smith, Locke, and Walker found that non-college-educated officers were more authoritarian than college-educated officers. They also found that older college-educated officers were more authoritarian than the younger, less college-educated officers; however, these older officers were still found to be less authoritarian than the non-college-educated officers (Smith, Locke, and Walker, 1967). A follow-up study by Smith, Locke, and Fenster found that police officers with a bachelor's degree were significantly less authoritarian than non-college-educated officers (Smith, Locke, and Fenster, 1970).

A 1975 study of the Royal Canadian Mounted Police examined, among other factors, the differences in authoritarianism between college graduates and non-college graduates. This study focused on the contention that the university-graduated officer was in some ways superior to the non-graduate, and that this was due to a different working personality between the two groups of officers. In contrast to the previous study, Dalley found that college-graduated officers were less authoritarian in addition to being less conservative and holding less rigid attitudes. Also, officers who had completed a college education were found to be less inclined to resolve incidents by arrests than were officers who were not college graduates (Dalley, 1975). Dalley concluded that the traditional working personality of the police officer is effectively hindered by a university education and that a college education acts as an inhibitor in the development of authoritarian, conservative, and rigid attitudes (Dalley, 1975:468).

A review of studies by Carter and Sapp indicates that while the evidence has not been conclusive, college education experience has a desirable effect on police officers. They found, in contrast to some of the studies discussed above, that college-educated officers were both less authoritarian and less cynical than non-college-educated officers (Carter and Sapp, 1990:62–63). Additionally, their 1988 research shows that more highly educated patrol officers were found to be more responsive to the public, were better decision makers, were more flexible and innovative in their ability to solve problems, showed a heightened level of empathy toward minorities and the disenfranchised, were more goal oriented, and overall were more "professional."

Hooper's study of the L.A.P.D. discussed earlier, while finding individual differences on various performance indicators dependent on the level of education of the officer, assessed that the overall level of performance did not differ despite educational differences of the officers. His specific findings were that college graduates were found to perform the highest in the training academy as well as being rated highest in report completion proficiency. The two-year college group was found to have the lowest incidence of complaints as well as to use the least amount of sick time (Hooper, 1988:94). Hooper's study concluded that there were "no appreciable differences across educational levels in the performance of police duties" (Hooper, 1988:114).

A recent study by Worden (1990), using both a cross-tabulation analysis and a regression analysis, found that citizen evaluations of officer performance were not related to the higher educational level of officers within the department. Although citizens who had been involved in interpersonal conflicts and similar incidents requiring the intervention of a police officer expressed a somewhat higher satisfaction with police officers holding bachelor's degrees, this difference was found to be statistically insignificant. Worden concludes, nonetheless, that citizens are somewhat more likely to be dissatisfied with decision-making and problem-solving skills of the less highly educated officers (Worden, 1990:586–88).

A more recent study by Shernock, discussed earlier, found that scores on several "professional" dimensions did not vary, regardless of the officers' educational levels. These dimensions include measure of commitment to the service ideal, self-regulation, suspicion of the outside world, exercise of discretion, efficiency of work, and obedience to superior officers (Shernock, 1992). Important controls such as psychological disposition, motivation, I.Q., and academic status were not used in the analysis since these data were not available (Shernock, 1992:83, n. 12).

Positive Relationship between Education and Indicators

As discussed previously, an early study by Niederhoffer (1967) found superior officers, supervisory officers including sergeants and lieutenants, with a higher level of education to be less cynical than superior officers with a lower level of education (Niederhoffer, 1967:185–88, 234). Smith et al. (1967, 1970) found police officer students with a higher level of college education to be less authoritarian than those with a lower level of education. Geary's (1970) study found police officers with a bachelor's degree as having a lower attrition rate and fewer disciplinary problems, as receiving more respect from the youths from the communities they served, and as being held in higher esteem by local citizens.

In a 1970 study for the Brookings Institute, Saunders reported that a sample of officers in Flint, Michigan, with at least sixty hours of college education received higher performance ratings for a six-month period than those officers who had no college education. The mean performance for the more highly educated group was 85.22 compared to a mean performance score of 76.35 for the lesser-educated officers.[36] Higher performance ratings for more highly educated officers were also found in studies by Finnegan (1976), Cascio and Real (1976), Cascio (1977), Weirman (1978), Roberg (1978), Wycoff and Susmilch (1979), Geary (1979), and Murrell (1982).

Finnegan's study of police officers in the Baltimore Police department included 113 police agents with a college degree and one year of street duty experience.[37] His comparison group consisted of 97 police officers with a high school education only and who had completed the required academy training. When comparing twenty-three traits from the performance evaluation instrument through a Mann Whitney U test analysis, Finnegan found that the supervisory performance ratings were positively correlated with a higher level of education. Finnegan concluded that college-educated police agents outperformed high school–educated officers in every evaluated item of the Baltimore Police Department performance rating instrument. Additionally, Finnegan found that data indicated that police agents with college degrees were found to receive promotions at a significantly higher rate than police officers with a high school education. The attrition rate also seemed to be lower for more highly educated officers, but this observation was not based on statistical analysis. However, more highly educated officers who did resign, did so in order to transfer to other law enforcement agencies or to return to college (Finnegan, 1976:62).

Cascio and Real's (1976) and Cascio's (1977) study of Dade County Police found not only higher performance for more highly educated officers but also found through path analysis and multiple regression procedures that officers with higher levels of education tended to have higher intelligence and higher motivation scores. The correlation between intelligence and education was found to be .37, between motivation and education .35, and between performance and education .27. Overall, a multiple regression model showed the joint contribution of these three variables on the dependent variable of officer performance was .30 (Cascio, 1977:93–95). Additionally, although the correlations were low, more highly educated officers were found to have fewer injuries by assault and battery, fewer disciplinary actions, fewer preventable accidents, fewer absences due to illness, fewer citizen complaints, fewer physical force violations, and fewer verbal discourtesy violations than officers with a lower level of education (Cascio and Real, 1976:55; Cascio, 1977:90).

Weirman's study of approximately 400 Michigan State Troopers found that more highly educated troopers scored higher on a performance rating instrument known as the Achievement Development Inventory, a forced choice personnel evaluation system that included subscales on job involvement, interpersonal relations with peers, interpersonal relations with the public, and clerical skills. In this study, Weirman also found that no differences on these ratings were found to exist between officers from different academic disciplines. A second important finding in this study was that more highly educated officers received higher grade point averages from overall examinations administered during recruit school (Weirman, 1978:35).

Roberg's (1978) study found a relationship between level of education and officer performance using the International Chiefs of Police twenty-three factor index. Roberg examined three hypotheses using zero, first, and second order correlation coefficients. This study also controlled for various factors, including that of academic status: whether an officer was a preservice student (college education acquired prior to entering the department), an in-service student (college education acquired after entering the department), or a continuing student (college education initiated prior to entering the department and continued after an officer's employment with the department).

Roberg examined the relationship between the educational level of the officer and the officer's level of dogmatism and found it to be negatively correlated at -.28.[38] Second, Roberg tested the relationship between level of dogmatism and officer performance and also found it to be negatively correlated at -.26. Third, Roberg found the relationship between level of education and performance to be positively correlated at .17. None of the control variables, including academic status, seriously affected the original relationships. Roberg concluded that level of education influenced an officer's open-mindedness and flexibility, which in turn affected an officer's overall performance as measured by the IACP performance index.[39]

Wycoff and Susmilch's 1979 study, discussed earlier, found a small but statistically significant relationship between an officer's level of education and supervisory rating. In addition, these researchers found that a negative relationship existed between an officer's level of education and the average number of sick days taken by the officer (Wycoff and Susmilch, 1979:29).

Geary's more recent doctoral dissertation (1979) examining the relationship between performance and level of education for officers within two large urban police departments also used the

IACP performance evaluation instrument. Using an analysis of variance technique, Geary tested seven hypotheses and found statistically significant differences in performance between high school graduate officers and two groups of college-educated officers as rated on the IACP instrument. Additionally, he also found no performance differences between Criminal Justice degree holders and degree holders from other disciplines (Geary, 1979:62).

In addition to differences in overall performance evaluations, Murrell's doctoral dissertation study also found significant performance differences between more highly educated officers and seven performance factors. Using a multiple regression technique, Murrell found that more highly educated officers achieved more superior work performance records for less sick leave, more departmental awards and commendations, fewer departmental reprimands, higher promotional test scores, more felony arrests, higher felony arrest filing rates, and a greater number of misdemeanor arrests (Murrell, 1982). As pointed out previously, he did not find any differences on discharge of firearms.

The U.S. Supreme Court has acknowledged the validity of results of studies that find a positive relationship between training academy performance and level of education.[40] Six studies examining the relationship between level of education and level of academy success (graduation from the training academy) found that a positive relationship exists between these two variables. Those studies finding a statistically significant positive relationship include Gross (1973), Sanderson (1977), Plummer (1979), Lester (1983), Copley (1987), and Hooper (1988). Both Sanderson's and Hooper's studies involved police officers at the L.A.P.D. training academy. No studies examining this relationship have reported negative findings.

In addition to a higher level of training academy success, Sanderson's L.A.P.D. study also found that higher levels of education for his sample of police officers resulted in lower absenteeism, a lower rate of attrition, fewer disciplinary problems, fewer sustained complaints, and more promotions. Hooper's L.A.P.D. study also found that a higher level of education resulted in higher report completion proficiency, fewer citizen complaints, and less sick leave.

In one of the earliest studies on the relationship between level of education and officer performance, Cohen and Chaiken (1972) found that for their sample of officers from the New York Police Department (N.Y.P.D.), level of education emerged as the most powerful predictor for several performance indicators. Using a multiple regression statistical analysis, Cohen and Chaiken found that inverse relationships existed for officers with some college (as opposed to no college education) and citizen complaints, which included allegations of abuse, discourtesy, ethnic slurs, and the unnecessary use of excessive force (Cohen and Chaiken, 1972:57–64). Education was inversely related to total number of complaints, total number of sustained complaints, total number of departmental charges, number of departmental disapprovals for injury time taken by an officer, and fewer sick leave days (Cohen and Chaiken, 1972:48, 64).

Cohen and Chaiken also found that officers with college education before joining the force were promoted faster than those officers who had not received college education before entering the department. Finally, of the total number of firearms removals as a result of improper usage, none of the officers involved included college graduates (Cohen and Chaiken, 1972:3, 65). Cohen and Chaiken concluded that officers at the N.Y.P.D. with at least one year of college education were superior performers compared to those without any college education; those with college degrees achieved even greater on-the-job performance than the other officers.[41]

Two other performance-related studies disclosed that more highly educated police officers engaged in more arrests overall in one study,[42] but they also engaged in fewer incidents of arrest in discretionary situations in another study (Finkenauer, 1975).

In studies examining the relationship between officers' psychological attitudes and level of education, Guller (1972), Parker et al. (1976), and Ledoux (1980) found more highly educated officers to be more open-minded than their less-educated counterparts. Guller also found more highly educated officers to have a greater sense of self-esteem, as well as a greater flexibility and adaptivity to the working environment. Dalley (1975) also found more highly educated officers to possess a more open belief system in that they were found to be less authoritarian, less conservative, and held less-rigid attitudes than their less-educated officer peers.

A longitudinal attitudinal study by Weiner (1976) found that the achievement of a higher level of education for a sample of in-service police officers from one city police department did not affect their attitudes overall. However, Weiner did find that the more education the police officer received, the more he was willing to accept blacks, Puerto Ricans, and Italians. Additionally, more highly educated officers were more approving of protests by blacks and expressed an understanding of black demands (Weiner, 1976:453).

Barry's (1978) study of criminal justice students and agency representatives found that the majority of respondents perceived the students' education as having positively influenced their abilities to perform their law enforcement jobs; they attributed better job performance to course work taken in college (Barry, 1978:354). Smith's (1978) study found that the more professional and highly educated the officer, the more favorably disposed he or she was found to be toward the U.S. Supreme Court.

As discussed earlier, a study by Carter and Sapp (1990) has shown that more highly educated police officers generally develop the following qualities: (1) achieve a broader base of information for decision making; (2) appreciate constitutional rights, values, and the democratic form of government; (3) are more creative and flexible in handling difficult or ambiguous situations; (4) have a fuller understanding of and appreciation for the roles of prosecutors, courts, and corrections; (5) develop a greater empathy for minorities and their discriminatory experiences; (6) respond to the service needs of the community with more civility; (7) are better able to perform policing tasks with little or no supervision; (8) develop better community relations skills; (9) are more stable and reliable employees; (10) are less authoritarian and less cynical in respect to the milieu of policing; and (11) are readily able to adapt to organizational changes (Carter and Sapp, 1990:62–63).

Worden's 1990 study not only finds several attitudinal differences dependent on the officer's level of education, but also finds differences between officers who receive a preservice college education as opposed to an in-service education. For academic status, those officers receiving degrees as in-service students were found to perceive their police roles more narrowly than those officers who received their degrees as preservice students. For differences in educational-level attainment, officers with degrees were found to have more positive attitudes toward legal restrictions than those without a degree. Officers with a degree expressed a greater preference for autonomy and were found to be "discretion-control-oriented" in carrying out their role, as opposed to being "command-control-oriented."[43] Additionally, officers with a college degree were less inclined toward rigid enforcement of the law; their attitudes inclined them to greater flexibility in applying the law (Worden, 1990:581–84).

Positive findings in Shernock's recent 1992 study on police officer professionalism indicate that more highly educated officers express less support for the insularity of the police than do their less-educated peers. Shernock also found that more highly educated police officers placed a higher value on the importance of ethical conduct generally (Shernock, 1992:84–86). In fact, Shernock found that the value of ethical conduct was enhanced by an officer's increasing exposure to a college education rather than actually receiving a bachelor's degree per se. When applied specifically to the misconduct of fellow officers, however, higher education did not affect ethical attitudes toward their colleagues. This seeming contradiction is attributed to an officer's competing demands between high ethical standards toward citizens and the upholding of personal commitments to fellow officers (Shernock, 1992:86).

Summary

An examination of the previous studies strongly suggests that there is ample evidence that college education positively affects various attitudinal and performance indicators of law enforcement officers. The majority of these studies support recommendations by the President's Commission on Law Enforcement and the Administration of Justice made in 1967 that college education should be required for police officers. The commission stated that

> The quality of the service will not significantly improve until higher educational requirements are established for its personnel. . . . Cities and counties which fail to recognize the vital necessity of upgrading the educational levels of their departments are . . . guilty of perpetuating ineffective police service and are not providing their citizens with adequate police service and protection. (President's Commission, 1967b:126)

NOTES

1. For an interesting account of police involvement in organized crime in Chicago and attempts by the Illinois Association for Criminal Justice to bring about reform, see Landesco, *Organized Crime in Chicago* (1968).

2. Vollmer's classical view of professionalism is acknowledged as the dominant view at that time by Price (1977:15), i.e., a view emphasizing an individual mastery and application of skills; Walker (1977:33), i.e., professional status consisting not only of managerial efficiency but also a crime prevention and social work role in which professionalized policing would change society by preventing crime; and Sykes (1989:287), i.e., a view emphasizing preprofessional classic education in the liberal arts and social sciences, scientific theory, and crime prevention in addition to professional training.

3. Greene (1989:353) and Walker (1977:170) point out however, that black activists found that this form of "professionalism," i.e., a preoccupation with "expertise" and "nonpartisanship," was essentially both rhetoric and a technique to hamper the legitimate claims of disenfranchised minority groups.

4. Upon the advisement of George O'Connor, International Association of Chiefs of Police, the President's Commission recommended that improvement in police performance could be achieved

by exposing police officers to higher education and training. The President's Commission recommended a baccalaureate degree for all personnel with enforcement powers (President's Commission, 1967b:216, 653–655).

5. A recent study by Carter and Sapp (1990:59–85) shows that only 14 percent of law enforcement agencies nationwide require education beyond that of a high school diploma. The Bureau of Justice Statistics (U.S. Department of Justice, 1992:5) has reported that by 1990, only approximately 6 percent of law enforcement agencies nationwide required at least some college education.

6. See Price (1977:20) for models.

7. This model is at variance with a model of professional work in which officer autonomy is derived from personal competence (Smith and Ostrom, 1974:76, n. 2). However, as Niederhoffer discusses the problem, the principles of the classical view of professionalism create an atmosphere in which only the professionally oriented officer can operate successfully. The majority of police officers at this low end of the hierarchy are tough-minded, authoritarian types who exalt the use of power and force and are contemptuous of the professionals (Niederhoffer, 1967:131).

8. As Price (1977:10) points out, one of the central issues of professionalism for police officers is the issue of officer discretion. The formalist model with its limitations on discretion is a barrier to police professionalism in that its decisions are made strictly according to rules and regulations. This contrasts with the expertise model or one-to-one medical model of professionalism in which autonomy, an internalized code of ethics, and professional knowledge influence ultimate decision making.

9. This typology of bureaucracies is somewhat comparable to those types of agencies examined by Wilson (1968) who distinguishes between the watchman, service, and legalistic style agencies. Wilson's typology and police officer styles resulting from them are discussed in chapter 4.

10. In addition to the development of a hierarchical military-type organization as well as an ambivalence toward higher education, two other conditions include the amount of political control or influence and organizational policies inhibiting the autonomy of the individual officers (Rudoni, Baker, and Meyer, 1978:454–60).

11. Nonetheless, as Woods points out, Chief Parker, as a veteran of one of the worst periods in American police history, was both aware of and deplored excesses of indifference, dishonesty, and brutality that

characterized a significant number of the old-time police officers. "He understood that much of the blame for public aversion to policemen rested on the officers themselves" (Woods, 1973:480).

12. According to Goldstein (1979:258), addressing the quality of the police product is the most effective way of achieving the original objectives or goals of police reform.

13. For a discussion of the development and quality of this body of knowledge, see Sherman and National Advisory Commission (1978) as well as Ward, Webb, and the Joint Commission on Criminology and Criminal Justice Education and Standards (1984).

14. It is only when this individualistic, subject-area expertise and certification has been acquired that legal autonomy to exercise discretionary judgment and authorized self-regulation based on a universally defined and maintained code of ethics can be legitimately granted by the public (Steinman, 1986:187–88).

15. As Menke, White, and Carey point out, the most important part of socialization in which the inculcation of basic social values occurs for most professions is during a lengthy period of higher education that individuals undertake (Menke, White, and Carey, 1982:86).

16. Citing the 1989 study of K. Feldman and T. Newcomb entitled *The Impact of College on Students.*

17. Although Sherman and the National Advisory Commission (1978) are critical of community colleges generally and their vocationally oriented emphasis as inadequate preprofessional preparation for police officers, a study by Leavitt (1989) finds that community colleges in California currently provide broad-based general education courses integrated into the criminal justice curriculum. Leavitt argues that such an approach enhances the student's awareness of historical, philosophical, psychological, and sociological influences which cannot be underestimated in importance in preparing criminal justice students for careers in law enforcement.

18. In fact, Skolnick (1966:94) points out that by rejecting a variety of Supreme Court decisions protecting the rights of individual citizens, the police community undermines its own professional status.

19. See Carter and Sapp (1990) on police executive views toward professionalism of officers and the need for higher education requirements. For a contrast to this view, Crank (1987) finds that more professional chiefs are as likely to reject the criterion of professionalization as they are to support it.

20. A similar profile is compiled by Trojanowicz and Nicholson (1976:58). They also provide a profile of the noneducated officer as viewing the law as fixed and inflexible; as preferring to follow a fixed schedule; as liking to take directions or preferring his or her supervisor to make the decisions; as being overly emotive and moving against an aggressor or counterattacking someone who is acting in a belligerent or aggressive manner; as being unimaginative or uncreative; and placing high value on conformity to directive leadership.

21. The empirical results of his study will be explored in the following section, Summary of Previous Studies.

22. Woods (1973:2) points out, however, that academicians trained in criminology, police science, and public administration deny that current practices constitute professional training. They urge that college education, including advanced degrees for ranking officers, be a mandatory professional requirement.

23. For Hahn (1971), one of the key characteristics necessary for a police officer's involvement in corruption is an officer's pervasive feelings of animosity toward the public. Such feelings have been identified by Niederhoffer (1967) as cynicism, which he saw as pervasive within the police culture. For Bittner (1974:40), not only are a large number of police officers contemptuous toward the people with whom they interact, but they also use force gratuitously coupled with prevalent vices in policing such as rudeness and bullying.

24. This model is better known as the sociological model of professionalism (e.g., Rudoni, Baker, and Meyer, 1978; Price, 1977:14). As Price (1977:92) points out, public recognition of the profession *must* occur before members can be considered as professionals.

25. The issue of police autonomy is perhaps the most controversial reform feared and criticized by the public at large. Ideally, professional autonomy accompanies monopoly status of the profession; members within the profession are responsible for maintaining entrance and performance standards, generating rules and regulations over its members, evaluating the performance of its members, and for generating the body of knowledge to be used by its members. In return for this power, professionals commit themselves to the service ideal, their activities directed toward the interests of the general public and not toward their own self-gain (Walker, 1977:ix–x). But as Smith and Ostrom point out, the dependence of the policing occupation on the public for its legitimacy as a profession implies the need for public evaluation and public sanction, a contradiction of one of the requirements for police autonomy (Smith and Ostrom, 1974:50).

26. A recent study by the University of Southern California found that cases under 42 U.S. Code, sec. 1983, involving constitutional law violations, which were granted financial awards, were decided against criminal justice agencies in approximately 29 percent of all cases filed and against individuals in 12 percent of them. Among its recommendations, an increased level of higher education and training, including education in the basic knowledge of public law was stressed (Bantz, 1988).

27. The issue of values as intervening variables between attitudes and performance is more fully discussed in chapter 4.

28. The concept and philosophy of cynicism are more fully discussed in chapter 4. Although Niederhoffer did not define cynicism per se, Regoli adopts the dictionary definition. Cynicism has been defined as (1) given to or affecting disbelief in commonly accepted human values and in man's sincerity of motive or rectitude of conduct; accepting selfishness as the governing factor in human conduct; (2) exhibiting feelings ranging from distrustfulness and doubt to contemptuous and mocking disbelief (Regoli, 1977:2).

29. In a separate essay on Jewish patrolmen, Niederhoffer explains that since their introduction into law enforcement after the Depression, Jewish officers have been highly educated and their verbal style in handling disputes and solving problems is not appreciated by the average patrol officer. Additionally, Jewish culture, while emphasizing the need for higher education, frowns upon policing as a career, Jewish parents desiring their sons to become medical doctors. Ironically, the colloquial expression of "cop son" in Yiddish signifies "a person who will never amount to anything." These cultural constraints combined with the achievement of a higher education may explain the higher mean cynicism scores for Jewish patrol officers as well as the higher means scores for the group of more highly educated patrol officers (Niederhoffer, 1985a).

30. A recent study by Anson, Mann, and Sherman (1986), while not testing for the effect of education, found that higher cynicism scores were related to higher supervisor performance evaluations. This finding is explained in relation to reference group theory, which holds that actors aspire to identify with the values and norms of the groups or subcultures in which they have the closest contact. Evaluation by like peers and supervisors are important in this respect (Anson, Mann, and Sherman, 1986:304). Small departments having a lower degree of professionalism or fewer more highly educated officers could help to explain the higher level of cynicism, expressed as frustration for the more highly educated officers in these departments. Nonetheless,

Anson, et al., also concluded that Niederhoffer's original scale was highly unreliable.

31. Milton, Halleck, Lardner, and Abrecht's 1977 study is cited in Sherman and Blumberg (1981:318).

32. Interestingly, Hooper points out that although the use of I.Q. scores is no longer permissible in the selection of officers, under his leadership Chief Parker had implemented a mandatory I.Q. score of 110 for new police recruits. Nonetheless, the mean I.Q. scores for Hooper's sample were 111.2 for high school graduates, 107.0 for A.A. degrees and 110.5 for bachelor degree holders (Hooper, 1988:94, 103–04).

33. One of the scales used in this present study is essentially a derivative of that scale used in a law enforcement related context, e.g., Regoli and Poole (1979).

34. However, as Cascio (1977) points out, the subjectivity of these ratings could be influenced by several factors such as propinquity, cooperative behavior by subordinates, and similarity of attitudes and values.

35. Hooper found no statistically significant differences between academic specialization among his educated officer sample and performance measures which included police academy scores, probationary officer evaluations, commendations, department incidents, sick time used and performance evaluations overall (Hooper, 1988: 114).

36. Letter from Chief James Rutherford, Flint, Michigan, 1968 (Saunders, 1970:88).

37. Police agents in Baltimore were members of a Police Agents Program, a program initiated by the Baltimore Police Department in 1969; these officers became eligible as agents only after serving a year on patrol (Finnegan, 1976:61).

38. Using the Rokeach dogmatism scale, dogmatism was defined as the "extent to which the person's belief system is open or closed" (Roberg, 1978:338).

39. Zelig (1980) has critiqued Roberg's analysis in that he argues that it is not the officer's college degree but his or her psychological flexibility that makes the difference in overall performance. Roberg's response is that his study has shown that whereas psychological flexibility does make a difference regarding officer performance, it is the officer's level of education that makes the difference in regard to psychological flexibility (Roberg, 1980).

40. The *Washington* v. *Davis* (1976) decision will be discussed in chapter 3.

41. But Cohen and Chaiken's overall results have been criticized by Goldstein (1977:291).

42. Study by Bozza (1973) cited in Sherman and Blumberg (1981:319–320).

43. These two groups are distinguished in that officers who are "discretion-control-oriented" determine desirable outcomes for events in which they engage, use latitude in engaging in these events, and follow these events to their conclusions. Those officers who are "command-control-oriented," in contrast, are primarily satisfied in adopting standards established by administrators, engaging in each event as a discrete intervention on their part, with minimal concern for the outcome of such events (Worden, 1990:576).

CHAPTER 3

Federal Court Decisions Concerning Validation of Higher Education as a Prerequisite to Employment as a Law Enforcement Officer

On November 21, 1991, President George Bush signed the new Civil Rights Bill (PL 102-166) into law, overturning eight Supreme Court rulings decided in the 1980s and one in 1991.[1] Although this new law shifts the burden of proof for employment selection criteria (such as objective tests or academic requirements as a "job-related business necessity") back to the employer, an open-ended provision of the law allows the courts, based on Supreme Court rulings prior to 1989, to decide or interpret "business necessity" standards.[2]

One of the main purposes of this chapter is to analyze the evolution of those federal court rulings interpreting the business necessity standard beginning with the Supreme Court decision in *Griggs* v. *Duke Power Co.* (1971). *Griggs* was the initial case deciding the constitutionality of academic requirements and standardized tests as a business necessity. The most recent U.S. Supreme Court case not overturned by the new civil rights legislation was decided in *Watson* v. *Fort Worth Bank and Trust* (1988), a case that accepted nationwide studies and reports, as well as expert testimony, as appropriate criteria for establishing a business necessity defense in Title VII disparate impact (nonintentional discrimination) challenges.[3]

To date, the Supreme Court has ruled on neither the constitutionality of a high school diploma nor college education requirements for law enforcement officers. However, the Supreme Court had ruled in 1971 that a high school diploma, as well as objective, standardized tests for industrial laborer positions must have "a manifest relationship to the employment in question."[4] Subsequent district and appellate court decisions have addressed educational requirements generally; have upheld high school diploma requirements for both police officers and corrections officers; and have upheld college requirements for specific positions, including that of law enforcement officers. However two district courts have failed to uphold a high school diploma requirement for fire fighters,[5] and the Eleventh Circuit Court of Appeals has failed to uphold a college degree requirement for professionals, such as scheduling, traffic, and systems analysts. (See discussion of individual decisions below.)

Legal History of Higher Educational Requirements

In 1971, the Supreme Court decided a case of nonintentional discrimination against minorities. The case at issue involved an employer who required applicants to pass an objective, standardized intelligence test as well as possess a high school diploma for certain industrial, manual positions. The Court in *Griggs* v. *Duke Power Co.* (1971) held that the Civil Rights Act of 1964 prohibited both overt, intentional discrimination as well as practices that were discriminatory in effect; that is, were "fair in form but discriminatory in operation" (*Griggs*, 1971:431). The Court then articulated the business necessity requirement in that even if an employment practice did not intentionally discriminate against blacks, if it were shown to discriminate in effect, the practice must be shown by the employer to be related to job performance in order to be upheld as constitutional.[6]

Through tracing the legislative history of the passage of the Civil Rights Act of 1964, the Court determined that the Equal Employment Opportunity Commission's requirement that employment testing be job related was consistent with congressional intent. However, although the Court stated that the facts of the case before it demonstrated "the infirmity of using diplomas or degrees as fixed measures of capability," (*Griggs*, 1971:433) it also noted that the provisions of Title VII of the Civil Rights Act of 1964 applied only to professionally developed ability tests and not to the high school diploma requirement (*Griggs*, 1971:433, n. 8).

Nonetheless, the job-relatedness of the educational requirements principle has been expressly recognized in cases following *Griggs*. If an agency or business is able to show that its educational requirement standards (although resulting in a disproportionately low employment or advancement rate of minorities) is necessary to the operation of its business, then such requirements are not in violation of Title VII of the Civil Rights Act.

In *Griggs*, the Court cautioned that congressional intent did not require that less-qualified minority candidates be given preference in employment over better-qualified candidates because of their minority status (*Griggs*, 1971:436).[7] Following *Griggs*, the Fourth Circuit Court of Appeals (in a challenge against age standards for police officers) ruled that the "claimed right to governmental employment is not per se a fundamental right" (*Arritt* v. *Grissell*, 1977:1272), and the First Circuit Court of Appeals held that each minority candidate does not have a constitutional right to employment as a police officer (*Castro* v. *Beecher*, 1972:735).

The Supreme Court seemed to have acknowledged the distinction between validated requirements for manual labor positions challenged in *Griggs* and those for public service positions challenged under the Fifth and Fourteenth Amendments' equal protection clause in *Washington* v. *Davis* (1976). In a challenge against a written employment test resulting in a disparate impact on black applicants, the Court upheld the test using a "rational relationship" standard pointing out that

> [I]t is untenable that the Constitution prevents the Government from seeking modestly to upgrade the communicative abilities of its employees rather than to be satisfied with some lower level of competence, particularly where the job requires special ability to communicate orally and in writing. (*Washington*, 1976:246)

The Court pointed out, however, that the rational basis for disparate impact challenges under the Constitution was inadequate for disparate impact challenges under Title VII of the Civil Rights Act, which required "a more probing judicial review of, and less deference to, the seemingly reasonable acts of administrators and executives. . . . " (*Washington*, 1976:247). In addition, the Court stated that such requirements must be validated in one of three ways (criterion, construct, and content validity) in relation to job performance, acknowledging that there was "no single method for appropriately validating employment tests for their relationship to job performance" (*Washington*, 1976:248, n. 13). In the case before it, however, the Court validated the verbal skills test due to its positive relationship to training course performance and not actual on-the-job performance of the police officer.

Arguing that its conclusion was not "foreclosed" by prior rulings, the *Washington* decision cited in a footnote the Civil Service Instructions on "Examining, Testing, Standards, and Employment Practices" in which effective job performance or success in training were only two of the "important job-related performance objectives identified by management."[8] In a concurring opinion, Justice Stewart agreed that this part of the majority decision was not inconsistent with prior holdings of the Court, stating that "as a matter of law, it is permissible for the police department to use a test for the purpose of predicting ability to master a training program even if the test does not otherwise predict ability to perform on the job" (*Washington*, 1976:257).

Educational Requirements Generally

As early as 1971, the New York district court, in an employment discrimination suit, had held that recommendations from national commissions should be given consideration when deciding the job-relatedness of educational requirements for public safety positions, such as fire fighters (*Vulcan Society of Westchester County, Inc.* v. *Fire Department of City of White Plains*, 1971:966–67). In 1973, a Texas district court had ruled that it was impermissible to impose educational requirements for any job unless such requirements were job related or constituted a bona fide business necessity (*Roman* v. *Reynolds Metal Co.*, 1973).[9] In 1976, a Mississippi district court was the first to acknowledge that educational qualifications served a compelling state interest and that such qualifications as recommended by the American Bar Association and the National Advisory Commission were vital to law enforcement officers in the discharge of their duties to protect life and property. The court also pointed out that states within the fifth circuit required at least a minimum of a high school degree, whereas the state of Texas required at least forty-five semester units of college (*Morrow* v. *Dillard,* 1976).

That same year the Virginia district court also acknowledged evidence that college-trained police officers made better police officers (*Ice et al.* v. *Arlington County et al.,* 1977). However, while acknowledging that educational qualifications were also evidence of superior abilities, the North Dakota district court in 1978 held that such qualifications were not proof of superior ability to perform in a given situation (*Eckroth* v. *Flasher Public School Dist. No. 39,* 1978). The Eighth Circuit Court of Appeals, however, in 1979 ruled that college degree requirements, despite disparate impact on minorities, were justified for public health employees for

> . . . tasks that are difficult and taxing and performance in a satisfactory manner requires maturity, "unshockability," persistence and tact, as well as an ability to communicate with others, frequently in a relatively sophisticated manner, and an ability to speak and write intelligibly and also where there was some risk to public health and safety in employment of unqualified representatives. (*Rice* v. *City of St. Louis,* 1979:797)

An Illinois district court had ruled in 1979 that for an employer to justify educational qualifications as a "business necessity" for public service workers, the employer must show that an ability to deliver services was improved as a result of formal education and that the "professionalism" required for such a position was linked with skills acquired through formal education (*Liberles* v. *Daniel,* 1979). The Fifth Circuit Court of Appeals in 1980 reiterated that educational requirements must meet the "business necessity" defense standards as well as be validated under EEOC guidelines on employee selection procedures (*Johnson* v. *Uncle Ben's, Inc.,* 1980).

Finally, in 1984, in a challenge against educational qualifications as not being reasonably related to requirements of a job as health code enforcer (thereby, not constituting a "legitimate" explanation for preferring another over plaintiff), the First Circuit Court of Appeals held that hiring a candidate with a superior education is a valid business practice. The court held that the lower court's finding that an "employer might reasonably regard applicant's *educational qualifications as indicating 'self-discipline and an ability to complete tasks and follow instructions'* was not clearly erroneous" (*White* v. *Vathally*, 1984:1040–41).

These cases have demonstrated that the courts have been more inclined to apply less-stringent standards to the relationship between the direct effects of educational standards and performance in public service and more professional positions than to other directly measurable objective employment criteria and performance in manual laborer positions. As one legal commentator has pointed out:

> When employment requirements bear a more tenuous relationship to ability to perform a job, the courts have been tolerant of such requirements when public safety depends to some extent on the quality of the defendant's employees, as with pilots or policemen. (Waintroob, 1979:118)

The following analysis of federal court cases will show that the courts have accepted both police officers and corrections officers as public service positions involving the public safety of citizens, and have upheld educational requirements for these positions. However, the courts have been reluctant to extend such rationale for fire fighter positions, thereby striking down educational requirements for them.

Cases Upholding High School Degree Requirements

As early as 1972, the First Circuit Court of Appeals upheld educational requirements for police officers in the Boston Police Department based upon the testimony of public reports, including that of the 1967 President's Commission on Law Enforcement and Administration of Justice's task force report on the police (President's Commission, 1967b). In *Castro* v. *Beecher* (1972) the court affirmed a district court decision that upheld a requirement that applicants for positions as Boston police officers must have obtained a high school diploma, a high school diploma equivalency certificate, or served three years in the armed forces. Although not a Title VII case, the court applied *Griggs* Title VII disparate impact standards, noting that 70 percent of police forces already imposed a high school degree requirement (*Castro*, 1972:735, n. 11). In ruling that such standards were valid and did not deny the constitutional rights of blacks or Hispanics, the court stated that

> Policemen . . . *unlike some other types of employees* . . . are in a calling in which book knowledge is an important element and there is a constant demand for the performance of intellectual as well as physical tasks. (*Castro*, 1972:739)

In this case, the court held that the high school diploma or equivalent requirement for employment as a police officer was significantly related to job performance, even though no validation study as to this relationship was made before or after the educational requirement had been adopted.

In 1975 the federal district court in Ohio also upheld a high school education or equivalent requirement for Akron police officers, although such a requirement disqualified more blacks than Caucasians. In *Arnold* v. *Ballard* (1975), the court referred to the "job related" precedent of the *Castro* decision and stated that

> It is somewhat arbitrary in nature but a high school degree does indicate a measure of accomplishment and ability which is *essential for initial training and performance as a police officer.* (*Arnold*, 1975:738; emphasis added)

A California federal district court in 1976 also upheld a high school requirement for police officers. In *League of United Latin American Citizens* v. *City of Santa Ana* (1976) the court decided that such a requirement did not have a "disparate impact" on Mexican Americans.[10] In addition, at this time the court urged that college education be considered for police officers. Quoting from *Task Force Report: The Police*, the court stated that,

> A policeman today is poorly equipped for his job if he does not understand the legal issues involved in his everyday work, the nature of the social problems he

> constantly encounters, the psychology of those people whose attitudes toward the law differ from his. Such understanding is not easy to acquire without the kind of general knowledge that higher education imparts. . . . Police candidates must be sought in the college, and especially among liberal arts and social science students. (*League*, 1976:883)

In 1980 the Second Circuit Court of Appeals affirmed a lower court ruling upholding high school education requirements following the reasoning of *Castro, Arnold,* and *League of United Latin American Citizens.* In *United States* v. *City of Buffalo* (1980), the court held that requirements for police department applicants to possess a high school degree or equivalency diploma had been validated by meaningful study of the relationship to job performance ability, referring to conclusions reached in the 1967 *Task Force Report, Challenge of Crime in a Free Society,* and the 1968 National Advisory Commission on Civil Disorders (*City of Buffalo,* 1980:628–29).

The Seventh Circuit Court of Appeals in 1985 affirmed a lower federal court ruling upholding high school educational requirements for correctional officers in Illinois. Noting that the position of correctional officer was comparable to that of a police officer, the court, in *Aguilera* v. *Cook County Police & Corrections Merit Bd.* (1985), also observed the potential for abuse inherent in both positions (*Aguilera,* 1985:848). Despite a finding that such requirements had a disparate impact on Mexican Americans, the district court ruled that a high school education requirement was sufficiently job related.[11] Although educational requirements were required to be substantially related to job performance or to be a business necessity, the court also held that educational requirements did not need to be validated in accordance with EEOC guidelines (*Aguilera,* 1985:847–48).

Cases Overturning Educational Degree Requirements

In a 1975 federal case involving the job-relatedness of high school requirements for fire fighters, the Ohio district court held that such standards were discriminatory against blacks and were not job related. In *Dozier* v. *Chupka* (1975), the court referred to

Griggs and found that since fire fighters continued to perform their duties effectively, without either a high school diploma or equivalent, the use of such requirements was prohibited.

A subsequent federal court case from the New York district, also found high school degree requirements for fire fighters invalid. Citing *Dozier* as precedent, the court in *United States* v. *City of Buffalo* (1980) struck down the high school degree requirements for fire fighters but, as discussed earlier, upheld such requirements for police officers.

In 1978, the Eleventh Circuit Court of Appeals in *Payne* v. *Travenol Laboratories, Inc.* (1978) did not extend the public safety rationale for the professional positions of systems, traffic, and scheduling analysts. In this case, the court found that college degree requirements had been recently adopted, rendering a disparate number of blacks ineligible for such positions. The court also found that evidence presented by the plaintiff was insufficient to show the relationship between college degrees and the jobs performed by the employees.

In a minority of cases, as shown above, several of the federal courts have refused to extend the public safety rationale to both fire fighter and a class of professional positions involving traffic safety, thereby striking down educational requirements. The following cases, however, indicate the court's willingness to uphold college education requirements for positions involving elements of public safety.

Cases Upholding College Degree Requirements

A year following the *Griggs* decision, the Tenth Circuit Court of Appeals distinguished between the type of positions at issue in *Griggs* and positions requiring successful performance tasks involving the health and safety of the public. *Spurlock* v. *United Airlines, Inc.* (1972) held that a college degree, inter alia, was job related within the meaning of *Griggs*. For positions requiring a small amount of skill and training, the court reasoned that the employer should have a heavy burden to demonstrate that the employment requirements are job related. However, for positions requiring a high degree of skill and where the economic and human risks involved in hiring an unqualified applicant are serious, the employer bears a lighter burden of showing job-relatedness. Therefore, the court suggested that courts should proceed with a degree of caution before permitting employers to lower employment standards for such positions (*Spurlock*, 1972:219).

In *Spurlock*, the challenged employment practice was that of college degree requirements for airline flight officers, an employment requirement that had been found to discriminate against blacks. However, the court held that the reasonableness requirement for college was satisfied since the court reasoned that college-educated employees were superior in their understanding and retention of concepts and information necessary for performing the job requirements provided during training and subsequent refresher courses. The court stated that

> . . . the possession of a college degree indicates that the applicant has the ability to understand and retain concepts and information given in the atmosphere of a classroom or training program. Thus, a person with a college degree, particularly in the "hard" sciences, is more able to cope with the training program and the unending series of refresher courses than a person without a college degree. (*Spurlock*, 1972:219)

The issue of college degree requirements for medical technicians was considered by the Second Circuit Court of Appeals in 1977. Approving of the public safety rationale in *Spurlock*, the court in *Townsend* v. *Nassau County Medical Center* (1977) upheld the college degree requirement stating that

> The requirement of a college degree, particularly in the sciences, seems to be in the modern day of advanced scientific method, a neutral requirement for the protection of the public. . . . The relative function of the academic prerequisites to job-relatedness varies inversely with the risk to the health and safety of the public who depend on the technology. (*Townsend*, 1977:120)

Although the court agreed in this case that such requirements could serve as pretexts for discrimination, the court also indicated that *Griggs'* application of population statistics in order to determine a prima facie case of discrimination could not be used in all disparate impact cases.

Here the court held that the *Griggs* criteria could not be applied to challenge college degree requirements (*Townsend,* 1977:117).[12]

In a 1978 federal case involving educational requirements for campus patrol officers, the Missouri district court in *Jackson* v. *Curators of University of Missouri* (1978) upheld a two-year college requirement as a business necessity. In this case, expert testimony presented to the court by a police chief was accepted in establishing a relationship between the college requirements and "hazardous duties performed without supervision or assistance by campus patrolmen" (*Jackson,* 1978:882).

College requirements for public health positions were upheld by the Fifth Circuit Court of Appeals in 1984. In *Walls* v. *Mississippi State Department of Public Welfare* (1984), the court found that such requirements had a disparate impact on blacks, in that greater than 85 percent of state welfare jobs requiring an educational minimum were held by Caucasians. However, in applying the job-relatedness standard of *Griggs,* the employer had established that educational requirements of a college degree for social worker and two years of college credit for eligibility worker were related to successful performance.

In 1985, the federal district court of Illinois conceded that college requirements could serve as pretexts for discrimination. Nonetheless, in *Equal Employment Opportunity Commission* v. *Chicago Miniature Lamp Works* (1985), the court held that college requirements for the position of data processing manager were not unreasonable even though such requirements were not an "essential prerequisite" for the job in objective terms (*Chicago Miniature Lamp Works,* 1985:1304–05).

One year after the Fifth Circuit Court of Appeals had upheld college requirements for public health positions, it also upheld college requirements for applicants to positions on the City of Dallas police force. In *Davis* v. *City of Dallas* (1985) the circuit court approved of the lower court's use of applicant flow and internal statistics in a finding of discrimination against blacks.[13] Nonetheless, the court upheld the lower court's ruling that applicants must have completed 45 semester hours of college credit with at least a C average at an accredited college or university, despite the requirement's statistically significant disparate impact upon blacks (*Davis,* 1985:208–10).

In *Davis,* the court accepted evidence of expert witnesses as well as national studies and reports as validation for the department's educational requirement. The court acknowledged that the position of police officer combined both aspects of professionalism and significant public risk and responsibility. It then adopted and discussed two distinct rationales in validating higher education standards for police officers—the public risk and responsibility rationale and the professional skills rationale.[14]

In 1987, a federal district court within the fifth circuit ruled on the validity of college education requirements for a social services position. In *Thompson* v. *Mississippi State Personnel Bd.* (1987) the district court cited *Davis* concerning professionalism and ruled that empirical evidence was not required to validate educational requirements for the position at issue, "in view of the professional nature of the position and public interest involved therein" (*Thompson,* 1987:213).[15]

In 1988, the Supreme Court adopted the more lenient standard of job-relatedness requirements generally for disparate impact cases, although the instant case involved disparate treatment analysis for a promotional discrimination claim. In *Watson* v. *Fort Worth Bank and Trust* (1988), the majority opinion approved of the more lenient standard in validating the business necessity defense approving of the Supreme Court's *Washington* v. *Davis'* method for police officers.[16] The Court pointed out, at least with reference to public safety positions, that

> Our cases make it clear that employers are not required, even when defending standardized objective tests, to introduce formal "validation studies" showing that particular criteria predict actual on-the-job performance. (*Watson,* 1988:2790)

In a concurring opinion, the Court acknowledged that the "proper means of establishing business necessity will vary with the type and size of the business in question, as well as the particular job for which the selection process is employed" (*Watson,* 1988:2795). The Court then proceeded to recognize validation methods used in the *Davis* v. *City of Dallas* (1985) decision (showing the job-relatedness of college education through nationwide studies and reports, presentation of expert testimony, and testimony of criminal justice scholars), stating that such methods "can be used, under appropriate circumstances, to establish business necessity" (*Watson*, 1988:2795).

The previous discussion has demonstrated that the majority of federal court decisions have upheld educational qualifications for various positions including college education requirements for police officers. Although two district court decisions and one circuit court decision have not recognized educational requirements (for fire fighters and systems, traffic, and scheduling analysts) the Fifth Circuit Court of Appeals has recognized that the role of police officer is a professional position requiring special qualities of judgment, maturity, and responsibility to effectively carry out a complex set of tasks affecting the health and safety of the public (*Davis* v. *City of Dallas*, 1985). The previous discussion also suggests that, if this discrimination challenge was decided by the court, the Supreme Court might uphold a college education requirement for police officer applicants even if college requirements resulted in a disparate impact on minority groups.[17]

Issue of Validating Educational Requirements

The 1971 Supreme Court decision in *Griggs* had adopted the criterion validation standard requirement for private employers, one of the three employment validation methods developed by the American Psychological Association and adopted by the Equal Employment Opportunity Commission. At that time, the Court stated that private employers should defer to the EEOC guidelines when devising standardized tests since the construction of these administrative guidelines is supported by legislative history, thereby expressing the will of Congress (*Griggs*, 1971:434).

District court decisions in the second, seventh, and ninth circuits, while accepting deference to the EEOC standards, nonetheless ruled that such requirements applied only to standardized tests and not to a high school educational requirement (*League of United Latin American Citizens* v. *City of Santa Ana*, 1976:901, referring to *Albemarle Paper Co.* v. *Moody*,

1975:431 and *Griggs,* 1971:433–34, n. 8; *United States* v. *City of Buffalo,* 1980:628–29, quoting *Griggs,* 1971:433, n. 8.; and *Aguilera* v. *Cook County Police and Corrections Merit Bd.,* 1985:847).[18] Additionally, several courts have noted that the *Griggs* decision applied solely to objective tests for manual, craftsman-type positions and was not applicable to a high school education requirement (*League,* 1976:901; *City of Buffalo,* 1980:628–29; *Aguilera,* 1985:847). Nonetheless, various courts have ruled on the validity of high school and college education requirements under the "business necessity" defense when discrimination against a minority group has in fact been shown under the EEOC guidelines' four-fifths rule.[19]

In addition, in *Albemarle* v. *Moody* (1975) the Court also discusses the EEOC guidelines for validating employment criteria (*Albemarle,* 1975:430–35). Referring to *Albemarle,* the Supreme Court the following year in *Washington* v. *Davis* (1976) further acknowledged that no single measure existed for appropriately validating employment tests for their relationship to job performance (*Washington,* 1976:247, n. 13).

Various district, appellate, and Supreme Court rulings have clarified and adopted three methods of validating both objective tests and subjective hiring criteria in accordance with EEOC guidelines. These cases and their relevance to the present study are discussed in the following section.

Validation Standards and Procedures

Two years following the landmark *Griggs* decision, a federal district court in the second circuit ruled on the legality of hiring criteria that had an adverse impact on minorities. In *Sontag* v. *Bronstein* (1973), the court permitted employers to use a significant amount of discretion in developing both minimal hiring standards and related performance tests, as long as such criteria could be shown to "bear a rational relationship to job performance." The court, however, cautioned at this time that judicial scrutiny of the use of such discretionary standards is warranted (*Sontag,* 1973:406).

A California federal district court in the ninth circuit explicated that employers were required to ensure that no qualified candidate, whether a minority or otherwise, was adversely affected by an over-demanding test. The court stated in *Western Addition Community Organization* v. *Alioto* (1973) that

> All that the law requires is that no minority job applicant, or white job applicant, who is otherwise qualified to perform a job, shall in effect be excluded from that job by an employment test that goes beyond the actual requirements of the job and thus adversely affects applicants, generally minorities, who, although able to do the job, lack the background and education to pass an over-demanding test. (*Western Addition*, 1973:79)

That same year, 1973, two federal district courts in the First and Ninth Courts of Appeals formally endorsed the EEOC uniform guidelines which specified the three distinct validation methods permissible in assessing the legality of employment procedures. In *Officers for Justice* v. *Civil Service Commission of City and County of San Francisco* (1973), the federal district court in the ninth circuit held that EEOC guidelines provided "persuasive standards" for evaluating claims of job-relatedness for public employment examinations challenged on the grounds of a denial of equal protection (*Officers for Justice*, 1973:1336–37).

The federal court, in *Bridgeport Guardians, Inc.* v. *Members of Bridgeport Civil Service Commission* (1973), determined that employment standards that are claimed to be discriminatory require only "some consideration" of EEOC standards. At this time, the court discussed the three validation standards: predictive, content, and construct validity. The Connecticut federal court then defined the criterion-related or predictive validity approach as involving "the identification of criteria reflecting successful job performance and test scores and correlation of same with performance ratings for predetermined criteria"; the content validity approach as involving "direct measurement of knowledge or skill needed for successful job performance"; and the construct validity approach as involving "an identification of 'constructs' or characteristics, followed by a test to measure the degree to which applicant possesses required characteristics" (*Bridgeport Guardians*, 1973:788–89).

In 1974, the First Circuit Court of Appeals affirmed a Massachusetts court ruling invalidating employment examinations that had not utilized the predictive validation approach. Striking down hiring criteria that were not predictive of job performance, the court, in *Boston Chapter, NAACP, Inc.* v. *Beecher* (1974), specified that empirical evidence rather than expert opinion was necessary to prove the legality of the challenged criteria. The court specifically stated that an

> . . . [e]mployer whose job qualifications are alleged to be discriminatory cannot operate from some expert point of view that the qualifications and tests are doing what they are supposed to do; rather empirical evidence to that effect must be obtained. (*Boston Chapter,* 1974:517–18)

A 1974 New York federal court decision in the second circuit, citing *Bridgeport Guardians* as precedent, endorsed the three validation methods of the EEOC guidelines for employment selection criteria. However, the court in *Kirkland* v. *New York State Department of Correctional Services* (1974) expressed its preference for the criterion or predictive validation method over the other two methods for a civil service examination for corrections sergeants positions. While defining validation as a "term of art designating the process of determining job-relatedness of selection procedures," the court expressed its view that criterion-related validation of an employment examination is not required if the examination can be validated by other means (*Kirkland,* 1974:1370). The court also discussed the construct validation approach as requiring the "identification of general mental and psychological traits believed necessary to successful performance of job in question" (*Kirkland,* 1974:1371–72).

In 1975, the New York federal district court also acknowledged the distinction between lower-level positions requiring an empirical validation approach and more professional, higher-level positions requiring subjective assessments as to the applicant's qualifications for a position. In *Pace College* v. *Commission on Human Rights of City of New York* (1975), the court ruled that while statistical data may show discrimination, subjective judgments have a proper role in employment considerations, and statistics have less significance than with respect to unskilled and semiskilled labor. The court stated: "In a professional or academic milieu, subjective judgments necessarily have a proper and legitimate role" (*Pace College,* 1975:885).

Also in 1975, a federal district court in the seventh circuit limited the appropriate job-relatedness validation methods to either the predictive or content validation approach (*Crockett* v. *Green,* 1975). This more restrictive validation approach was also adopted by the Missouri federal court in the eighth circuit the following year (*United States* v. *City of St. Louis,* 1976).

Shortly after these cases had been decided, a New York district court acknowledged that there was no single method for properly validating the relationship of employment tests to job performance, citing the newly decided *Washington* v. *Davis* (1976) Supreme Court decision as precedent. However, as with the prior federal court decision, the court in *Jackson* v. *Nassau County Civil Service Commission* (1976), continued to endorse the predictive validation approach over the other methods as the most desirable method for determining on-the-job performance, citing the *Kirkland* decision (*Jackson,* 1976:1169).

After the 1976 *Washington* decision by the Supreme Court, federal courts in the sixth, seventh, ninth, and eleventh circuits formally adopted the three validation methods of the EEOC guidelines in disputing disparate impact discrimination challenges (*Harless* v. *Duck,* 1976; *Detroit Police Officers Association* v. *Young,* 1978; *United States* v. *City of Chicago,* 1978; *Scott* v. *City of Anniston Alabama,* 1979; and *Blake* v. *City of Los Angeles,* 1979). The Ninth Circuit Court of Appeals, however, in *Blake,* while acknowledging that no single method was appropriate in validating employment criteria, also acknowledged the importance of the public safety factor in selection criteria for police officers. The court stated that

> . . . it is not enough that the device selects characteristics that may have some rational relationship to job performance; rather, a discriminatory employment practice must be shown to be necessary to safe and efficient job performance. (*Blake,* 1979: 1377)

The Ninth Circuit Court of Appeals in 1981 also ruled that EEOC guideline validation requirements, although not mandatory, were entitled to deference when deciding Title VII discrimination challenges. The court in *Contreras* v. *City of Los Angeles* (1981), however, went one step further in its decision, cautioning that employers who disregarded EEOC validation guidelines shouldered a "heavier than usual burden of job-relatedness" when challenged in the courts (*Contreras*, 1981:1281).

When confronted with the issue of legally validating educational requirements, the Second, Fifth, Seventh, and Ninth Circuit Courts of Appeals have been hesitant to require EEOC guideline standards for positions involving public safety. These cases are primarily critical of the strict empirical validation approach in Title VII discrimination challenges and endorse a relaxed standard of scrutiny for higher education requirements as employment criteria.

In 1976, a California federal district court upheld high school requirements for police officers despite an adverse impact on Mexican-American applicants. Ruling that prior decisions of *Griggs* and *Albemarle* did not apply to educational standards, the court, in *League of United Latin American Citizens* v. *City of Santa Ana* (1976), stressed the importance of national reports as validation devices in discrimination challenges. The court stated:

> This court . . . is reluctant to accept the idea that education requirements must be empirically validated. To accept that concept would be to adopt the proposition that empiricist's methods of arriving at truth are the only acceptable ones. It would involve the categorical rejection of reports of Presidential Commissions on the basis that they were "unscientific." It is one thing to say that paper and pencil tests must be validated by prevailing concepts of educational measurement . . . it is quite another to say that the common sense judgment and reasoning of expert observers cannot be considered as relevant to the assessment of the value of institutional education to the increasingly complicated tasks of the police officer in an urban environment. (*League*, 1976:901)[20]

In 1980, the Second Circuit Court of Appeals affirmed a lower federal court opinion upholding educational requirements for police officers. Using national studies as validation standards, the federal court in *United States* v. *City of Buffalo* (1980) held that high school requirements did not violate Title VII provisions. The court wrote that

> . . . the Supreme Court has found the EEOC guidelines to be applicable to tests only and not to the high school diploma requirement under 42 USC sec. 2000e-2(h). Therefore, the standard to be applied here is not as rigid as that required for tests. (*City of Buffalo*, 1980:628–29)

While acknowledging the potential for employers to require higher credentials than is appropriate (outside of a public-safety position context), a federal district court in the fifth circuit endorsed a relaxed standard of validation for college education requirements. In differentiating employment tests from educational requirements generally, the court, in *Vuyanvich* v. *Republic National Bank of Dallas* (1980), discussed the lesser potential of abuse for educational requirements by employers than for employment tests. In fact, the court acknowledged the educational institution's superior ability to assess a person's competence over that of the employer, at least in terms of subjective qualifications. The court stated:

> A college degree reflects the judgment of a comparatively neutral institution, better qualified [than the employer] and with greater opportunity than the employer to assess an individual's credentials, that the recipient has reached a threshold level of competence in a given field. (*Vuyanvich*, 1980:371)

Finally, the District of Columbia federal court in 1980, in *Reynolds* v. *Sheet Metal Workers Local 102* (1980), accepted the construct validation approach in determining the legality of high school education requirements for positions within a blue-collar context. In accepting the contentions of employers that high school graduates could be expected to master classroom training exercises and successfully apply this new knowledge to the demands of the actual job, the court ruled that professional validation studies correlating the relationship between the completion of a high school degree and performance in an apprenticeship were required (*Reynolds*, 1980:971). At this time, the court determined that the validation of educational requirements using the construct validation method involved a two-step process: (1) that the construct must be suitably related to the position at issue and (2) that the selection criteria must reflect the construct (*Reynolds*, 1980:971–72).

More recent federal cases in the fifth and seventh circuits, decided in the 1980s, have accepted all three of the EEOC guidelines' validation methods. Moreover, the more recent cases of *Gillespie* v. *State of Wisconsin* (1985), *Thomas* v. *City of Evanston* (1985), and *Evans* v. *City of Evanston* (1988), while defining the three methods, explicitly state that no one validation method is preferred over the others. *Davis* v. *City of Dallas* (1985), while accepting the need for at least one study using the EEOC validation method, primarily applied the more lenient standard of expert testimony and national commissions' recommendations in deciding the legality of college education requirements for police officer applicants of the Dallas Police Department.

A more recent fifth circuit case has upheld the validity of the use of correlation coefficients between tests and cognitive abilities. Accepting general cognitive abilities as important job performance elements rather than the actual specific job duties themselves, the court, in *Bernard* v. *Gulf Oil Corp.* (1988), ruled that a relationship derived from a study using those elements could be used to establish a relationship between tests and job performance (*Bernard*, 1988:564–66).

The immediately preceding discussion has shown that any one of three validation methods may be used in affirming the relationship between employment criteria and successful job performance. Discussion of those cases from the various federal courts has also shown that no method is currently preferred over any other. However, for positions involving more professional or public safety positions in which employers require a minimum level of educational attainment, several circuits have adopted the more relaxed validation standard that has included accepting the recommendations of national reports and expert testimony.

Although several courts have expressed the view that EEOC validation methods are not applicable to educational requirements, a more recent fifth circuit decision (while accepting expert testimony and national commission recommendations) has also stipulated the need to utilize at least one empirically validated study in deciding the legality of college education requirements. The most recent fifth circuit decision, however, has authorized the construct of cognitive ability as an acceptable substitute for actual performance in validating a correlation between employment criteria and actual on-the-job performance.

Analysis of the rationale in the previously discussed cases supports the position taken and validation methods utilized in the present study. The logic in the current approach is that (1) officer professionalism is an important construct in determining safe and effective performance in a public safety position when directly working with the public; (2) the construct of professionalism is an acceptable alternative equivalent for actual on-the-job performance; (3) a significant relationship can be established between higher education and the construct of professionalism; therefore such validation also legally validates a relationship between education and performance; and (4) at least one traditional validation approach, for example, measuring the correlation or relationship between education and an actual performance indicator as well as between one performance indicator and the construct of professionalism, empirically validates the relationship between education and the construct of professionalism.

Rationales for Upholding College Education Requirements

Two major lines of reasoning have been advanced by the various courts in upholding the legality of college education requirements in Title VII discrimination challenges. The first is the public risk and responsibility rationale that was advanced in 1972, the same year provisions of the 1964 Civil Rights Act were extended to apply to public agencies. The second is the professional skills rationale, legal reasoning developed by the Fifth Circuit Court of Appeals in *Davis* v. *City of Dallas*. The final part of this section discusses the evidence accepted by the federal court in *Davis*, validating college education requirements for police officer applicants in the city of Dallas.

Public Risk and Responsibility Rationale

Approving college education requirements for flight attendants in *Spurlock* v. *United Airlines, Inc.* (1972),[21] the Tenth Circuit Court of Appeals recognized the hazardous risks associated with under-qualified employees in positions dealing with the public. The court in *Spurlock* set the stage for the development of the public safety rationale when it stated:

> When the job clearly requires a high degree of skill and the economic and human risks involved in hiring an unqualified applicant are great, the employer bears a correspondingly lighter burden to show his employment criteria are job-related. (*Spurlock,* 1972:219)

In 1974, the Seventh Circuit Court of Appeals in an age discrimination challenge, upheld age requirements for bus driver positions on the grounds of safety to the public. *Hodgson* v. *Greyhound Lines, Inc.* (1974), approving of *Spurlock,* announced that when employees are "entrusted with the lives and well-being" of the public, the employer "must continually strive to employ the most highly qualified persons available" (*Hodgson,* 1974:863). For the position of inner city bus driver, the court held that the employer

> . . . need only demonstrate . . . a minimal increase in risk of harm for it is enough to show that elimination of the hiring policy might jeopardize the life of one more person than might otherwise occur under the present hiring practice. (*Hodgson,* 1974:863)

The Fifth Circuit Court of Appeals in 1976 essentially recognized and followed this rationale for its bus driver positions. The court in *Usury* v. *Tamiami Trail Tours, Inc.* (1976), while not specifically approving of *Spurlock,* recognized the same general principle in the context of cases involving the issue of bona fide occupational qualifications, approving of a lighter burden of job-relatedness when the safety of a third person is involved. The circuit court specifically stated that

> The greater the safety factor, measured by the likelihood of harm and probable severity of that harm in the case of an accident, the more stringent may be the job

qualifications designed to insure safe driving. (*Usury*, 1976:236)

In 1977, federal courts in the District of Columbia as well as in the Second and Eighth Circuit Courts of Appeals approved of the rationale advanced in both *Spurlock* and *Hodgson*. In *Kinsey* v. *First Regional Securities, Inc.* (1977), the court distinguished the position of a securities sales representative from that of a flight officer "who ultimately is responsible for the safety of passengers as well as costly aircraft." For the position at issue in *Spurlock*, the court stated that the "public interest is paramount and justifies high employment standards" (*Kinsey*, 1977:837).

In another flight officer discrimination challenge, the Eighth Circuit Court of Appeals upheld height requirements found to be discriminatory against women. The court decided in *Boyd* v. *Ozark Air Lines, Inc.* (1977) that because of the "human risks being involved, the court cannot agree that empirical validation is required here" (*Boyd*, 1977:54). In *Townsend* (1977), a decision discussed earlier, the Second Circuit Court of Appeals announced that for the position of a medical technician, a college bachelor's degree was a "neutral requirement for the protection of the public" (*Townsend*, 1977:120).

Subsequent rulings in the Fifth, Sixth, Ninth, and Eleventh Circuit Courts of Appeals also approved of the prior holdings of the circuit courts. The Eighth Circuit Court of Appeals in 1979 affirmed a lower court ruling in *Rice* v. *City of St. Louis* (1979:142) citing *Townsend* and *Spurlock* and agreed that academic requirements of employees were inversely related to the health and safety of the public who depended on the expertise acquired through such education. Additionally, the Ninth Circuit Court of Appeals in *Harriss* v. *Pan Am. World Airways, Inc.* (1980), citing previous decisions as controlling and acknowledging safety factors as a business necessity defense, stated that the "Federal Courts have uniformly recognized the relevance of the safety factor in assessing whether an employment policy is justified as a B.F.O.Q." (*Harriss*, 1980:675, n. 4).

In 1981, the Sixth Circuit Court of Appeals decided a challenge to truck driver qualifications. *Chrisner* v. *Complete Auto Transit, Inc.* (1981), while approving of *Spurlock's* public interest in safety, construed *Spurlock* as creating a "job demands" spectrum in which an employer "must be allowed more latitude in structuring the requirements which could effect [*sic*] the performance of a primary business objective" (*Chrisner*, 1981:1262). The court went on to state that

> The important public interest in safety . . . is sufficiently weighty to convince us that [the requirement for the present job] . . . is manifestly related to the safe and efficient operation of its business. (*Chrisner*, 1981:1263)

That same year, however, the Sixth Circuit Court of Appeals, in *Equal Employment Opportunity Commission* v. *Ball Corp.* (1981), also announced that the public safety standard of *Spurlock* was to be applied narrowly and to those positions that greatly implicated human safety, such as airline pilots or truck drivers (*EEOC* v. *Ball*, 1981:541, n. 10). This view was also followed by the Eleventh Circuit Court of Appeals in *Walker* v. *Jefferson County Home* (1984), the court noting that the position before the court was distinguishable from *Spurlock*. The court wrote:

> In determining whether the employer has met its burden [to prove business necessity] the Court looks at the amount of skill required for the position and the economic and human risks involved. When consequences for hiring an unqualified applicant are insignificant . . . the employer should have a heavy burden to demonstrate component criteria are related. (*Walker*, 1984:1558)

Finally, the Fifth Circuit Court of Appeals upheld a lower court decision agreeing on, inter alia, 45 units of college education for police officer applicants to the Dallas Police Department. Basing its decision on the emerging doctrine of the public safety factor, the court, in *Davis* v. *City of Dallas* (1985:215), equated the position of police officer in a major metropolitan area with other positions that the courts had found involved "important public interests in safety" (*Chrisner*, 1981:1263), in carrying "responsibility for the safety of the public" (*Hodgson*, 1974:853), and involving "risks to . . . safety and even life" (*Rice*, 1979:853). The court agreed that a lighter standard of job-relatedness was warranted for metropolitan police officers than *Spurlock* required for flight officers because of the degree of public risk and responsibility involved in the duties of police officers. In upholding the constitutionality of educational requirements despite their disparate impact on African-Americans (i.e., by using internal, applicant flow statistics), the court concluded that

> . . . [f]ew professionals are so peculiarly charged with individual responsibility as police officers. Officers are compelled to make instantaneous decisions, often without clearcut guidance from the Legislature or departmental policy, and mistakes of judgment could cause irreparable harm to citizens or even to the community. (*Davis*, 1985:215)

Professional Skills Rationale

In addition to the public safety factor rationale, the court, in *Davis* v. *City of Dallas* (1985), advanced a professional skills rationale, concluding that the professional nature of a Dallas police officer's position distinguishes it from other positions challenged under Title VII in cases before the Supreme Court (*Davis*, 1985:216). The court pointed out that, for police officers, "factors that combine to produce a qualified police officer . . . are far less susceptible to precise definition and to identification and quantification in individual cases" (*Davis*, 1985:216). The court also pointed out that

> . . . concepts such as maturity, judgment, and the ability to handle pressure, among others, are difficult to precisely define or to break down into component skills making "formal validation" through the use of empirical evidence "a virtual impossibility." (*Davis*, 1985:217)

Because of the "professional nature of the job" (in addition to the risk factors), the court concluded that empirical evidence was not required to validate job-relatedness, although it did accept the findings of a criterion-validated report by one of its expert witnesses. The court then held that

> . . . the responsibility and potential for danger and abuse inherent in the position make the question of what constitutes a *minimally* qualified "adequate" police officer

> a less appropriate standard for selecting members of the force than would be the case in most other job positions, let alone the positions this Court has had occasion to examine in the context of a Title VII suit. (*Davis,* 1985:217 referring to *Hodgson,* 1974:863 and *Chrisner,* 1981:1262–63)

The court did point out, however, that it was not suggesting that validation methods of expert testimony and high-caliber national reports were any less reliable than the methods recommended by the EEOC guidelines. In effect, the Fifth Circuit Court of Appeals at this time endorsed the views and more lenient validation standards recommended by and applied in *League* (1976) and *Aguilera* (1985).[22]

Fifth Circuit Validation of Educational Requirements

Both the *League* (1976) and *Aguilera* (1985) federal court decisions had validated high school diploma requirements for police officers based on the recommendations of national commissions. *Davis* (1985) agreed with the logic behind these court decisions and upheld college educational requirements for Dallas police officers. The court's decision was based, however, not only on the recommendations of commissions but also on the testimony and recommendations of experts in the field of criminal justice and members of professional organizations, as well as upon empirical studies showing the relationship between education and officer performance conducted by one of the court's expert witnesses (*Davis,* 1985:218–23).

At this time, the court acknowledged that higher educational requirements had been recommended as early as 1931 by the National Commission on Law Observance and Enforcement. In 1967, the President's Commission on Law Enforcement and Administration of Justice report, *The Challenge of Crime in a Free Society,* urged all police departments to establish departmentally the long-range goal of a baccalaureate degree for sworn officers. The 1971 Advisory Commission on Intergovernmental Relations, 1972 American Bar Association, and 1973 National Advisory Commission of Criminal Justice Standards and Goals also made similar recommendations for police departments. Arguing that a high school degree was an inadequate and inferior level of education due to the essential tasks performed by officers (including preservation of constitutional guarantees and the exercise of discretion involving life and death decisions), the National Advisory Commission had stated that

> The need for police officers who are intelligent, articulate, mature, and knowledgeable about social and political conditions are apparent. . . . A college education develops and imparts that requisite level of knowledge. (*Davis*, 1985:219)

Additionally, the court accepted as valid evidence the testimony of the following expert witnesses: David Patrick Geary, Associate Professor of the Administration of Justice, a former police officer and chief of police; Julius Debro, Chairman of the Department of Criminal Justice and Criminology, Atlanta University; Gerald Lynch, President of John Jay College of Criminal Justice, City University of New York; and Lawrence Redlinger, Professor of Sociology and Political Economy and Acting Dean of the School of Social Sciences at the University of Texas at Dallas.[23]

Professor Geary provided testimony to the court that his empirical studies in 1978 and 1979 examining the relationship between college education and overall officer performance, statistically confirmed the relationship between the two. Studies supplying the type of statistical evidence provided by Professor Geary essentially fulfill the EEOC criterion validation requirements in Title VII cases challenging employment practices as discriminatory. Additionally, Geary also pointed out to the court that no significant differences were found between criminal justice majors and officers studying in other fields (*Davis*, 1985:219).

Professor Julius Debro had located, reviewed, and analyzed all studies that had been done on the subject of police education for the Joint Commission on Criminal Justice Educational Standards. Agreeing with the recommendations of the commission urging a minimum of a bachelor's degree for police officers, Professor Debro told the court that college education provided police departments with the advantages of improved performance by officers, improvement of race relationships with ethnic groups throughout the community, less-authoritarian officers, less-stressed officers, and overall improvement in professionalism. In noting that the National Association of Blacks in Criminal Justice also recommended a college degree for the entry-level officer, he discussed numerous studies showing that departments with college education requirements had superior overall performance records to those lacking such a requirement (*Davis*, 1985:221–22).

Dr. Gerald Lynch also testified before the court, essentially supporting the job-relatedness educational requirement and recommending a bachelor's degree as a requirement for police officer applicants. Dr. Lynch's recommendations were based on the recommendations of the national commissions. Although he pointed out the problems in validating education as a requirement due to difficulties in correlating more abstract and subtle performance indicators with education, he also relied on studies indicating that police officers act in a less authoritarian and more open-minded manner if they have a college education. Dr. Lynch then rejected the notion that college might be required at some point later on in an officer's career rather than at the entry level, reasoning that once officers graduate from the training academy

> they have a gun . . . the full responsibility as a police officer, and . . . the full capacity to . . . wound or kill whomever they think should be wounded or shot . . . [as well as] all the stress of police work from the very beginning. (*Davis*, 1985:220–21)

Professor Lawrence Redlinger argued that the variable of 45 hours of college course work is a surrogate variable for comprehension, intelligence, and the ability to deal with complex and ambiguous situations (*Davis*, 1985:220). In response to the issue of the "costs and consequences" of accepting applicants without college education, Professor Redlinger stated that education provides maturity, knowledge of the operation of American government, knowledge of the history of the country and its laws, and allows for more flexibility in handling ambiguous, discretionary situations. Therefore,

> . . . [i]nsofar as those things are desirable, then not having them is a cost not only to policing but to the society. And that's a cost hard to measure, but one which, nevertheless, is a real cost. (*Davis*, 1985:220)

Based on the expert testimony presented to the district court as well as the studies introduced as evidence, the appellate court concluded that 45 units of college education were job related. Additionally, the court concluded that compliance with the EEOC guidelines did not present an obstacle due to the fact that

> . . . [t]he extraordinary risk posed by an officer who is *not* adequate for the job is such that the city is justified in requiring applicants for positions on the police force to possess "the professional maturity gained through education. . . ."It "is enough to show that elimination of the hiring policy might jeopardize the life of one more person than might otherwise occur under the present hiring practice." (*Davis*, 1985:223, citing *Hodgson*, 1974:863)

Recommendations of the various commission reports urging police departments to implement higher educational requirements for their officers have been criticized by some scholars as being based upon rhetoric and intuition rather than on empirical evidence (Shernock, 1992:73). However, the prior discussion has shown that the Fifth Circuit Court of Appeals has validated the arguments of these commission reports concerning the value of higher education through the presentation of the testimony of scholarly experts in the field of criminal justice. These experts, involved in both small- and large-scale studies concerning the relationship of education, officer performance, and professionalism in policing, all concurred with the recommendations of the commissions and the need to upgrade educational requirements for police officers nationwide.

Affirmative Action, the Law, and College Requirements

The concept of affirmative action, like that of equality, is a concept in dispute. The application of affirmative action rulings has brought consternation to many Americans, especially to those individuals who have been adversely affected by the rulings.[24] Affirmative action "can mean different things to different people"; however, the meaning and application of equality embodied within affirmative action policies can be demarcated into three ideologically defined categories: equality of opportunity, equality of condition, and equality of result (Stephenson et al., 1992:136).

The year congress extended the provisions of the Civil Rights Act of 1964 to public service positions at the local, state, and federal levels, President Richard Nixon spoke of the progress America had made in assuring equal opportunity to minority members.[25] Nixon's conservative approach to affirmative action was intended to remove barriers that had existed for minorities, affording them "an equal place at the starting line" in life's competitive struggle. Legal application of this equal opportunity approach prohibited employers from intentionally discriminating against minorities, providing remedies for aggrieved minorities when discrimination was shown to exist.[26]

A more moderate approach is that of equality of condition, in which affirmative action policies eliminate barriers as well as address the lingering effects of discrimination (Stephenson et al., 1992:136). Politically, affirmative action policies under this approach would allocate economic resources into Head Start programs in minority neighborhoods and provide minority scholarships to eligible college applicants.

The U.S. Supreme Court in *Griggs* applied this concept in its "disparate impact" approach toward minorities as a group, essentially addressing the lingering effects of employment discrimination. The court at that time cautioned that unqualified minorities were not to be given preference over qualified minorities; however, it did recommend that qualifications excluding a disparate number of minorities needed to be validated in accordance with EEOC procedures.

The more liberal approach of equality of result to affirmative action policies has caused strong reactions in segments of both the majority and minority communities.[27] Because of the pervasive effects of inequality, this view holds that in order for equality to be achieved by minority groups, because the competitive race is perceived as grossly unfair the government must "carry some runners to the finish line if they are to get there at all" (Stephenson et al., 1992:136). Politically, policies established to achieve this form of equality would result in special preference or preferential treatment of protected groups, such as veteran and minority preference in hiring and promotion. Legally, laws discriminating against protected classes would be subject to "strict judicial scrutiny," whereas laws giving preferential treatment to protected minority groups would not. Mandatory hiring or set-aside quotas would be considered appropriate remedies in findings of discrimination.

The U.S. Supreme Court did not accept the type of remedy endorsed in this approach in its ruling in *Regents of the University of California* v. *Bakke* (1978). At that time, the Court ruled that a reservation of a fixed number of seats for minority students was unconstitutional in that such an admissions policy unnecessarily denied other persons an equal chance to be considered. The Court did rule, however, that the university could use race as one factor or characteristic in its admissions process when comparing minority applicants with all other applicants, in its efforts to assure cultural diversity.

The Ninth Circuit Court of Appeals endorsed this approach in 1979 in *Blake* v. *City of Los Angeles* (1979) and *United States* v. *City of Los Angeles* (1979). The holdings in these companion cases resulted in consent decrees whereby the L.A.P.D. would hire agreed-upon percentages of minorities and women within an established time period. Other law enforcement agencies in major cities in the United States have also been attempting to comply with similar court rulings.[28] Subsequent to these rulings, the U.S. Supreme Court upheld the constitutionality of consent decrees for fire fighters in its 1986 *Local Number 93, International Association of Fire Fighters* v. *Cleveland* (1986) decision.

In California, law enforcement agencies presently require at least a minimum of a high school degree or a general education diploma for employment as a police officer. A total of forty-six police departments and sheriff's offices require some level of college education in addition to or as a supplement for basic training (California Commission on Peace Officer

Standards and Training, 1990:5–39). Some of these agencies are mandated to comply with consent decree requirements in order to achieve "equality of results" for minority groups whereas others are not.[29]

The dilemma for the L.A.P.D. is that, while it continues to require a minimum of a high school education for police officer applicants, it attempts to hire and promote officers with a college education. However, consent decree requirements mandating the hiring of a predetermined percentage of members of minority groups has precluded the L.A.P.D. and other similarly situated agencies from raising their P.O.S.T. certified minimum educational standards of a high school or equivalent degree.[30]

Although police departments nationwide are experiencing difficulties in staffing their sworn officer positions, (e.g., see Guffey, 1991), several studies have pointed out that the practice of raising educational standards has resulted in an increased pool of applicants for police officer positions overall.[31] The L.A.P.D., however, due to its current state of affairs,[32] may experience problems in attracting highly qualified college-educated minority recruits. If the L.A.P.D. were to adopt higher educational requirements for its police officer applicants, it would need to intensify its present recruitment strategies[33] in order to both attract sufficient numbers of college-educated minority recruits and comply with consent decree mandates.

Blake, and the *City of Los Angeles* companion case, has adopted local total labor force participation rates (which includes unskilled laborers) as the formula base in determining whether or not discrimination existed. These two cases had determined that nonvalidated hiring criteria used by the L.A.P.D. (e.g., height and weight requirements) resulted in a disparate impact on both minority groups and women. It is not quite clear whether the U.S. Supreme Court would adopt and apply this same formula in employment discrimination challenges for educational requirements. Subsequent to *Blake,* the Fifth Circuit Court of Appeals in *Davis* has utilized internal statistics and applicant flow data in a determination of employment discrimination, while at the same time distinguishing "professional" police officer positions from manual, unskilled labor positions. Prior to the *Davis* ruling, however, the Fourth Circuit Court of

Appeals in 1977 had ruled that for those positions requiring special qualifications, the correct disparate impact formula to be applied was the ratio of qualified minorities in the appropriate labor force rather than the ratio of the gross percentage in the total labor force, which included unskilled laborers. The Fourth Circuit Court of Appeals reasoned that in any discrimination case, "one element which remains essential is that a minority applicant be qualified for the position for which he applies" (*EEOC* v. *United Va. Bank/Seaboard National*, 1977:405–406).

If either the Ninth Circuit Court of Appeals or the Supreme Court were to follow the methods and rationale of previous circuit court rulings, it would seem that (1) a finding of disparate impact and hence, discrimination, most likely may not be supported,[34] and (2) a college education, nonetheless, would be considered a bona fide occupational qualification exception for police officer positions.

NOTES

1. For a discussion of the passage of the new law see Fessler et al. (1991) and Biskupic (1991b; 1991c).

2. Five 1989 cases overturned by the law include (1) *Wards Cove Packaging Co.* v. *Atonio*—burden of justifying selection criteria with disparate impact shifted back to the employer; (2) *Martin* v. *Wilks*—spells out rules in which third parties can challenge consent decrees in antidiscrimination cases; (3) *Patterson* v. *McLean Credit Union*—prohibits racial harassment occurring after a person has been employed; (4) *Price Waterhouse* v. *Hopkins*—prohibits employment decisions based on race, religion, sex, national origin, whether or not other factors also motivated the decision; (5) *Lorance* v. *AT & T Technologies*—allows challenges to a discriminatory seniority system when adverse impact is experienced rather than when policy is adopted. Four additional cases include: (1) *Equal Employment Opportunity Commission* v. *Arabian American Oil Co.* (1991)—allows American workers employed outside the U.S. to sue their U.S. employers for discrimination; (2) *Library of Congress* v. *Shaw* (1986)—allows successful challengers in discrimination cases under Title VII against the federal government to recover interest in delayed

cases; (3) *Grove City College* v. *Bell* (1984)—reverses that decision which had restricted the reach of four civil rights laws; and (4) *Crawford Fitting Co.* v. *J. T. Gibbons Inc.* (1987)—permits successful parties to recover costs of hiring experts under the damages provision of the bill.

3. The Court stated that "[t]he proper means of establishing business necessity will vary with the type and size of the business in question, as well as the particular job for which the selection process is employed." It also specifically acknowledged the results of nationwide reports showing job-relatedness of the college degree requirement as well as criminal justice scholars' testimony explaining the job-relatedness of college degree requirements for law enforcement officer positions (*Watson*, 1988:2795).

4. The Court continues that "[t]he facts of this case demonstrate the inadequacy of broad and general testing devices as well as the infirmity of using diplomas or degrees as fixed measures of capability. . . . Diplomas and tests are useful servants, but Congress has mandated the commonsense proposition that they are not to become masters of reality." (*Griggs*, 1971:432).

5. The courts in these cases, however, have upheld educational requirements for law enforcement officers.

6. The Court pointed out that the company implemented the new requirements in order to improve the overall quality of its work force. However, neither the high school degree requirement nor the intelligence test was "shown to bear a demonstrable relationship to successful performance of the jobs for which it was used." (*Griggs*, 1971:431).

7. The Court also stated that "Title VII is designed only to eliminate discrimination and not requiring the hiring of unqualified personnel" (*Griggs*, 1971:434). This caveat seems to have been ignored by employers when mandated by court decisions to fulfill affirmative action goals. The issue of race "norming" of testing scores in order to fulfill mandates has stirred controversy and reaction by aggrieved white male candidates. The new Civil Rights Act essentially would prohibit the "racial norming" or adjustment of testing scores for minority candidates (Biskupic, 1991a).

8. Other "important job-related objectives" may include capability, reduced turnover, *or* job satisfaction (*Washington*, 1976:251, n. 16).

9. The court had held that educational requirements were impermissible if intended to maintain a high quality of personnel or to ease advancement (*Roman*, 1973:50).

10. Approximately 40 percent of the high school student population in the city was Mexican American, whereas the total population of the city was only 25 percent Mexican American. This evidence was accepted by the court that educational requirements for employment as patrolmen (as well as fire fighters) would not have an adverse impact on Mexican Americans. The court did not, however, take into consideration the high school attrition rates nor the graduation rates of Mexican American students (*League*, 1976:883).

11. In contrast to the *League of United Latin American Citizens* decision, census data showing that 70 percent of white residents had completed a high school education compared to 35 percent of Mexican Americans was accepted by the courts in determining that such a requirement resulted in a "prima facie" case of discrimination against the minority group (*Aguilera*, 1985:846).

12. The issue of applying general population or census data for appropriate statistical comparisons was adopted by *Griggs* for laborer positions and by *Dothard* v. *Rawlinson* (1977) for correctional officer positions. See discussion in Palombo, 1992.

13. This method of statistical comparison was approved in *Albemarle Paper Co.* v. *Moody* (1975). In *Davis*, the court compared the applicant flow of qualified blacks (22 percent of the applicant pool) with the number of blacks hired during a specific time period.

14. At this time, the court determined that professional positions required "skills or abilities which are extremely difficult to define with precision and even harder to test for or measure" (*Davis*, 1985:213–218). The two rationales used by the court will be discussed more fully in a following section of the present chapter.

15. The court found that the state personnel board's requirement that applicants for social work positions have a college degree or two years of college with experience was sufficiently job related to justify its continued application, in view of public interest in the livelihood of the public and welfare of children, in which the supervisory position was involved (*Thompson*, 1987:210–11).

16. *Washington* (1976) held that the job-relatedness requirement was satisfied when it was demonstrated that a written employment exam was related to police academy success, regardless of its relationship to on-the-job performance.

17. Waintroob discusses three methods of statistical comparisons applied by the courts in determining prima facie cases of discrimination: (1) census data or general population statistics (2) relevant (qualified) labor market comparisons; and (3) applicant flow or internal statistics.

(Waintroob, 1979:69–103). It is not clear as to what method of statistical comparison would be applied by the court or whether a resultant finding of discrimination would be made.

18. "Therefore, standard to be applied here is not as rigid as that required for tests."

19. *Uniform Guidelines on Employee Selection Procedures* 29 CFR 1607.4(D), "Adverse Impact and the Four-Fifths Rule." This rule is based on applicant flow or internal statistics in which the overall selection or hiring rates for applicants from protected groups must be at least 80 percent of the hiring rate for the dominant group in order for a hiring practice not to be found discriminatory. Nonetheless, as noted in note 17 above, the federal courts have used at least three distinct methods in determining adverse impact for professional-type positions.

20. The reasoning in this decision is cited as controlling, in *Aguilera* v. *Cook County Police & Corrections Merit Bd.* (1985), a Seventh Circuit decision upholding educational requirements for corrections officers.

21. Discussed in previous section entitled *Cases Upholding College Degree Requirements.*

22. *Davis* (1985:218) endorsing the view of the *League* (1976:901) and *Aguilera* (1985:847), which quotes *League.*

23. Shernock has expressed skepticism of validation through expert witness testimony, footnoting in a recent study that expert opinion by social scientists who serve on national commissions has been questioned by James Q. Wilson, in that they "fail to distinguish what they believe as citizens and what they know as scholars." (Shernock, 1992:73, n. 2). However, it is apparent that he has not reviewed the actual testimony given and that his criticism would not be warranted in this decision.

24. For an overview of recent publications on the perceived adverse effects of affirmative action policies see Lynch (1989); Chavez (1991); Carter (1991); Steele (1990).

25. For text of President Nixon's speech, see *Blake* (Felkenes et al., 1990:11–12, vol. 1).

26. Legislation protecting blacks against "disparate treatment" forms of discrimination dates back to the Reconstruction Era, falling within the provisions of the Fourteenth Amendment.

27. For a limited discussion of the effects of affirmative action see Monroe (1991).

28. For an overview of these rulings, see Walker (1983 and 1990).

29. One statewide law enforcement agency has adopted an informal affirmative action employment policy, seeking to hire more minorities and women so that the ethnic composition of officer force is comparable to the makeup of the general population. In order to accomplish this goal, the agency periodically closes its application process to Caucasian males. The effect has been that minority applicants with no prior experience or higher educational qualifications are being hired; Caucasians with law enforcement experience and college education are being denied the opportunity to compete for employment! (Personal conversation with Training Officer Steve Larson, California Highway Patrol, June 13, 1992.)

30. P.O.S.T Standards are minimum standards. A representative from the Commission on Peace Officer Standards and Training has written that local law enforcement agencies are permitted to establish higher educational standards than those mandated by P.O.S.T. (Personal correspondence with Kathy Delle, Staff Services Analyst, Commission on Peace Officer Standards and Training, December 4, 1990.)

31. Petersen (1979:3) and Saunders (1970:58–59) have shown that departments that have raised their educational standards have experienced an increase in the number of qualified applicants. Additionally, they also provide an example of one agency in Maryland that, when it lowered its minimal requirements to that of an eighth-grade education, experienced a declining trend in the number of applications over the next ten years. Hoover (1975:27) discusses the "Gresham's Law" or self-fulfilling prophesy in recruitment in that an agency attracts persons whose educational attainment rarely exceeds an agency's minimum qualifications required by that agency. He cites a 1968 P.O.S.T. Commission study showing that increasing numbers of college-educated recruits were attracted to police departments in San Jose and Berkeley because these departments increased their educational requirements. Sherman and the National Advisory Commission on Higher Education for Police Officers (1978:183) believe that, given the favorable salary levels in many metropolitan police departments, agencies should experience little difficulty in recruiting college-educated applicants without the need to increase entry-level police salaries.

32. For example, see *Christopher Commission Report*.

33. For an overview of recent L.A.P.D. recruitment strategies to attract minorities and women, see *Blake* (Felkenes et al., 1990:12–18, vol. 2).

34. If the Ninth Circuit Court of Appeals or Supreme Court applied the applicant flow statistical formula approach used in *Davis* (1985), a finding of discrimination would result only if the ratio of minorities hired by a department was less than four-fifths of the total number of the educationally qualified minorities who applied for positions within the department.

CHAPTER 4

Models of Policing Styles

> Advocates of professionalism stress the qualities of police integrity rather than mere performance. . . . Professionals are introducing a new ethic into the modern police force which is undermining the old norms and loyalties. . . . The professional wants to transform and eventually control the system—this hope keeps him from cynicism. (*Niederhoffer*, 1967:71, 95)

In our complex, democratic American society, police officers are confronted with multifaceted role demands in the performance of their duties. These oftentimes conflicting tasks not only include enforcement of the law but also order maintenance and social service activities. Studies have shown, however, that a minimal amount of a patrol officer's time is devoted to law enforcement or violence-related activities, whereas approximately 80 to 90 percent of an officer's time is related to maintaining order or to handling various social services (e.g., see Roberg, 1978:336). Even a patrol officer within the L.A.P.D. can expect to engage minimally in law enforcement duties; for example, an officer may "detect a burglary no more than once in every three months and a robbery no more than once in every 14 years" (Bittner, 1974:25). A realistic estimate of crime-related matters is that the average officer makes approximately twenty-six arrests annually, with slightly more than five of those involving more serious crimes (Bittner, 1974: 25).

Although Chambliss and Seidman portray the working world of the patrol officer as a subculture of deviance primarily involving aggressive crime control and violations of constituted rules of due process (Chambliss and Seidman, 1971:365), Hoover stresses that an accurate portrayal of the role of the police officer primarily involves order maintenance or management of conflict situations. The problem for police officers in performing this order maintenance function is due to the presence of two conflicting value systems or techniques utilized to accomplish this goal: law enforcement and social service work.[1]

The majority of studies on the function or role of the police indicates that police officers presently engage in a number of diverse operations, many of these having little or nothing to do with law enforcement or crime control (e.g., see Petersen, 1979; Brooks, 1989:123; Goldstein, 1979:242). Many of these nonenforcement, service-related tasks are critical to the role of professional policing. These various services, however, involve competence unique to law enforcement and are rarely shared by any other occupation in society. As Bittner points out, the extraordinarily serious, necessary, and important matters which get accomplished by an individual officer depend on that officer's "perspicacity, judiciousness, and initiative" (Bittner, 1974:39). Viewing the enforcement of criminal law as an incidental part of police work, Bittner also believes that few officers possess the "perspicacity and judiciousness" necessary for their work (Bittner: 1974:40–41).

Police officers themselves have identified important components or dimensions necessary to professionalism within policing.[2] The ten key factors identified by Brown and Vogel (1983) include higher education and specialized knowledge and training, as the most important.[3] Second in importance is the ability to cope with a wide range of problems in the myriad of discretionary situations in which officers are involved. Serving and protecting the public, as well as honesty in their work, are determined as next highest in importance. The remaining six factors include pride in appearance; dedication to work; setting themselves as a public example; impartiality in engaging in their work; proper cheerful, compassionate, but cautious attitudes; and self-discipline or control of emotions in encounters with citizens (Brown and Vogel, 1983).

The models of policing styles discussed in the present chapter acknowledge the diverse and conflicting demands contemporary police officers are required to perform in their day-to-day performance of duties. These models also take into account the attitudes and discretionary choices officers make outside the confines of a bureaucratic, administrative environment. However, in this discussion, styles or modes of adaptations by police officers are considered within the larger context of the value of professionalism. In so doing, the various "ideal" styles of policing adopted by police officers will be identified and distinguished as either professional or nonprofessional.

Development of Modes of Behavior

In 1893, French sociologist Emile Durkheim first analyzed the process of urban social change generally from that of a premodern rural, agricultural society to that of the modern, urban industrial society (Durkheim, 1965). Durkheim argued that the rapid transition accompanying the modernization process from one form of society to the other would result in a type of social pathology or a breakdown in social norms or rules which he labeled as "anomie." A society in such a state would produce a variety of social maladies in its inability to control the natural appetites of individuals; such a society would be accompanied by an attendant rise in social deviance of all types.

American sociologist Robert Merton revised Durkheim's original conception of anomie and applied his typologies of behavioral adaptations of anomie to the American society in 1938 (Merton, 1968). For Merton, American culture defined the values and goals worth striving for, the most prominent being the acquisition of wealth. Additionally, American society also defined the institutionally accepted means or acceptable methods for accomplishing highly valued goals. These socially acceptable means consisted of the Protestant work ethic, also known as middle-class values, including such values as honesty, education, hard work, and deferred gratification (Merton, 1968:187).

In contrast to Durkheim, Merton conceived anomie as representing a contradiction between cultural goals and socially approved means in American society. For Merton, anomie resulted from an overemphasis on the achievement of cultural values (which also included status and prestige) and the social structure limiting the possibility for individuals in the lower social strata to use socially legitimate means to accomplish these goals. Merton also believed that anomie was a permanent feature of American life, and due to the inequality embedded in the social structure in American society, disproportionately more individuals in the lower socioeconomic strata were affected by anomie. The resultant strain on this class would cause more persons to deviate than those in the upper social strata.

According to Merton's theory, individuals respond in various ways to the problem of anomie, depending upon an individual's attitudes to the dominant cultural goals and access to institutionalized means for accomplishing them. These modes of adaptation include conformity, innovation, ritualism, retreatism, and rebellion. Educated persons who adopted middle-class values, in Merton's view, would choose conformity to societal values through legitimate means. Most deviance and crime would take the form of innovation, an adaptation in which persons mostly from the lower-class social strata would aspire toward dominant social values but would be structurally prohibited from achieving them through legitimate means. Hence, they would engage in socially unapproved means to obtain the culturally approved goals.

Persons who have achieved a minimal amount of success through legitimate means and are fearful of losing it, "play it safe" and engage in the third adaptation, ritualism. Merton hypothesized that persons from the lower middle class, such as bankers or bureaucrats, fit well into this mode of adaptation, retaining allegiance to the institutional means but giving up aspirations for cultural values. Those who dropped out altogether may be committed to society but realize the impossibility of achieving success; such people engaged in the fourth adaptation, retreatism. Last, the adaptation of rebellion is one in which persons replace old values with new ones and seek out an alternate religious, political, or social culture.

Merton pointed out that the four modes of deviant adaptation referred to role behaviors of individuals in specific types of situations and not to personality types (Merton, 1968:194). He also distinguished between rebellion as a mode of adaptation and "ressentiment," which he considered superficially similar but essentially different from rebellion. Whereas rebellion involved a genuine change in values, ressentiment did not. Ressentiment, according to Merton, involves a "sour grapes pattern which asserts merely that desired but unattainable objectives do not actually embody the prized values" but that one also "condemns what one secretly craves" (Merton, 1968:210). Ressentiment also consists of three interrelated elements: diffuse feelings of envy, hatred, and hostility; a powerlessness in expressing such feelings toward persons or social stratum evoking them; and a continual experiencing of impotent hostility (Merton, 1968:209–10).

Merton suggests that this group of "resentfuls" originates primarily in the lower socioeconomically depressed strata. The problem for society when institutional and social dislocations become acute is that the resentfuls can be easily organized into a revolutionary group by successful members of the rebellious rising class (Merton, 1968:210–11).

At the time Merton developed his theory of social structure and anomie, American law enforcement was predominantly a low social status occupation consisting of officers from the lower working class social strata of American society. It was during this era that the professionalism movement in law enforcement was in its infancy stage and policing was in a transition from a corrupt, brutal, blue-collar occupation to that of an effective middle-class, respectable, law enforcement profession. As a result of this continuing transition, policing generally has experienced a breakdown in occupational norms or normlessness that continues to exist today.[4] However, whereas Merton's typology may be able to account for the corruption within law enforcement prior to the rise of early twentieth-century "progressivism," his typology cannot account for the rise of professionalism within law enforcement throughout the twentieth century.

Examining behavioral adaptations in the context of social change, Dubin critiqued and extended Merton's original analysis, creating a typology consisting of fourteen categories of modes of deviant behavior. Its importance in the present context is that Dubin's concern is with the institutional setting in which

Merton's cultural norms become institutional goals or guides for behavior within a social institution (Dubin, 1959). Whereas Merton classified innovation as the most prevalent mode of adaptation resulting in criminal behavior and other forms of deviance, Dubin's typology involves innovation as a constructive invention in institutions in which it occurs. Whereas Merton's paradigm permitted little room for institutional, behavioral, or value change or reform (other than outright rebellion), Dubin's model posits not only behavioral innovation or invention but also value innovation or invention within institutions generally.

Behavioral innovations within institutions (institutional inventions) include such practices as collective bargaining and joint decision-making as positive adaptations to reformist strains within an institution. Innovation in this sense is positive and beneficial to society rather than harmful and destructive as in Merton's model. Such innovations may assist in explaining the goals of reform in policing in that they

> . . . take place when new standards of legitimacy come to be accepted, governing newly developed . . . behaviors. The historical point of invention of an institution occurs when the new norms achieve legitimacy and the behaviors conforming to them are practiced. (*Dubin*, 1959:150)

A second form of innovation introduced by Dubin is that of "normative invention," a form of deviant adaptation in which new norms replace old ones but the institutional setting remains the same. In this mode of adaptation, the norm of "might makes right" is replaced by a new norm in which competency necessary in decision-making is valued, justifying the employment and authority of highly educated and trained individuals.

In contrast to the adoption of new norms and modes of behavior of the innovator, the adaptation of ritualism takes into account persons whose behavior and ideas reject the new norms or institutional requirements. Such individuals, while failing to form substitutes for the old rejected norms, may respond in several ways. They may overconform and become the institutional moralist, e.g., an autocratic chief of police who espouses democratic decision-making within the organization (Dubin, 1959:157–58). Or such individuals can become organizational automatons or bureaucrats who perform their duties strictly "by the book" (Dubin, 1959:158).[5] Other responses include that of the "demagogue," a mode of behavior in which "the end justifies the means" becomes the guiding philosophy; the normative opportunist; and the means opportunist (Dubin, 1959:159–61).[6]

Finally, the concept of the ressentiment, suggested by Merton as a subjective prelude to involvement in revolutionary activity, is considered by Dubin to be a prelude to retreatism rather than rebellion. In this view, ressentiment as hostility, envy, and anger would result in resignation or suicidal tendencies rather than involvement in a violent or deviant subculture. It is Merton's concept of ressentiment rather than Dubin's that is developed by both Niederhoffer and Regoli in explaining the prevalence of cynicism, the antithesis of professionalism, within the police culture.

Neither Merton's nor Dubin's typologies of adaptations or part-theories have been examined empirically. The differences between the two sets of theories is that whereas Merton's typology is grounded in sociological laws of interaction within the social structure, Dubin's typology is developed within the framework of social psychological theories of the interaction process. More contemporary research on anomie theory and its attendant modes of behavior have shown that anomic responses by the individual are governed by cognitive and personality factors that are attitudinal, intellectual, social, or psychological in nature (e.g., see McClosky and Schaar, 1965:14–28).

Despite the relatively limited guidance in the literature as to the best means for empirically capturing policing styles, it is this latter approach or response to anomie by officers as individuals that provides the groundwork for the personality types or theoretical models of policing styles used in the present study.

Policing Styles within an Organizational Context

Various studies of policing as an institution have argued that the professionalization movement within American policing was a phenomenon primarily committed to changes at the organizational level. This view emphasizes the centralization of administrative authority and bureaucratic effectiveness as well as the enhancement of central administrative control over the patrol officers' exercise of discretion at the street level. The first typology of police officer styles was constructed at this organizational level of analysis, in which the predominant style of policing adopted by officers is determined by the demands of the organizational hierarchy.

In his work on operational styles, James Q. Wilson essentially argued that various types of police departments encouraged a dominant style of policing that ultimately affected an officer's discretionary behavior. The issue of discretionary officer behavior was important for Wilson because in the law enforcement hierarchy, in contrast to other political institutions, as one moves down the institutional hierarchy, the amount of discretion increases (Wilson, 1968:7). In his analysis of eight American law enforcement agencies, Wilson determined the existence of three distinct types of agencies. Each type of agency in turn determined a unique type of operational style in its officers. These included the "watchman style," the "legalistic style," and the "service style" of policing.

For agencies adopting the watchman style of policing, officers primarily are concerned with the maintenance of order over that of the enforcement of the law or the provision of public services. In this role, police ignore many minor violations and selectively enforce the law, although they believe that serious crimes "should be dealt with seriously" (Wilson, 1968:141). Aggressive in their pursuit of both order maintenance and serious crimes, officers apply "street justice" or "curbstone justice" selectively and prejudicially against juveniles, as well as against members of minority and deviant groups.[7] Since the objectives for officers adopting this mode of policing is to do the least amount of work possible, when time permits, officers selectively provide public services to friends and political supporters. Although this model of policing was the target of police reformers in the early twentieth century, it still exists in cities today (Pursley, 1991:193; also see Slovak, 1986).

The legalistic style of policing was seen as a "professional" response in larger urban agencies to the corrupt watchman style of the earlier era. Emphasizing aggressive police work aimed at arresting criminal offenders, a high arrest rate for all types of offenses, and nonselective treatment of individuals constitute the major components of the legalistic style. In contrast to the watchman style, law enforcement activities are emphasized over order maintenance behaviors, and involvement in public or social services is nonexistent. Currently labeled the "old professionalism," an officer adapting to this model is

> . . . not especially interested in hearing from the lay public, including businessmen, to say nothing of representatives of minority groups. [He] saw himself as someone who had received advanced training in the intricacies of the penal code, search-and-seizure law, use of firearms, interrogation tactics, and the fine points of when and how to apply the baton. His training did not, he thought, require additional input from members of the community. (Skolnick and Bayley, 1986:212)

The service style of behavior was found by Wilson to exist within more-affluent suburban areas. Since the overall goal of this style is heightened and impartial service to the community as well as positive police–community relations, an emphasis on a large number of arrests is avoided and juveniles and less-serious offenders are diverted to social service agencies. The type of police agency adopting this mode stresses informal rather than formal, punitive sanctions. This style has more recently been labeled the "new professionalism" in which police

> . . . serve, learn from, and are accountable to the community. Behind the new professionalism is a governing notion: that the police and the public are co-producers of crime prevention. (Skolnick and Bailey, 1986:212–13)

Overall, Wilson's typology of operational styles suggests not the absence of conflicting operational styles within a particular agency, but the general resolution of that conflict in favor of the organizational demands. Such a resolution, then, would lead to a homogeneity of styles within agencies and a heterogeneity of styles across agencies. Additionally, despite the ambiguities of Wilson's original policing styles, his descriptions of these styles have acknowledged crime fighting and criminal apprehension, at least in the watchman and service styles, as a minor facet of the overall demands of police work.

Slovak (1986) empirically tested Wilson's organizational thesis as to the dominant types of officer styles within individual agencies. Comparing the operational styles in three eastern cities, Slovak found that the larger the police agency, the greater the amount of discretion exercised by its officers on patrol. Additionally, the larger the police department, the less legalistic or the more watchman-like were the officers within these agencies in comparison to the smaller agencies examined (Slovak, 1986:29).[8] More important, Slovak also found that dominant operational styles varied within law enforcement agencies; adoption of the various styles was dependent upon the size of the police agency and the status of the locality or neighborhood served within the agency's jurisdiction. However, he also found one agency adopting a "mixed style" of policing, "doing a little bit of everything in nearly every neighborhood it serves" (Slovak, 1986:164).

In Slovak's study, the problem of anomie within law enforcement was not assessed as a result of the normlessness within agencies in a state of transition from the old style to the new style of policing. Anomie, in his view, was a product of the environment of the central business district, areas in which few permanent residents were able to act as informal agents of social control. As a result, policing within these districts was required to be more legalistic and aggressive than styles adopted within the residential neighborhoods (Slovak, 1986:180).

Results of Slovak's study support the thesis that neighborhood or environmental variables rather than the organizational context primarily influence policing styles. However, Slovak also acknowledges that external social and political factors, as well as individual personality factors, influence the operational styles and quality of police service. At least at the street level, patrol officers' decisions are only "imperfectly" controllable by police administrators and managers, and a style adopted by an officer "is essentially a response negotiated by individual officers . . . to the various demands placed upon them, and therefore a response that will vary notably across different groups or categories of officers" (Slovak, 1986:110, 183).

Professional Values and Policing Styles

One of the major problems associated with the determination of just what constitutes a professional police officer is that, according to Brown and Vogel, "virtually all practices and procedures in policing have been cited as evidence of professionalism" (Brown and Vogel, 1983:17). Confusion abounds as to its conceptualization. Nonetheless, the discussion in the previous chapter has shown that the courts consider professionalism a prerequisite to "safe and efficient" law enforcement but also admit that, as a construct, professionalism is extremely difficult if not impossible to measure. As a result, expert testimony rather than empirical evidence has been accepted by the courts as evidence of the relationship between higher education and police professionalism.

Much of the prior research on police officers has focused on various attitudes, such as dogmatism, authoritarianism, open-mindedness, and flexibility. However, as critics have pointed out, attitudes in and of themselves do not necessarily determine behavior. Tentative conclusions in the attitudinal studies are that attitudes, in some way, may influence officer behavior.

The study of police officer values in general, or the value of professionalism in particular, as theoretical concepts has been given considerably less attention. Over the past half century, social scientists generally have focused more on the development of theory and measurement of attitudes than on those of values (Rokeach, 1973:17). Nonetheless, the results of one study measuring the "police values" of a sample of Caucasian male police officers suggested that postrecruitment socialization was not a determinant of an officer's values. Personality and social backgrounds, in contrast, were found to be important determinants of those values (Rokeach, 1973:151–52). The factor of education, however, was not taken into account or given consideration as a form of prerecruitment socialization of those values.

In his study of human values generally, Rokeach posits that the values an individual incorporates into his or her personality are distinguishable from his or her attitudes toward certain objects or situations. For Rokeach, a value or specific belief occupies a more central position than attitudes within an individual's personality structure and cognitive system; therefore, values are determinants of both attitudes and behavior. More specifically, a value is

> . . . an enduring belief that a specific mode of conduct and end-state of existence is personally or socially preferable to an opposite or converse mode of conduct or end-state of existence. . . . [A value] concerns a desirable mode of behavior or end-state that has a transcendental quality to it, guiding actions, attitudes, judgments, and comparisons across specific objects and situations and beyond immediate goals to more ultimate goals. (Rokeach, 1973:5, 18)

A value, like all beliefs, has three distinct components: cognitive, affective, and behavioral. In the context of professionalism, to say that a police officer has incorporated that value into his or her personality is to say that that officer "cognitively knows the correct way to behave or the correct end-state to strive for" (Rokeach, 1973:7). Additionally, the value of professionalism is affective in that an officer can feel emotional about it: feel strongly for or against it, approving of those who exhibit positive instances of that value and disapproving of those officers who exhibit negative incidents of it, for example, exhibiting nonprofessionalism in their duties. Last, the behavioral component within the value of professionalism is considered an intervening variable; it "leads to action when activated" (Rokeach, 1973:7).

Conceived within this framework, police professionalism, at least at the individual officer level, is an enduring value incorporated within the officer's personality guiding the rightness of his or her actions. Although this value may be mediated by the organizational constraints and factors in the working environment, the core value of professionalism is incorporated into the officer's personality and influenced by socialization factors, such as education, prior to recruitment into law enforcement. Additionally, strong positive emotional feelings would be exhibited toward those who incorporate this value into their personality and negative feelings toward those who do not. Finally, the cognitive knowledge of the "correct way" to respond would result in situational behavior leading toward the end-state or goal of professionalism.

Arthur Niederhoffer engaged in the first major study empirically examining, not professionalism, but what he perceived to be the antithesis to professionalism within policing. Niederhoffer identified the problem of cynicism as a deeply entrenched "ideological plank" within police departments, a state in which officers lose faith in people, society, and themselves; a state in which officers adopt a Hobbesian view of the world in which crime, brutality, and corruption represent the norms of society; a problem leading to frustration, resentment, pessimism, and misanthropy (Niederhoffer, 1967:9).

Building upon Merton's original concept of anomie or normlessness in the social structure, Niederhoffer postulated that cynicism was a by-product of social anomie, which unless mediated, could lead to personal "anomia" or an absence of values in police officers. He also identified three elements of anomie within police work, which included a loss of faith in people, a loss of enthusiasm for the high ideals of police work, and a loss of pride and integrity (Niederhoffer, 1967:91).

Cynicism, according to Niederhoffer's model, resulted in a two-step process or movement away from a value of commitment to either failure, frustration, or disenchantment with the social system and its values. Once this last step of cynicism has been reached, officers may adapt in three ways: return to a commitment of professional values; join a deviant subculture that in turn reinforces a set of values dedicated to a philosophy of cynicism;[9] and remain a loner, which could lead to psychological anomia or suicide (Niederhoffer, 1985:208–09; 1967:95).

Niederhoffer validated his cynicism scale and empirically examined the extent of cynicism within a large Eastern police department.[10] Using bivariate analytical techniques, he found cynicism, a noncommitment to professional values, to be as prevalent as he had hypothesized. However, his hypothesized inverse relationship between professionalism and cynicism, a continuum model in which professionalism represented scores on the low end and cynicism represented scores on the high end, was not empirically examined. Nonetheless, his personal experience and expertise within the police culture provided an analytical insight into the police professionalism movement generally and the conflict between the professionals and nonprofessionals during this transition. Niederhoffer observed that a primary consequence of professionalization was a shift in values from that of an "ideal tough cop" to an "ideal of social scientist police officer" (Niederhoffer, 1967:28). He also observed that

> The doctrine of the professional movement advocates education, a non-punitive orientation, strict legality in every phase of police work, and most important of all, good public relations. These principles create an atmosphere in which only the professionally directed police officer can operate successfully. On a lower plane within the hierarchy exists the tough minded, authoritarian working class of the police society. Conditions at this level foster an outlook that exalts power and force, and is contemptuous of the so-called unrealistic, soft-minded, and even submissive ideas of the professionals. (Niederhoffer, 1967:131)

Within this working-class world of the police culture, cynicism manifested itself in feelings of anger, envy, impotent hostility, and "ressentiment" among patrol officers. The adoption of an aggressive form of cynicism, which was a by-product of ressentiment, largely depended on whether or not an officer remained a loner or joined a subculture of cynicism.[11] For middle-class patrol officers, cynicism was represented by frustration (as a result of the police culture), a feeling that Niederhoffer found mediated or intervened the effects of the relationship between higher education and professionalism (Niederhoffer, 1967:236). He did not explain, however, how frustrated officers could return to the stage of commitment to professionalism although, intuitively, involvement in professional organizations most likely would assist an officer toward this direction.

Following in the footsteps of Niederhoffer, Regoli and associates built upon Niederhoffer's original cynicism study by empirically exploring the relationship between cynicism and professionalism (Regoli, 1977; Regoli, 1976b; Regoli, 1976a; Lotz and Regoli, 1977; Regoli and Poole, 1979; Regoli, Poole, and Hewitt, 1979; Regoli, Crank, and Culbertson, 1987a; Regoli, Crank, Culbertson and Poole, 1989; Regoli, Crank, and Culbertson, 1987b). In his initial study, Regoli, like Niederhoffer before him, built upon Durkheim's and Merton's theoretical foundation of anomie and applied it to the police culture. With the "professionals" taking over control from the "old core," a state of transition of old values being supplanted by new values created a state of police normlessness. Officers within the lower ranks (including patrol officers) are seen as being caught between contending forces, facing both a confusion of norms and a conflict of loyalties. The diffusion of anomie is considered a result of this state of confusion (Regoli, 1977:4).

In addition to this problem, according to Regoli, the public's refusal to confer professional status on the police as an institution contributes to frustration of the officers and leads to a greater chance for anomie (Regoli, 1977:5). Cynicism is the primary adaptation to this state of anomie within the police culture, cynicism having all the characteristics of Merton's ressentiment (Regoli, 1977:6–7). Cynicism does not necessarily represent an acting out of hostile feelings but, for Regoli, is a "stage of psychological latency" resulting from the strain or conflict in the police organization and the individual officer's personality. However, quoting Coser, if such aggressive feelings are not released or acted out, resentment arises and officers will openly degrade the professional values they despise and those persons who espouse them (Regoli, 1977:6).

In his pioneering study, Regoli considered both cynicism and professionalism as attitudes although he defined professionalism as an "ideology" found in occupations whose members aspire toward professional status (Regoli, 1977:25). The major importance of Regoli's study, however, is that he empirically examined Niederhoffer's hypothesized inverse relationship between cynicism and professionalism and found his empirical results to support Niederhoffer's original hypothesis.[12] Additionally, and more important for this study, the results of his examination of the relationship between the construct of professionalism and college education (as a dichotomous variable) for large urban agencies were inconclusive (Regoli, 1977:96). However, he did suggest that the less-educated officers defended themselves from the organizational value conflict by joining a subculture of cynicism and scoffing at professionalism within policing. Therefore, the professional culture and the cynical culture within police organizations were considered to be two diametrically opposed cultures in conflict with each other.

Typologies Based on Police Personalities

Professionals, Enforcers, Avoiders, and Reciprocators

The first scholarly and qualitative research study to examine and identify unique typologies of police personalities or policing styles was that of William Muir (1977). Through the use of in-depth interviews and observations of various officers while they were engaged in street-level work, Muir distinguished four operational styles of police officers. He considered only one of these styles to be that of the police "professional" and representative of the "good" police officer; the other three styles theoretically represented "nonprofessional" police officers (Muir, 1977:54).

In formulating his typologies and his "professional political model of the good policeman," Muir used Max Weber's professional political model of the "mature man" as his foundation (Muir, 1977:47). This professional political model incorporates the notions of understanding human conduct, a comprehension of human suffering, sensitivity to the individual's yearning for dignity, and a faith in people generally. Muir considered police officers as "politicians" in the narrow sense in that a central feature of the officer's role is the coercive, necessary, and oftentimes violent use of power. "Professional" referred to the fact that coercive encounters occurred so frequently that they were routine. The routine use of such power easily became a corrupting mechanism.[13] In Weber's model, two characteristics or "virtues," identified as "passion" and "perspective," in combination reduced the chances of cynicism and corruption (Muir, 1977:50).

These two virtues of passion and perspective are important in Muir's model of policing styles in that they determine the responsible use of coercive power by police officers. The problem of the use of force and coercion, the relationship between cruel means and worthwhile ends, plays a large part in the development of an officer's outlook on the world. The virtue of passion essentially enables an officer to establish an ethic of the use of principled violence as a means to an end. Passion determines the extent to which officers are able to morally reconcile the need for using coercive power in order to accomplish worthwhile goals.

However, Muir also believed that a moral ethic or calm could be achieved while rejecting the ethical concerns of society; therefore cynicism and corruption were possible. The second necessary virtue of perspective, described as intellectual "objectivity," a sense or inner knowledge of a "tragic" perspective, provided officers with the capacity to objectively understand and empathize with the circumstances of others (Muir, 1977:50–51). The secret of avoiding corruption or cynicism through the use of coercive power was the ability to combine passion with perspective. The combination of both of these virtues is characteristic of the professional police officer.

> If he felt morally reconciled to using coercion and at the same time he reflected empathetically upon the condition of mankind, he measured up to being a professional, a good policeman. (Muir, 1977:54)

The professional political model also generated three unique types of nonprofessional police officers. Whereas the professional officer has acquired both passion and perspective to reconcile the demands of his or her complex role, the others have not. Unlike the professional or good police officers, all three of these nonprofessional types are unable to reconcile the two virtues of passion and perspective in responding to their complex role demands, which in effect makes them prone to cynicism.

"Enforcers" possess passion, which enables them to use coercive force in carrying out law enforcement tasks, but lack perspective or the tragic sense, and hence are unable to empathize and provide positive assistance to citizens. "Reciprocators" possess a tragic perspective but lack passion, or a moral equanimity with regard to the use of coercion in their law enforcement tasks, therefore, they are unable to use coercive force at all. "Avoiders" lack both passion and a tragic perspective and are therefore unresponsive to the human condition and especially vulnerable to adopting a cynical perspective (Muir, 1977:54).

In his work, Muir discusses at length characteristics of twenty-eight officers, which assist in the construction of his four unique police officer profiles. An analysis of his discussion of those attitudinal and behavioral characteristics for each officer profile indicates not only a distinction between these groups in the application of aggression or force relative to law enforcement duties, but also a distinction in initiative or the resourceful carrying out of those tasks. Analysis also reveals a distinction in attitudes toward and performance of tasks not directly related to law enforcement dependent on the personality profile of the officers. Selectivity or prejudicial bias in enforcing the laws or providing public support services is also found to be a distinguishing characteristic between the groups. Classification of these types is shown in table 2 at the end of the chapter.

Overall, Muir's professional police officer is able to reconcile the contradictions inherent in the police officer role. The professional, while taking initiative in controlling the situation, does not alienate citizens through aggression or intimidation. He or she places as much importance on service-related and order maintenance tasks as on enforcement of the law. He or she uses the color of his or her authority to impartially enforce the law within the framework of the law. He or she also uses knowledge and skills to provide services to citizens that fall beyond the definition of law enforcement per se.

As a result of their moral and intellectual differences, these four types of officers differ in how they perform their roles. The professional remains legalistic while at the same time also giving importance to the full range of tasks necessary to the fulfillment of his or her role. The enforcer, adopting the traditional view of aggressive "crime fighting" as his or her true role, rejects any tasks outside this domain. The reciprocator is considered a social service worker in the true sense of the word, rejecting coercive law enforcement duties as inherently immoral. The avoider, because of his or her inadequacies, avoids all tasks as much as possible. However, when forced to perform (to bring up his or her grades), the avoider resorts to aggression and oftentimes brutality in enforcing the law in order to "produce."

Muir's typologies of policing styles are instructive in that they place primary emphasis on the characteristics, values, and behavioral styles of officers. In contrast to Wilson's organizational model, Muir's model reveals the contradictory and conflicting styles adopted by officers in a midsize police department under the leadership of an autocratic chief of police. Attempts to replicate Muir's psychological model, however, have been unsuccessful (e.g., see Snipes and Mastrofski, 1990).

Old Style, Clean Beat, Professional, and Service Types

Brown's typology of policing styles in two L.A.P.D. divisions as well as in two suburban Los Angeles police departments is not so much concerned with the problem of normlessness or anomie and cynicism but with the amount and types of discretionary choices officers make in their day-to-day decision-making. For Brown, professionalization in policing in recent decades has been primarily an organizational phenomenon, focusing on the centralization of both executive authority and control over the exercise of street-level discretion of patrol officers (Brown, 1981). Similar to Wilson, Brown has argued that a positive relationship exists between the amounts of officer discretion and the size of the police agency: the larger the police agency, the more freedom the patrol officer exercises in his or her discretionary encounters with citizens.

By using field observations and attitudinal survey data, Brown establishes four typologies of officer behavior based primarily upon an officer's attitudes or orientations in his or her understanding and use of discretionary behavior. According to Brown, the beliefs officers hold toward their jobs, the law, the people, and the situations they confront in the daily course of their work shape the succession of choices they make in responding to an actual encounter with citizens, for example, decisions on the appropriateness of service or order maintenance activities and crime control preoccupation. However, Brown also acknowledges other factors, such as occupational socialization and organizational and environmental characteristics, influencing such choices (Brown, 1981:34–41). He points out that the matter of an officer's operational style "is clearly more complex than Wilson's argument would suggest" (Brown, 1985:203).[14]

Brown's operational styles are differentiated in terms of two main characteristics: aggressiveness and selectivity. For Brown, aggressiveness refers to the use of coercive force, which legitimizes the use of illegal tactics, and the use of initiative on the street to handle matters related to criminal events. He distinguishes between "high aggressiveness" as being extremely aggressive, whereas "low aggressiveness" represents not passivity but the quality of being active and flexible, that is, taking initiative. Selectivity essentially refers to priorities in enforcing the criminal codes. Selective officers choose to focus on felonies, giving misdemeanors lower priority, whereas others believe that all laws should be enforced so far as possible.

Brown points out that his five operational styles—the "old style crime fighter," the "clean beat crime fighter," the "professional," the "negative service style," and the "positive service style"—are analytical types highlighting "the distinctive characteristics of a particular approach to police work." Only a few of the officers observed perfectly exemplified any one of these styles (Brown, 1985:196). In his study, Brown also clarifies differences between the styles in terms of general characteristics of the officers he observed. His observations take into account not only typical responses to various encounters but also related attitudes associated with each style. The distinct styles he describes are similar to Wilson's and Muir's types in certain characteristics but different in others.

An analytical comparison of Brown's five types of operational styles with Wilson's and Muir's reveals similarities in important areas. Like Muir's professional type, Brown's professional style takes initiative in law enforcement and order maintenance events, but is not overly aggressive, staying within the framework of the law, rules, and regulations. Both are nonselective in enforcement of laws in that they give equal consideration to both serious and not so serious crimes, while at the same time trying to be impartial in applying the criminal codes. Importance is also placed on non-law enforcement–related tasks, such as calls for service and domestic problems, and such calls are not treated with scorn or disdain. Taking into account the nature of the human condition, a sense of empathy guides officers falling within these groups to handle such events either informally or formally, being judicious, impartial, and fair in attempting to resolve conflicts.

Brown's conceptual type of professional is also similar to Wilson's combination of legalistic/service-oriented officer. Wilson's legalistic type takes initiative in enforcing the law without being abusive; this type is also nonselective in carrying out law enforcement and order maintenance tasks. The downside of this type is that it rejects any involvement in social service–related activities. However, when the legalistic and service types are combined, they represent the "best that the police have to offer," the "new professionals" identified by Skolnick and Bayley (1986). They also represent the professional style of officer that was found by Brown to exist within the L.A.P.D.

Brown's old style crime fighter, a vestige from the old school of law enforcement, apparently resembles Muir's enforcer type and Wilson's watchman style in some respects, the main differences being that Muir's enforcer rejects outright any involvement in service-related activities. Although the old style crime fighter treats such services with disdain, he or she performs them in a selective manner in conformance with the officer's individual moral code, quite similar to Wilson's watchman type. These three types are also similar in that they are highly aggressive in handling serious criminal conduct and highly selective in handling order maintenance events.

Brown's clean beat crime fighter operational style represents the "worst of all worlds," the personified "robocop" of modern policing. Officers adopting this style represent the height of cynicism. This type of officer, like Wilson's legalist and Muir's professional, may take initiative in handling law enforcement duties; however, like Wilson's watchman and Muir's enforcer, as well as Brown's old style crime fighter counterpart, he or she also adopts overly aggressive tactics in crime suppression. In performing these tasks, the officer does so quite selectively and rejects any involvement in service-related duties, having narrowly defined the role of the contemporary police officer.

The two distinct service operational styles are both assets and liabilities to contemporary policing. The negative service style totally avoids involvement in any type of activity, doing just enough to get by. However, when involved in the less time-consuming, service-related activities, this type of officer does so selectively in a self-interested manner, much like Muir's avoider and reciprocator, and Wilson's watchman. In contrast, the positive service style attempts to inculcate a new humanistic philosophy in policing, emphasizing the selective enforcement of more serious and violent crimes while downplaying the seriousness of vice-related crimes and misdemeanors or infractions of the law. This type of officer places a major emphasis on and takes an initiative in providing extralegal services to the community, stressing the importance of implementing crime prevention–type programs, such as neighborhood watch and drug awareness programs.

Enforcers, Zealots, Social Service Agents, and Watchmen

Pursley (1991) divides police behavior into four operational types, based upon secondary analysis of prior studies. He identifies these distinct types as the "enforcer," the "zealot," the "watchman," and the "social service agent," while disclaiming that none of these types is strictly inclusive.

Analysis of the characteristics discussed by Pursley suggests that the watchman style falls within the nonprofessional classification of operational styles, and the social service agent is directly comparable to Wilson's service style of policing, therefore falling within the professional classification of operational styles. However, Pursley's two remaining operational styles are not directly comparable to Wilson's, Muir's, or Brown's professional or nonprofessional types.

Much like Brown's clean beat crime fighter, Pursley's zealot takes initiative and is both aggressive and nonselective in law enforcement–related tasks. The zealot, like the clean beat crime fighter, also rejects service-related activities because of the need to spend time and scarce resources on more primary law enforcement–related tasks. However, unlike the clean beat crime fighter, the zealot is not aggressive to the point of "craziness" and takes the due process rights of the citizens into account when performing this aspect of his or her role. The zealot is more legalistic than the clean beat crime fighter, but less legalistic (using illegal tactics when the situation warrants) than either Muir's or Brown's professional officer.

Pursley's enforcer is aggressive and nonselective in handling law enforcement–related tasks, primarily functioning in a reactive-type capacity. Proactivity or initiative used by Muir's and Brown's other types is not used by this enforcer, who rejects the preventative type of law enforcement activities. The enforcer also rejects outright social service–related activities, characteristics placing this enforcer in the nonprofessional classification. Unlike Wilson's combination legalistic/service style officer and Muir's and Brown's professional officer, none of Pursley's types of officer styles fit well into the present professional classification model.

POLICEwomen and policeWOMEN

Susan Martin's examination of the effectiveness of women as patrol officers in the Washington, D.C., Police Department essentially recognizes two distinct operational styles adopted by female patrol officers (Martin, 1980). Martin identifies these two types as POLICEwomen and policeWOMEN. It is clear from her study that despite the role ambiguities these women face in the day-to-day encounters in their work, many of the female officers she observed fit well within the professional model of policing styles.

POLICEwomen adapted well to the complex and strenuous demands of patrol work, and Martin found that these women succeeded and found satisfaction in their jobs by stressing overachievement in both law enforcement and service-related duties, assertiveness in the more dangerous aspects of their encounters with citizens, and strict adherence to department rules and policies. Despite the fact that POLICEwomen were primarily enforcement oriented, they also stressed their desirability to display empathy, compassion, and a willingness to provide services beyond the enforcement function. Essentially, they considered "professionalism" to be an important component of their patrol officer role.

Overall, POLICEwomen expressed their comfortableness with working the streets as patrol officers, enjoying the variety of duties and the opportunity to meet new people. They also recognized that the physical aspect of patrol work is overemphasized and that the key to success in effective patrol work primarily involves astute mental acumen and the development of verbal and nonverbal communication skills (Martin, 1980:186–93).

PoliceWOMEN, in contrast, were found to adopt traditional feminine behavior and were clearly apathetic and disinterested in their occupational demands, except as a source of income. PoliceWOMEN primarily adopted a service-oriented role perspective; in their role as law enforcer, they showed little initiative, responding only to calls to which they were dispatched and making few arrests. Martin found that policeWOMEN expressed extreme unhappiness or discomfort on patrol, stressing their physical limitations, avoiding dangerous, confrontational situations while on duty, or relying on male officers to handle the situation (Martin, 1980:194–99).

Martin's qualitative analysis of the two diverse operational styles adopted by female police officers demonstrates that the POLICEwoman type coincides with Wilson's combined legalistic/service-oriented officer type, as well as with Muir's and Brown's professional officer styles. POLICEwomen possess both the initiative and nonselectivity in enforcing the law by "going by the book" as well as taking initiative and being nonselective in providing extralegal social services.

PoliceWOMEN, on the other hand, fall short of falling within the professional classification developed in the present study. Although this type of officer does take initiative in service-style encounters, like the other nonprofessional types, they avoid, when possible, participating in law enforcement and order maintenance–related duties.

Professional/Nonprofessional Classification of Policing Styles

The previous discussion initially presented the various modes of behavioral adaptations that have assisted in the development of specific typologies or styles of police behavior. The operational styles identified in this discussion are analytical types, based primarily on theoretical and qualitative, observational research techniques. None of these "ideal" types has been empirically validated or replicated in subsequent research.

The goal in this present chapter has been to trace the development of the specific operational styles formulated by previous researchers. Second, an analysis and comparison of these various styles has been made as to whether they conform to either the professional or nonprofessional theoretical categories of operational styles developed in the present study. Classification of styles is primarily based upon individual characteristics gleaned from the studies of police professionalism, consisting of certain "virtues, qualities, or characteristics" necessary for the multifaceted and complex role of patrol work in contemporary policing.

If a specific operational style has been assessed as incorporating qualities of initiative and impartiality in law enforcement and order maintenance tasks as well as initiative and impartiality in performing service-related activities, then that particular type has been classified as professional. In contrast, if a distinct policing style has been shown to be representative of both aggression and selectivity in performing law enforcement and order maintenance tasks, as well as exhibiting an outright rejection of or selectivity in providing extralegal social service–related activities, then the operational style has been defined as nonprofessional. Table 2 depicts the final results of this effort.

An empirical examination and replication of the various operational types identified by researchers discussed in this chapter is not possible in the present study. Unfortunately, the proper empirical data are not available at the present time to accomplish such an undertaking. The professional model developed here, however, is based upon the theoretical cynicism/professional continuum model initially explored by Niederhoffer and followed up and reformulated by Regoli and associates.

Several assumptions concerning this professional continuum model are being made at this time. First, patrol officers who score high or above the mean on the cynicism/professional continuum scales empirically examined in this study exhibit more professional attitudes and are more likely than not to adopt a professional policing style identified by either Wilson, Muir, Brown, or Martin.

Second, patrol officers who receive a low score, a score below the mean on the cynicism/professional continuum scales, exhibit more cynical attitudes and are more likely than not to fit into one of the nonprofessional typologies identified by these prior researchers.

Third, if, as the following chapter will show, education is determined as being significantly related to higher professionalism scores, then one can feel fairly confident that officers fitting within the operational styles identified as professional value both higher education and officer professionalism. Those who fit into one of the nonprofessional types more likely than not reject the values of professionalism toward citizens, the police organization, their own role as police officers, and other social institutions. Additionally, such officers can be expected to reject higher education as a prerequisite for successfully fulfilling the officer role.

TABLE 2

MODELS OF POLICING STYLES

	Professional			
	Law Enforcement/Order Maintenance Activities		Public/Social Service Activities	
	Initiative	Nonselective	Initiative	Nonselective
Wilson, 1968	Legalistic	Legalistic	Service	Service
Muir, 1977	Professional Enforcer	Professional	Professional	Professional
Brown, 1981	Professional Clean Beat Old Style Positive Service	Professional Clean Beat	Professional Positive Service	Professional Positive Service
Pursley, 1991	Zealot	Zealot Enforcer	Social Service	Social Service
Martin, 1980	POLICEwomen	POLICEwomen	POLICEwomen policeWOMEN	POLICEwomen policeWOMEN
	Nonprofessional			
	Law Enforcement/Order Maintenance Activities		Public/Social Service Activities	
	Aggressive	Selective	Reject	Selective
Wilson, 1968	Watchman	Watchman	Legalistic	Watchman
Muir, 1977	Enforcer Avoider	Enforcer Avoider Reciprocator	Enforcer	Avoider Reciprocator
Brown, 1981	Clean Beat Old Style	Old Style Positive Service	Clean Beat	Old Style Negative Service
Pursley, 1991	Zealot Enforcer		Zealot Enforcer	
Martin, 1980		policeWOMEN		

NOTES

1. Hoover also states that most police officers resolve the conflict by rejecting a social work self-image and conceiving of themselves exclusively as crime fighters. Whenever this occurs, the ability of a police officer to resolve conflict situations without invoking the criminal process is diminished (Hoover, 1975:9).

2. Brown and Vogel asked a sample of police officers open-ended questions concerning their views on criteria vital to professionalism (Brown and Vogel, 1983).

3. Skolnick points out in his study of police officers that those with less formal higher education and legal training consider themselves as belonging to a different type of organization, i.e., view themselves as "craftsmen" rather than as "professionals." He believes that these officers react more adversely to having their actions and opinions challenged in a court of law (Skolnick, 1966:233).

4. For a history of this transition, see primarily Walker (1977:1980) for general information and Woods (1973) for the L.A.P.D.

5. According to Dubin, persons from the lower socioeconomic strata make up this group. Such persons are disinterested in education and nonfinancial incentives for work. Such persons are pessimistic in their appraisals of opportunities for "getting ahead" generally (Dubin, 1959:158, n. 28). The point here is that these typologies seem to coincide with typologies of operational styles such as the clean beat patrolman and the legalist to be discussed later in the text.

6. For these three responses, individuals who reject institutional norms or means, center society's attention on the espousal of certain values, e.g., the traditional family. The point here is that several of these modes of adaptation are comparable to deviant policing styles developed by Muir (1977) such as the enforcer, the reciprocator, and the avoider, to be discussed shortly.

7. Wilson points out that watchman style organizations primarily recruit officers from the working class who use rough language and a gruff manner in dealing with certain types of citizens; however, these officers learn not to antagonize more "respectable" members of the community. Their informal style of maintaining order includes physical aggression, physical abuse toward disrespectful and minority juveniles, as well as "roughing up" disenfranchised citizens and blacks (Wilson, 1968:145–70).

8. Slovak suggests that the reason for this finding is that larger agencies have greater levels of autonomy and flexibility in defining their missions other than that of pure law enforcement–related activities.

9. Although Niederhoffer did not explain the philosophy of cynicism, he stated that a subculture adopting such a philosophy incorporated a specific set of core values. Although he did not address what these alternate values were, it is clear that cynicism consists of three distinct themes. First, according to the Greek philosopher Diogenes, cynicism denies the brotherhood of man and within this perspective the world is divided into two classes: the vulnerable and the invulnerable. Second, cynicism adopts a one-dimensional world view in that society consists of injustices in which the "foolish" lack the self-control to endure pain whereas "the virtuous" possess the strength to submit without admitting pain. Third, adherents to cynicism adopt a belief in extreme individualism, keeping the cynic invulnerable to the influences of others. This belief insulates the cynic from moral conflict and disavows standards of civility, thereby eliminating personal guilt and pain (Muir, 1977:174–76).

10. His method of validating the cynicism questionnaire through presentation of the items to experts in the field of law enforcement is somewhat similar to the method of constructing a Thurstone scale. Despite the involvement of experts in validating his scale, however, Niederhoffer believed that his final scale grossly underestimated the amount of cynicism within the department (Niederhoffer, 1967:189).

11. Although Niederhoffer did not discuss the behavior and norms of these deviant groups of officers, others describe such groups as blue-collar militants. For example, see Kronholm (1972). According to Toch, militant police officers or blue-power advocates react with the premise that they can no longer operate within the system; they represent radical dissenters while most officers are moderate critics of the system (Toch, 1972:198–99).

12. This relationship was confirmed in two subsequent studies. See Lotz and Regoli (1977) and Regoli and Poole (1979).

13. Muir identified three forms of power used by police officers: (1) threat and coercion—power of the sword or gun; (2) trade and reciprocity—power of the purse; and (3) "truth" and exhortation—power of the "word" (Muir, 1977:47).

14. In a footnote Brown states, "The significance of operational style for police discretion clearly suggests that the psychology of the individual policemen and the link between psychological traits and an operational style, ought to be investigated in more depth than it so far

has been. The question must remain open for the moment, for I have neither the data nor the expertise to pursue it here" (Brown, 1985:207, n. 9).

CHAPTER 5

L.A.P.D. Officers on Patrol: Examining Relationships between Education, Probationary Performance, and Professionalism

> Educational qualifications provide a rough but important index of intelligence, competence, and capacity to absorb professional training. . . . Low educational attainment may not necessarily reflect on an individual applicant's intelligence, although it is likely to signal other problems of personal or social adjustment. (Saunders, 1970:43)

Introduction

Quite generally, the question raised and answered in this chapter is whether L.A.P.D. patrol officers with a college education are more professional than their less-educated counterparts. For our present purposes, a more professional officer is one who scores higher on the cynicism/professionalism continuum, as briefly described in the previous chapter and more fully discussed below. Furthermore, this chapter discusses the results of a model examining the relationships between college education, early performance indicators, academic status of officers, and professionalism scores for a sample of L.A.P.D. patrol officers.

Results of prior studies linking the relationships of higher education achievement and police officer performance indicators have been equivocal, although, as chapter 2 has shown, these relationships are primarily positive ones. The main validation method for testing such relationships has been through the application of a criterion validation approach, a method that empirically examines the presence or absence of a direct relationship between officer performance and level of education. Sherman (1980:76) has pointed out, however, that some of these prior studies have serious flaws; they have been poorly designed.[1]

In contrast to the criterion validation approach, an alternative validation method has been approved by the federal courts, a method that was discussed in chapter 3. This construct validation approach has been used to examine the relationships among level of education, the probationary performance indicators of department commendations and citizen complaints, academic status, and the construct of professionalism, a construct that had been empirically examined by Regoli and Poole in relation to Niederhoffer's original cynicism index (Regoli and Poole, 1979). That study by Regoli and Poole also validated Niederhoffer's assumption that the construct of cynicism was in fact, the opposite of the construct of professionalism. The results of this "newer" construct validation approach are discussed here.

Arthur Niederhoffer originally conceived the construct of cynicism as reflecting negative attitudes on one extreme end of a single continuum of police attitudes, the opposite extreme being that of professionalism. However, the effect of higher education and its relationship to the construct of cynicism (by studies using Niederhoffer's original index) has not been consistently demonstrated.[2]

Niederhoffer suggested that behavioral manifestations of cynicism included envy and hostility toward other officers, supervisors, and the public. Professional officers, on the other hand, while at times experiencing frustration, behaved respectfully toward their coworkers and the public. Niederhoffer did not, however, empirically examine this theoretical relationship between behavior and attitudes in his groundbreaking study.

Subsequently, Regoli and Poole constructed a professionalism scale, consisting of three subscales, in which higher scores on the scale indicated a strong support for professionalism, and lower scores indicated a lower level of support. Through factor analysis of Niederhoffer's original index and subsequent multiple regression and correlation analyses, they constructed three subscales (consisting of thirteen questions) from Niederhoffer's original twenty-item index and found them to explain more variance than the original cynicism index (Regoli and Poole, 1979). They also found that as professionalism scores increased, cynicism scores decreased. A positive relationship between Regoli and Poole's professionalism scale with Niederhoffer's revised cynicism/professionalism index is also determined here in addition to their relationships with the levels of education, academic status, and probationary performance for L.A.P.D. officers.

The persistent problem as to what constitutes effective patrol officer performance has been a controversial one. Two self-reported probationary performance indicators as measures of patrol performance during an officer's field training period are examined and results reported shortly. The logic of department commendations as one measure of performance seems straightforward in that the more highly valued activities by an officer while on duty are rewarded by the organization. In contrast, citizen complaints, as Van Maanen has pointed out, are "unavoidable occupational hazards," which officers go to great lengths (at least in his review) to ensure will be unfounded (Van Maanen, 1974:110). Nonetheless, in his early research on scandals within police departments, Sherman discusses the problems citizens generally experience in filing complaints. Additionally, he discusses how the officers view complaints as an attack on the department and how they resist accepting complaints by citizens (Sherman, 1978:148–155). More recently, and perhaps even more important, the Christopher Commission has documented the difficulties citizens have experienced when attempting to file complaints against an officer within the L.A.P.D. (Indepedent Commission, 1991:xix).[3]

When viewed from the perspective of the quality of police services received by the citizenry, those complaints that are filed under such extreme conditions merit consideration as well-founded complaints.[4] Therefore, it seems highly appropriate to consider citizen complaints filed against an officer prior to the Christopher Commission investigation as an important and viable indicator of performance during an officer's probationary period.[5]

The importance of the concept of the academic status of police officers was discussed by Sherman in his research on the quality of police education (Sherman and the National Advisory Commission on Higher Education for Police Officers, 1978:139–150). Sherman distinguished the value differences between preservice education and in-service education, a debate that Roberg points out has developed within the criminal justice field as to whether or not academic status influences the attitudes of police personnel (Roberg, 1978:338). Generally, a preservice education for police officers is thought to have a positive influence on the professionalization process for individual officers prior to their entrance into a police agency. Such officers are found to be more critical and innovative in their professional roles as officers. In-service officer students, in contrast, largely develop unique working styles prior to entering the higher educational arena, a factor that is thought to inhibit important changes necessary for the professionalizing process.[6]

In his examination of the relationship between education, dogmatism, and performance of police officers, Roberg used academic (student) status (grouped into preservice, in-service, and continuing) as one of several control variables. As a control variable, academic (student) status was found to have no effect on the original relationships between education, dogmatism, and performance. He attributed this absence of a finding to the fact that all officers in his sample with some college had attended or were attending the same land-grant university, which provided an interdisciplinary curriculum (Roberg, 1978:342).

In contrast to Roberg's model (Roberg, 1978; 1980), the present model includes academic status grouped into four categories: nonservice—no college education; preservice—college education acquired prior to entering policing; in-service—college education acquired only after being appointed as a police officer; and continuing—some college acquired prior to entering policing and continued or completed after being appointed to the agency. It has been hypothesized that in addition to level of education, academic status significantly influences officers' professional attitudes. The theoretical model of relationships between level of education, performance, academic status, and professional attitudes is more fully explained and diagrammed in appendix A.

This present model suggests that a police officer's higher level of education prior to his or her appointment to the department influences (1) the officer's probationary performance, (2) the officer's academic status once employed by the department, and (3) professional attitudes exhibited by the officer completing the survey. Second, probationary performance, as an intervening variable, is thought to influence an officer's academic status as well as subsequent professional or nonprofessional attitudes as measured by several indicators. Third, based upon tentative findings of previous studies, academic status as an intervening variable is also thought to influence professional or nonprofessional attitudes of officers (with nonservice or in-service status having little or no influence but with preservice and continuing status having positive, professionalizing influences). Finally, this model suggests not only that the higher level of education is important in determining the professional performance and attitudes or values of officers, but also that the timing of an officer's higher education is important in this process, with college education received prior to becoming an officer, as well as continuing thereafter, having a more positive influence than no higher education or higher education initiated only subsequent to employment as a police officer.

Analyses of L.A.P.D. Officer Data

Descriptive statistics of the sample of L.A.P.D. officers on patrol are discussed in the first portion of this section, followed by a description of the Professionalism Indexes. Then the General Functional Model, which has been developed through hypothesis testing, is explained, followed by an examination of each of the six hypotheses. This general functional elaboration model is illustrated, and the results of hypothesis testing are summarized in figure 1.

FIGURE 1

GENERAL FUNCTIONAL ELABORATION MODEL

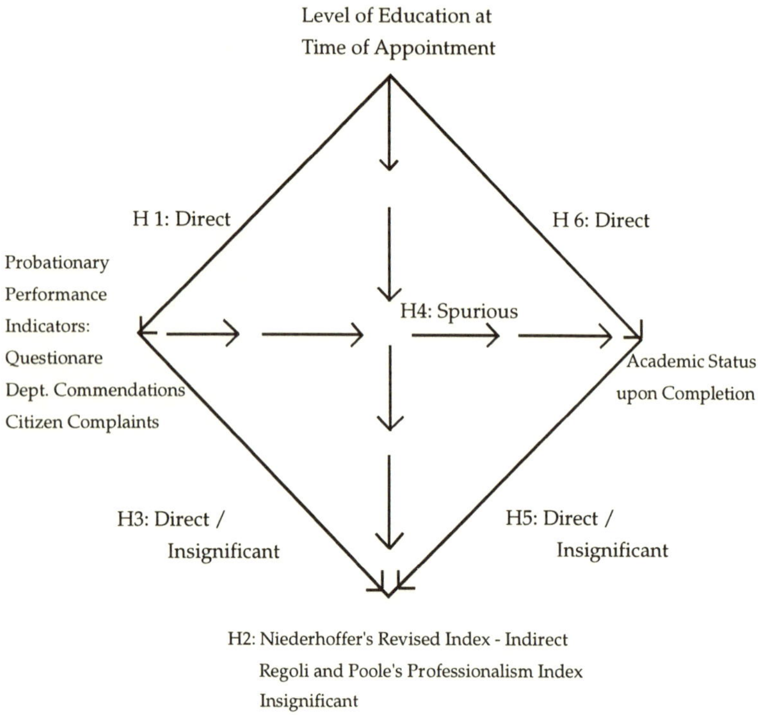

Statistics for Education and Academic Status

In order to be adequately represented in the L.A.P.D. survey, both female and minority officers were oversampled. As a result, the value of responses by these groups of officers would be artificially inflated because of this procedure. Therefore, in order to address the potential bias for these groups, data for all responses have been "weighted" so as to deflate the values of responses for oversampled groups and to inflate the values of responses for the undersampled groups, males and Caucasian officers.[7]

For the total weighted sample of 397 (missing = 2) L.A.P.D. officers on patrol, 37.4 percent had received no college education prior to entering the L.A.P.D., and 62.6 percent had at least some college education or above. For the weighted sample of 351 males, 38 percent had received no college education, whereas 62 percent had received at least some college education. The female patrol officer sample (n = 44) shows 30 percent with no prior college education and 70 percent with some college or above. The differences in college education between males and females is not statistically significant ($\chi^2 = 2.265$, $p = .687$). These figures seem to dispel the myth that female patrol officers, at least in the L.A.P.D., are much more highly educated than their male officer counterparts.

When broken down by ethnic status, 53 percent of the Latino patrol officers did not have any college prior to their appointments to the L.A.P.D., whereas 47 percent of Latinos had at least some college education. For African-American patrol officers, approximately 35 percent had no college education prior to entering the L.A.P.D., whereas 65 percent had received at least some college education prior to appointment to the L.A.P.D. For Caucasians, 32 percent had no prior college education, whereas 68 percent of these officers had at least some college prior to appointment. For patrol officers in the "Others" category (Filipinos, American Indian, and Asian), 29 percent had no college prior to appointment, whereas 71 percent had received at least some college education prior to appointment to the L.A.P.D.

A statistical testing of the relationship between ethnicity and education at time of appointment shows an absence of a relationship between these two variables at the .05 level of significance (χ^2 = 20.29, p = .062; Cramér's *V* = .1309). However, the results approach significance, and observation of the results comparing the actual number of cases in each category with the expected number of cases reveals a greater number of Latinos with no college prior to appointment as well as fewer Latinos with a bachelor's degree prior to appointment. Conversely, there are fewer African Americans, Caucasians, and "Others" in the no-college grouping and more in the bachelor's degree classification.

An analysis of academic (student) status at the time of questionnaire completion by 388 patrol officers (missing = 9) indicates that, for the total sample, 11.2 percent (*n* = 43) did not acquire any college education either before or subsequent to their appointment to the L.A.P.D. (nonservice). Officers acquiring their education prior to their appointment (preservice) amounted to 46.3 percent of the sample (*n* = 179); those acquiring it only after joining the force (in-service) represent 26.5 percent (*n* = 103). Patrol officers who began their college education prior to appointment and continued while with the L.A.P.D. (continuing) represent 16.1 percent of the sample (*n* = 63).

For the sample of male officers (*n* = 344), 11 percent are nonservice, 27 percent are in-service, 45 percent are preservice, and 16 percent are continuing students. For female officers (*n* = 44), 10 percent are classified as nonservice, 19 percent as in-service, 55 percent as preservice, and 16 percent as continuing. A chi-square statistic (χ^2 = 1.91, *p* = .592) and Cramér's *V* (.0757) reveal that no significant relationship exists between gender and academic status at the .05 significance level.

Statistical analysis of current academic (student) status by ethnicity reveals a relationship between the two. A chi-square statistic (χ^2 = 21.18, *p* = .011), a Cramér's *V* (.1353), and a comparison of the actual number of cases in each category with the expected number of cases show more Latinos in the in-service category and fewer in the continuing education category. African Americans, Caucasians, and "Others," in contrast, are fewer in the in-service category and greater in the continuing education category.

For Latino patrol officers, 11 percent fall within the nonservice category, 43 percent in the in-service category, 40 percent in the preservice category, and 6 percent in the continuing education category. For African-American patrol officers, 16 percent fall in the nonservice category, 19 percent in the in-service category, 49 percent in the preservice category, and 16 percent in the continuing education category. Results for Caucasians show 11 percent as nonservice officers, 22 percent as in-service officers, 48 percent as preservice officers, and 19 percent as continuing education officers. For "Others," 6 percent are nonservice officers, 23 percent are in-service, 48 percent are preservice, and 23 percent are continuing education officers.

Statistics for Probationary Performance Indicators

A frequency distribution for department commendations received by officers while on probationary status indicates that 11.4 percent of the weighted sample of 369 patrol officers (missing = 28) received no commendations. Of the remaining 330 officers, 20 percent received one commendation; 17.8 percent received two, 16 percent received three; 10.6 percent received four; 12 percent received five; 4.3 percent received six; 2.3 percent received seven; and 8 percent received eight commendations.

For number of citizen complaints received while on probationary status, 66.2 percent (260 of 393 officers, missing = 4) reported receiving none. The remaining 133 officers reported receiving the following: 19.6 percent received one complaint; 6.9 percent received two; 5.9 percent received three; less than 1 percent (.08) received four; and less than 1 percent (.08) reported receiving five citizen complaints. These statistics reveal that 33.8 percent of the officers in this sample received at least one complaint filed against them while serving his or her probationary period.[8]

A Pearson correlation coefficient testing the strength of association between number of department commendations and number of citizen complaints during probationary period was calculated to be a -.1452, a weak but statistically significant inverse relationship (p = .003) at the .05 significance level. The two variables have only 2 percent of their variance in common.

Descriptions of Professionalism Indexes

A frequency distribution for Niederhoffer's Revised Cynicism/Professionalism Index shows scores ranging from a low of 15.5 (representing a *high* level of cynicism) to 60.5 (representing a *low* level of cynicism). Niederhoffer had hypothesized that the midpoint response of 3 for each question, representing a 39 for this revised index, indicated a neutral response. The mean response reported here for 334 officers (missing = 63) is 42.34, indicating a less cynical or more professional response overall for the L.A.P.D. patrol officer group.

Patrol officer responses for Regoli and Poole's Professionalism Index (originally consisting of three subscales: Attitudes toward the Public, Attitudes toward the Officer Role, and Attitudes toward the Organization) range from a low of 14.5 to a high of 38.5 (n = 383; missing = 14). A mean of 28.20 (considering that the midpoint for this eleven-item index is 27.5, and low scores mean low professionalism and high scores mean high professionalism) indicates that the mean score falls within the neutral to the more professional range. These results, therefore, parallel the Niederhoffer results.

Niederhoffer's index had been broken down into three subscales by Regoli and Poole through a factor analysis procedure. Regoli and Poole found Niederhoffer's three subscales (Attitudes toward Others Effects on Police Work, Attitudes toward Ideals Concerning Police Work, and Attitudes toward Conduct Involved in Police Work) to be independent of each other and more reliable in predicting their three professionalism subscales than the original Niederhoffer Cynicism Index. These subscales have been retained for statistical analysis and hypothesis testing.

Descriptive statistics for Attitudes toward Others Effects on Police Work, a five-item subscale, indicate a range of twenty, from a low of five to a high of twenty-five. Officer mean response (n = 369, missing= 28) of 13.61 fell below the midpoint of 15, indicating a less professional response, more toward cynicism.[9] For Attitudes toward Ideals Concerning Police Work, a subscale consisting of three items, the mean score is 12.17 for 373 officers (missing = 24), falling above the midpoint of nine and representing a more professional response overall. Responses for this subscale range from a low of three to a high of fifteen. For Attitudes toward Conduct Involved in Police Work, officer responses (n = 371, missing = 26) range from a low of five to a high of twenty-five, with a mean of 16.82. Since for this subscale the mean falls above the midpoint of 15, this finding indicates a more professional response overall.

For Attitudes toward the Public, the mean response for 395 patrol officers (missing = 2) is 9.86, just below the midpoint of 10, representing neutral but leaning toward cynical attitudes by the officers. Scores range from a low of four to a high of fourteen for this four-item scale. Officer responses (n = 387, missing = 10) for Attitudes toward the Officer Role range from a low of four to a high of sixteen, with a mean of 11.11 for the four items. Since the mean for this subscale falls above the midpoint of 10, this indicates neutral but leaning toward professional attitudes. For Attitudes toward the Organization, officer responses (n = 396, missing = 1) range from a low of three to a high of twelve. A mean of 7.21 for this three-item scale, having a midpoint of 7.5, indicates a neutral, but leaning toward cynical response overall.[10]

These results have shown that overall, L.A.P.D. patrol officers (without taking into account an officer's educational background) are measured as being more professional than cynical when using both Niederhoffer's and Regoli and Poole's professionalism indexes. Mean responses for the six individual subscales making up these indexes, however, show that this group scores as neutral but leaning more toward the cynical range for their Attitudes toward Others Effects on Police Work, Attitudes toward the Public, and Attitudes toward the Organization. In contrast, this group of officers scores in the professional range on Attitudes toward Ideals Concerning Police Work, Attitudes toward Conduct Involved in Police Work, and Attitudes toward Officer Role.

A General Functional Elaboration Model

The General Functional Elaboration Model as illustrated in figure 1 has been developed from the results of hypothesis testing. This model deviates from the general theoretical model discussed and illustrated in appendix A in that the hypothesized relationships between (1) level of education and professionalism, as measured by two professionalism indexes and (2) the probationary performance indicators (department commendations and citizen complaints) and academic status, were found to be more complex than initially conceptualized. Nonetheless, the General Theoretical Model and the General Functional Elaboration Model developed from empirical results are conceptually quite similar. Table 3 explicates the statistical results.

TABLE 3

RESULTS OF STATISTICAL TESTS

H1:	Direct Relationship between Level of Education and Department Commendations: Eta = .1688 Eta^2 = .0285	Inverse Relationship between Level of Education and Citizen Complaints: Eta = .2426 Eta^2 = .0589
H2:	Indirect Relationship between Level of Education and Niederhoffer's Revised Index: Eta = .2101 Eta^2 = .0442 Pearson r = .1834 Pearson r^2 = .0336 When Controlling for Academic Status: Pearson r = .0212 (n.s.)	Insignificant Relationship between Level of Education and Regoli and Poole's Index: Pearson r = .1107 Pearson r^2 = .0123 F Score = 1.80 (p = .127, n.s.) Eta^2 = .0188

H3: Direct Relationship between Department Commendations/ Complaints and Niederhoffer's Revised Index: Multiple R = .33 Adj. R^2 = .11	Insignificant Relationship between Department Citizen Commendations/ Citizen Complaints and Regoli & Poole's Professionalism Index: Adj. R^2 = .11 When Controlling for Niederhoffer's Index: Pearson r^2 = .0019 (n.s.)
H4: Spurious Relationship between Department Commendations and Academic Status: Pearson r = .1286 Pearson r^2 = .0165 When Controlling for Level of Education: Pearson r = .0308 (n.s.) Pearson r^2 = .0009 (n.s.)	Spurious Relationship between Citizen Complaints and Academic Status: Pearson r = -.2137 Pearson r^2 = .0457 When Controlling for Level of Education: Pearson r = -.0912 (n.s.) Pearson r^2 = .0083 (n.s.)
H5: Direct Relationship between Academic Status and Niederhoffer's Revised Index: Eta = .281 Eta^2 = .079 Pearson r = .261 Pearson r^2 = .068	Insignificant Relationship between Academic Status and Regoli & Poole's Index: Eta^2 = .052 Pearson r^2 = .024 When Controlling for Niederhoffer's Index: Pearson r^2 = .0000 (n.s.)
H6: Direct Relationship between Level of Education and Academic Status: Gamma = .798; Pearson r = .642 Pearson r^2 = .412	

The purpose for developing this model has been twofold. First, in utilizing a construct validation approach, which examines the relationship between college education and the construct of professionalism, six hypotheses have been tested empirically and generally supported the existence of a relationship between level of education and professionalism. Additionally, the present model not only establishes a relationship between higher education and the construct of professionalism, it also establishes a relationship between level of education and performance-related variables, as well as a relationship between performance-related variables and the construct of professionalism. This procedure has satisfied the construct validation requirement as adopted by the U.S. Supreme Court: empirically validating a relationship between college education and at least one performance-related variable. (See chapter 3 for discussion.)

Second, the development of a functional, rather than a causal, elaboration model, that takes into account the influence of important antecedent, intervening, and concurrent test variables, challenges the prevailing notion that a simple, direct association or relationship exists between higher levels of college education and patrol officer professionalism. Empirical findings of the six hypotheses generally revealed the anticipated results, but these results also take into account the influence of critical variables that affect these original relationships. These results of hypothesis testing are discussed in depth in the following sections.

Relationship between Level of Education and Probationary Performance Indicators

The relationship of or correlation between level of education and department commendations was found to be a positive one in that the zero-order correlation coefficient of .1642 is significant at the .01 level of significance. The first-order partial correlation coefficients measuring the relationship between these two variables, when the common variances for each of the *control* variables of gender, ethnicity, and prior occupation are extracted, remain essentially the same as the unadjusted coefficient and are significant at the .01 level of significance. Therefore, gender, ethnicity, and prior occupation have no statistically significant effect on the original relationship between level of education and department commendations.

This original relationship also remains stable and significant when the influence of number of citizen complaints (which has been shown to be statistically correlated with department commendations) is included in the analysis. This finding suggests that, despite the positive relationship between both probationary performance indicators, the original relationship between level of education and department commendations is a positive and direct one, as illustrated in the elaboration model in figure 1.

Similarly, for the relationship between level of education and number of citizen complaints, a zero-order coefficient of -.2268 is also significant at the .01 significance level, but the relationship is an inverse one. As level of education increases, the mean number of citizen complaints decreases. When gender, ethnicity, prior occupation, and number of department commendations are taken into account, the original relationship between level of education and citizen complaints remains inverse and statistically significant.

The hypothesis that a significant relationship exists between level of education and probationary performance as measured by department commendations and citizen complaints is confirmed, although the direct relationship between level of education and department commendations amounts to just 3 percent of the variance. The inverse relationship between level of education and citizen complaints amounts to 5 percent of the explained variance.

A one-way analysis of variance for level of education and department commendations confirms the original relationship found in the zero-order correlation analysis, with an F value of 2.67, a significance level of .032, and an Eta^2 coefficient (similar to the squared zero-order correlation coefficient) amounts to .028, explaining approximately 3 percent of the variance between level of education and department commendations. Within-cell variances are shown to be equal (p = .584), and a Student-Newman-Keuls multiple range test comparing significant differences in group means shows that the average number of department commendations for the no college group is significantly *lower* than for the A.A. degree or equivalent, bachelor's degree, and graduate work or graduate degree groups. Two-way analysis of variance procedures testing for any interaction effects between level of education and department commendations, with gender, ethnicity, or prior occupation, are not significant at the .05 significance level.

One-way analysis of variance for the relationship between level of education and citizen complaints revealed an *F* value of 6.04 and a significance level of .000. The amount of explained variance for the relationship between these two variables is approximately 5 percent (achieving an Eta^2 coefficient of .059) However, the Bartlett-Box *F*-test reveals that the within-cell variances are not equal (.000 significance). Therefore, a nonparametric Kruskal-Wallis one-way ANOVA (analysis of variance) was run, and a Chi-square statistic of 22.99 indicates that group means are significantly different at the .01 significance level. A Student-Newman-Keuls multiple range test comparing significant differences among group means shows that the average number of citizen complaints for the no college group is significantly *higher* than for the some college, A.A. degree or equivalent, bachelor's degree, and completed graduate work or graduate degree groups, as shown in figure 2.

When level of education was dichotomized into two groups (i.e., officers with no college education and those with at least some college), results of Student *t*-tests support the existence of group differences between level of education and both mean number of department commendations and citizen complaints. For both of these probationary performance indicators, the group means for those with college and those without college were significantly different at the .05 significance level.

For department commendations, officers with at least some college scored above the total mean of 3.05, having a group mean of 3.28 commendations. In contrast, those officers with no college received a mean number of commendations of 2.64, falling below the overall mean score. For citizen complaints, the group of officers with no college received a group mean of .85, higher than the overall mean of .57. Conversely, those with at

FIGURE 2

MEAN PROBATIONARY PERFORMANCE INDICATOR SCORES BY LEVEL OF EDUCATION

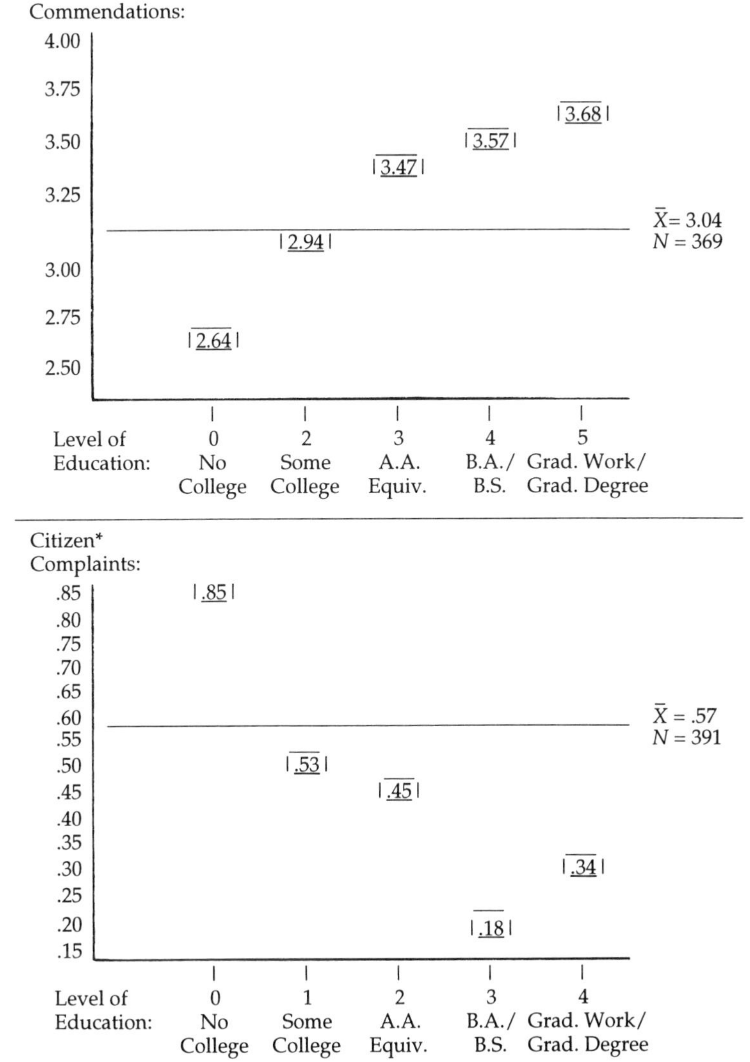

*Lower score indicates better performance in terms of interactions with citizens.

least some level of college received a group mean of .41, lower than the overall mean.

The preceding analysis of the results of empirical testing has confirmed the hypothesis that the level of education prior to appointment to the department is weakly but significantly correlated with department commendations and citizen complaints. These results confirm that a direct positive relationship exists between level of education and department commendations, and an inverse relationship exists between level of education and citizen complaints.

These results suggest that L.A.P.D. patrol officers with at least some college education prior to entering the department perform better during their probationary periods, at least in terms of department commendations and citizen complaints as reported here. Officers with at least some college education receive a statistically significant higher level of department commendations and a statistically significant lower level of citizen complaints than officers without any college education prior to entering the department.

Relationship between Level of Education and Professionalism Indexes

When examining the relationships between level of education and each of the professionalism indexes, a zero-order correlation coefficient of .1834 for level of education and Niederhoffer's Revised Index reveals a positive significant relationship with level of education, explaining approximately 3 percent of variance of the index. Although the zero-order correlation between level of education and Regoli and Poole's Professionalism Index is significant but extremely weak at the .05 significance level, a correlation coefficient of .1107 represents approximately only 1 percent of the explained variance.

When gender, ethnicity, age, rank, prior occupation, and years of experience are taken into account in the first-order partial correlation analysis between level of education and Niederhoffer's Revised Index, the original direct, positive relationship remains stable and significant at the .01 significance level. When gender, ethnicity, age, rank, prior occupation, and years of experience are introduced into a first-order partial correlation analysis with level of education and Regoli and Poole's Professionalism Index, the original relationship remains relatively constant and statistically significant but weak at the .05 significance level.

The main study variables were also introduced into first-order partial analyses for level of education and each of the professionalism indexes in order to elaborate the original relationship: to determine what, if any, impact the main study variables as antecedent, intervening, or concurrent test variables have on the original relationships. For the statistically significant relationship between level of education and Niederhoffer's Revised Index, the introduction of the main study variables of department commendations (as an intervening test variable) and Regoli and Poole's Professionalism Index (as a concurrent test variable) have little, if any effect on these two variables when included in a first-order partial analysis. When academic status (as an intervening test variable) and citizen complaints (as an intervening variable) are included in a first-partial correlation analysis, the original direct positive relationship between levels of education and Niederhoffer's Revised Index is no longer significant at the .01 significance level.

When introducing academic status (as an intervening variable), probationary performance indicators (as intervening variables), and Niederhoffer's Revised Index (as a concurrent variable) into the first-order partial analysis between level of education and Regoli and Poole's Index, department commendations exercise the least influence on the original relationship, decreasing the correlation to .0895, significant at .05 level. However, when the variables of citizen complaints and academic status are introduced into the analysis, the original, direct relationship drops to insignificance, achieving first-order partial correlation coefficients of .0405 and .0161, respectively.

When Niederhoffer's Revised Index is included in the partial-correlation analysis between level of education and Regoli and Poole's Professionalism Index, the original direct, positive relationship between level of education and Regoli and Poole's Professionalism Index no longer exists; the relationship decreases to insignificance. This particular finding suggests that Niederhoffer's Revised Index seems to be a more stable and valid measure of professional attitudes than Regoli and Poole's combined Professionalism Index, since the original relationship between level of education and Regoli and Poole's Professionalism Index no longer holds when the influence of Niederhoffer's Revised Index is taken into account. Additionally, the relationship between level of education and Niederhoffer's Revised Index remains constant when the influence of Regoli and Poole's Professionalism Index is taken into account in partial-correlation analysis.

In terms of an elaboration model of relationships between variables, control or test variables either replicate, explain, interpret, or specify the conditions of the original relationship between two variables. Here, the variables of academic status, as a statistically significant intervening variable between level of education and both professionalism indices, and citizen complaints, as a statistically significant intervening variable between level of education and Regoli and Poole's Index, do not deny the existence of the original relationship between level of education and professional attitudes. In elaboration, academic status and citizen complaints as test variables assist in interpreting the conditions through which the original relationship occurs: they clarify the process through which the original relationship functions.[11] Therefore, level of education does have a significant relationship with "professional attitudes" or professionalism through the intervention of an officer's academic status as well as through the amount of citizen complaints an officer has received during his or her probationary, field training period. Figure 1 illustrates that the original statistically significant relationships are no longer direct relationships between level of education and the two professionalism indexes as measured here, but rather an indirect one for the variables of level of education and Niederhoffer's Revised Index, as a result of the intervention of those test variables, which significantly influence the original relationship.

A one-way analysis of variance between level of education and Niederhoffer's Revised Index confirms the relationship between the two variables, with an F value of 3.77 indicating that the means between the groups are significantly different (p = .005). Eta^2, a statistic showing the amount of relationship between the two variables, indicates that 4.4 percent of the variance in the professionalism scores is explained by level of education. The within-cell variances, however, are determined to be unequal as a result of a Bartlett-Box F score of 4.78 (p = .001), and a nonparametric Kruskal-Wallis one-way ANOVA with a chi-square statistic of 5.76 fails to confirm the statistically significant original relationship between the two variables (p = .2170). Nonetheless, the results of the parametric one-way ANOVA are illustrated in figure 3 below in which the average professionalism score of 39.87 for no college falls below the

FIGURE 3

MEAN PROFESSIONALISM SCORES BY LEVEL OF EDUCATION

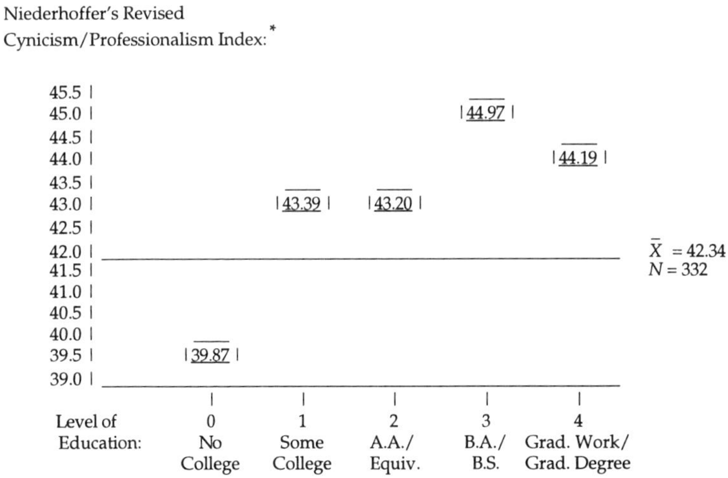

*The higher the score, the more professional the attitudes; the lower the score, the more cynical the attitudes. Although between group means have been determined to be different statistically (at .05 significance level), group variances have been determined to be unequal.

overall sample mean of 42.34, whereas the average scores for some college, A.A. degree or equivalent, bachelor's degree, and completed graduate work or graduate degree all fall above the overall sample mean achieving scores of 43.39, 43.20, 44.97, and 44.19, respectively. All of these average scores, however, fall above the midpoint of 39.00 for the professionalism variable as measured by Niederhoffer's Revised Index, indicating that they fall within the more professional range of scores.

For the individual subscales comprising the Niederhoffer Index, only Attitudes toward Others Effects on Police Work is significantly related to level of education, achieving an *F* value of 4.89 ($p = .001$). The strength of this relationship is significant with an Eta^2 of .051 (approximately 5 percent of the variance is explained). A Bartlett-Box *F* score of .47 indicates that within-cell variances are equal ($p = .760$).

A Student-Newman-Keuls multiple range test comparing differences among group means shows that the average score for the no college group (12.50) is significantly less than the average scores for the some college (13.68), A. A. or equivalent (14.21), bachelor's degree (14.90), and completed graduate work or graduate degree (15.65) groups. Figure 4 illustrates the differences between these average scores on Attitudes toward Others Effects on Police Work, with the average score for no college (12.50) falling below the overall sample mean score of 13.61, and the remaining groups falling above the overall sample mean score. Since the average scores for all of these groups fall above the midpoint of 12.00, this indicates that these scores all fall within the more professional range of scores. These results reveal, however, that as level of education increases, attitudes toward legitimate institutional influences (i.e., university, media, citizenry, the department, and the courts) on the police institution become more professional or positive.

When level of education is dichotomized into two groups, no college and at least some college, a Student's *t*-test of difference between group means for Niederhoffer's Revised Index reveals that the average score of 39.87 for the no college group falls below the overall average score of 42.34, whereas the average score of 43.74 for the at least some college group falls above the overall average score. A *t*-test score of -3.49 for these two groups indicates that the difference between group means is significant (p = .000). Similar results are also found for the individual subscales comprising Niederhoffer's Revised Index. The results of the Student's t-tests confirm a relationship between level of education and Niederhoffer's Revised Index when the variable of level of education is separated into those officers without college prior to entering the department and those with at least some college, even though the group variances have been determined to be unequal. Additionally, although the subscales making up Niederhoffer's index are not mutually exclusive of each other, similar statistically significant results have been determined for each of these subscales.

A one-way ANOVA between level of education and Regoli and Poole's Professionalism Index disconfirms a relationship between the two variables, because an F value of 1.80 indicates that means between the groups are not significantly different (p = .127). Eta^2, examining the amount of relationship between the two variables, reveals that less than 2 percent of the variance in the professionalism scores of the Regoli and Poole Professionalism Index is explained by level of education. The within-cell variances are determined to be unequal as a result of a Bartlett-Box F value of 3.46 (p = .008).

An analysis of variance for each of the three subscales comprising Regoli and Poole's Professionalism Index shows that two of these subscales, Attitudes toward the Public and Attitudes toward the Organization, are significantly related to level of education with F values of 3.09 and 3.08, respectively (p = .016 for each). An Eta^2 score of .031 for each of these two subscales indicates that level of education explains approximately 3 percent of the variance for each subscale.

A Bartlett-Box F value of 4.00 (p = .003) for Attitudes toward the Organization indicates that within-cell variances are unequal. However, a nonparametric Kruskal-Wallis one-way ANOVA with a resulting chi-square statistic of 10.15 (p = .0381) confirms the statistically significant relationship between level of education and Attitudes toward the Organization.

FIGURE 4

MEAN PROFESSIONALISM SUBSCALE SCORES BY LEVEL OF EDUCATION

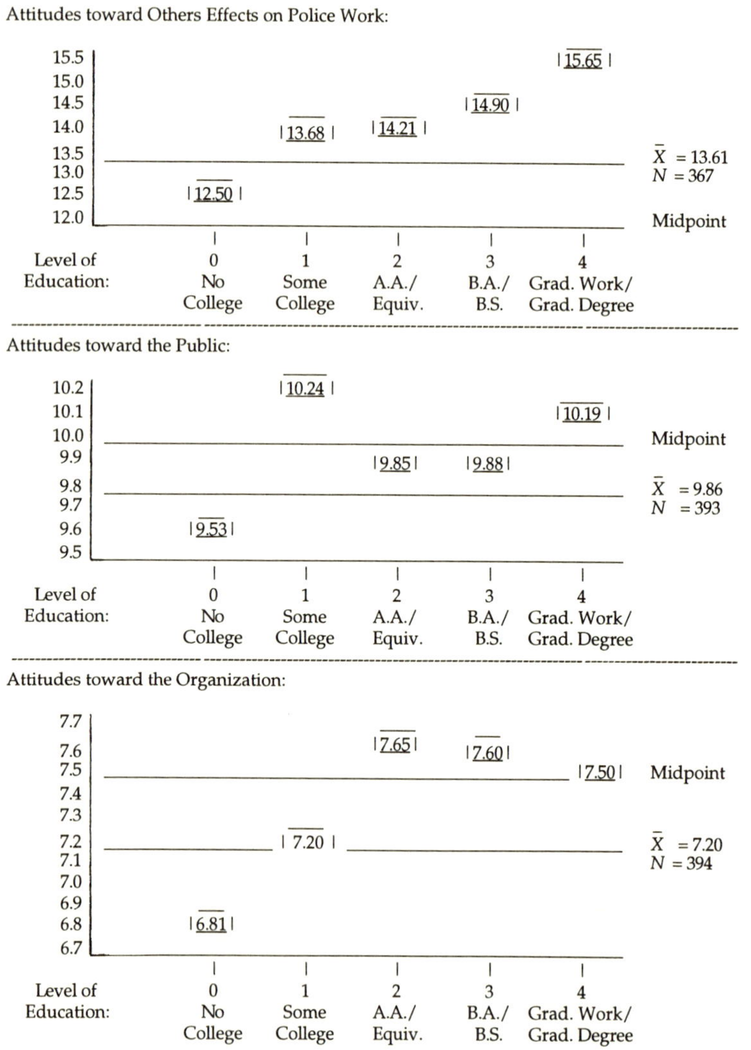

A Student-Newman-Keuls multiple range test comparing differences among group means shows that for Attitudes toward the Public the average score of 9.53 for the no college group is significantly less than the average score of 10.24 for the some college group. For Attitudes toward the Organization, a Student-Newman-Keuls multiple range test shows that the average score of 6.21 for the no college group is significantly less than both the average score of 7.65 for the A.A. degree or equivalent group and the average score of 7.60 for the bachelor's degree group.

Figure 4 also illustrates the differences between these average scores on Attitude toward the Public and Attitudes toward the Organization. Although the group mean for no college (9.53) for the Attitudes toward the Public subscale is significantly lower than only one other group (the some college group), it is the only score falling below the group mean of 9.85, a finding that represents more cynical attitudes overall for this no college group. The remaining four groups all fall above the mean with scores of 10.24 for some college, 9.85 for A.A. degree or equivalent, 9.88 for bachelor's degree, and 10.19 for completed graduate work or graduate degree. Essentially, both the some college group and the completed graduate work or graduate degree group have highly professional attitudes toward the public, those with an A.A. degree or equivalent or a bachelor's degree have neutral attitudes toward the public, and the no college group has the least professional or most cynical attitudes toward the public.

For Attitudes toward the Organization, the average score for the no college group (6.81) is significantly lower than the average scores for both the A.A. or equivalent (7.65) and the bachelor's degree (7.60) groups, thereby representing less professional or more cynical attitudes for the no college group. The group mean for no college falls below the overall sample mean of 7.20, the group mean for some college falls on the overall sample mean of 7.20, and the higher educational groups fall above the overall sample mean. These results suggest that the three highest levels of education (the A.A. degree or equivalent and above groups) express positive, professional attitudes toward the organization, the group with some college expresses neutral attitudes, and the group with no college expresses more negative or cynical attitudes toward the organization. These results may assist in clarifying a prior discussion.[12] It seems that the groups with lower levels of education lack confidence in the administration more so than those groups with higher levels of education. Subsequent discussion will show that academic status of the officers further clarifies or mediates this original relationship.

When level of education is dichotomized into two groups, no college and at least some college, a Student's *t*-test of difference between group means for Regoli and Poole's Professionalism Index reveals that the average score of 27.51 for the no college group falls below the overall average score of 28.21, whereas the average score of 28.61 for the at least some college group falls above the overall average score. A *t*-test score of -2.38 for these two groups indicates that the difference between group means is significant at the .05 significance level ($p = .018$). Similar results are also found for the Attitudes toward the Public and Attitudes toward the Organization subscales. The results of the Student's *t*-test confirm a statistically significant relationship between level of education and Regoli and Poole's Professionalism Index when the variable of level of education is separated into those officers without college prior to entering the department and those with at least some college, even though the group variances have been determined to be unequal. Additionally, although the subscales making up this professionalism index are not mutually exclusive of each other, similar statistically significant results have been determined for Attitudes toward the Public and Attitudes toward the Organization.

This discussion has shown that the direct zero-order correlation, establishing a relationship at the .01 level, between level of education and Niederhoffer's Revised Cynicism/ Professionalism Index has been supported by one-way analysis of variance testing. However, the relationship between level of education and Regoli and Poole's Professionalism Index has not been supported and has been disconfirmed by parametric ANOVA testing. Students' *t*-tests examining the relationship between these two professionalism indexes when level of education has been dichotomized into two groups, officers with no college prior to entry with the department and those with at least some college prior to entry, indicate that a statistically significant relationship does, in fact, exist.

One-way analysis of variance testing for associated subscales has also shown that one of the subscales included in Niederhoffer's Index, Attitudes toward Others Effects on Police Work and two of the subscales included in the Regoli and Poole Index, Attitudes toward the Public and Attitudes toward the Organization, are significantly related to the level of education of officers prior to entry into the department. Interestingly, the mean scores for these three subscales, as explained in the earlier section, "Description of Professionalism Indexes," fell within the neutral to more cynical range of scores. However, this analysis has determined that for the subscales of Attitudes toward Others Effects on Police Work and Attitudes toward the Organization only the no college group falls within the cynical range, whereas those with some college or more fall within the professional range of scores. For Attitudes toward the Public, results are ambiguous; the no college and A.A. or equivalent groups fall below the mean, whereas the other three college groups fall above the mean within the professional range. Nonetheless, the no college group achieves the lowest score of all the groups.

This section has shown that a statistically significant zero-order correlation has been established for level of education and Niederhoffer's Revised Cynicism/Professionalism Index at the .01 significance level. Also, a statistically significant zero-order correlation has been established for level of education and Regoli and Poole's Professionalism Index. One-way analysis of variance tests has confirmed the original relationship between level of education and Niederhoffer's Revised Index, but has failed to confirm the statistically significant relationship between level of education and Regoli and Poole's Professionalism Index.

When both control test variables and main test variables were included in a first-order partial correlation analysis with level of education and Niederhoffer's Revised Index, the main intervening test variable of academic status was found to reduce the original relationship to insignificance. As a result, the original direct relationship between level of education and professionalism (as measured by Niederhoffer's Revised Index) was found to be an indirect one in that academic status interprets the nature of the original relationship (figure 1 above).

Three subscales, Attitudes toward Others Effects on Police Work, Attitudes toward the Public, and Attitudes toward the Organization, were also found to be significantly related to level of education in that each of these subscales received statistically significant *F* values, at the .01 level of significance. For Attitudes toward Others Effects on Police Work, as the level of education increased, the average group professionalism score also increased. For Attitudes toward the Public, the no college group received the lowest professionalism score (the most cynical), and the some college group received the highest average professionalism score. The completed graduate work or graduate degree group received the second highest average score for this subscale, with the bachelor's degree and A.A. degree or equivalent group receiving the next highest scores, respectively. For Attitudes toward the Organization, the A.A. degree or equivalent received the most professional average score, followed by the bachelor's degree, completed graduate degree or graduate work, and the some college groups. The no college group received the lowest or most cynical score, which was found to be lower statistically from the A.A. degree or equivalent and bachelor's degree group scores.

Generally, then, a relationship is shown to exist between an L.A.P.D. officer's acquired level of college education and professionalism. However, this original relationship is mediated by whether an officer began his or her college prior to entering the department in addition to whether this education was begun or continued after appointment to the department.

Relationship between Probationary Performance Indicators and Professionalism Indexes

In order to examine these relationships statistically, zero-order correlation coefficients for the two probationary performance indicators, department commendations and citizen complaints, and the two professionalism indexes, Niederhoffer's Revised Cynicism/Professionalism Index and Regoli and Poole's

Professionalism Index, revealed statistically significant relationships at the .01 level of significance. An unadjusted correlation coefficient of .2012 for department commendations and Niederhoffer's index amounted to 4 percent of the total variance; an unadjusted correlation coefficient of .1419 for department commendations and Regoli and Poole's index amounted to 2 percent of the total variance.

The relationships between citizen complaints and both of these indexes were found to be inverse ones; as the number of citizen complaints increased, the professionalism scores for each of the indexes decreased. For citizen complaints and Niederhoffer's index, an unadjusted correlation coefficient of -.2876 amounted to 8 percent of the total variance; for citizen complaints and Regoli and Poole's index, an unadjusted correlation coefficient of -.3133, amounted to 10 percent of the total variance. These empirical results show that significant relationships exist between each of the two probationary performance indicators (department commendations and citizen complaints) and the two professionalism indexes.

To determine whether these direct relationships remain significant when the control variables of gender, ethnicity, age, rank, prior occupation, and years of experience are included in the analyses, first-order partial correlation analyses were conducted. Results show the original relationships remain statistically significant. Additionally, when level of education, as an antecedent test variable, and academic status, as an intervening test variable, are included in each of the first-order correlation analyses, these original direct relationships also remain stable and statistically significant. These findings indicate that neither level of education nor academic status influenced the original direct relationships between the two probationary performance indicators and the professionalism indexes. Also, despite the significant relationship between department commendations and citizen complaints (r^2 between the two variables is .02) when these variables are included in a first-order correlation analysis as concurrent main variables, their effects on each other's relationship with each of the measures of professionalism is minimal.

When Regoli and Poole's index is included in a first-order partial correlation analysis with each of the two probationary performance indicators in Niederhoffer's Revised Index, the original relationship between Niederhoffer's Revised Index and department commendations decreases to .1442, but remains statistically significant at the .01 significance level. The relationship, however, between Niederhoffer's Revised Index and citizen complaints is reduced to -.0900, but remains statistically significant at the .05 significance level.

When Niederhoffer's Revised Index as a test variable is included in a partial-correlation analysis between each of the two probationary performance indicators and Regoli and Poole's Professionalism Index, the original relationship between citizen complaints and professionalism (as measured by Regoli and Poole's index) decreases to -.1780, but remains statistically significant. However, the original relationship between department commendations and professionalism (as measured by Regoli and Poole's index) no longer exists; the relationship decreases to .0009 and is no longer statistically significant. This particular finding, which is similar to the finding in hypothesis two, suggests that Niederhoffer's Revised Index seems to be a more stable and valid measure of professional attitudes than Regoli and Poole's Professionalism Index. This essentially means that Niederhoffer's Revised Index, as an instrument to measure professionalism, may be a more valid predictor of professionalism than Regoli and Poole's index.

Stepwise multiple regression analyses of the relationships between department commendations and citizen complaints as predictor variables, and each of the two professionalism indexes as criterion variables, confirm the significance of the relationships of these probationary performance indicators with each of these indexes.

For Niederhoffer's Revised Index, citizen complaints emerges as the stronger predictor, achieving an F value of 28.91 (p = .000) and an R of .2908, which explains approximately 8 percent of the total variance of the professionalism index. Although the variable of department commendations is also a significant predictor, this variable adds less than 3 percent to the predictive equation, achieving a significant F value of 18.91 (p =

.000) In combination, citizen complaints and department commendations achieve a Multiple *R* score of .3288, together predicting approximately 11 percent of the total variance of Niederhoffer's Revised Index. The control variables of years of experience and age were found not to be statistically significant predictor variables since each of these variables achieved insignificant *F* and *t*-values (p = .808 for years experience; p = .463 for age). The final multiple regression predictive equation is: Score for Niederhoffer's Revised Index = 42.03 - 2.38 (value of citizen complaints) + .62 (value of department commendations). This equation indicates that approximately 11 percent of the total variance of Niederhoffer's index score can be predicted by knowing the values of complaints (complaints having an inverse relationship) and department commendations (commendations having a positive relationship).

For Regoli and Poole's Professionalism Index, citizen complaints also emerges as the stronger predictor, achieving an *F* value of 39.80 (p = .000) and an *R* of .3181, which explains approximately 10 percent of the total variance of the professionalism index. Once again, although the variable of department commendations is also a significant predictor, it adds less than 1 percent to the predictive equation, achieving a significant *F* value of 21.90 (p = .000). In combination, citizen complaints and department commendations achieve a Multiple *R* value of .3366, together predicting approximately 10.5 percent of the total variance of Regoli and Poole's index. Additionally, the control variables of years of experience and age were found not to be statistically significant predictor variables since each of these variables once again achieved insignificant *F* and *t*-values (p = .725 for years experience; p = .719 for age). The final multiple regression predictive equation is: Score for Regoli and Poole's Index = 28.37 - 1.29 (value for citizen complaints) + .17(value for department commendations). This second equation indicates that approximately 10.5 percent of the total variance of Regoli and Poole's index score can be predicted by knowing the values of complaints (complaints having an inverse relationship) and department commendations (commendations having a positive relationship) with Regoli and Poole's Professionalism Index scores.

Both variables of department commendations and citizen complaints are significant predictor variables for the subscales of Attitudes toward Others Effects on Police Work, Attitudes toward Ideals Concerning Police Work, and Attitudes toward the Organization. In each case, citizen complaints emerges as the stronger predictor. For Attitudes toward Conduct Involved in Police Work, Attitudes toward the Public, and Attitudes toward the Officer Role, department commendations is no longer a statistically significant predictor variable. Age and years of experience are not statistically significant for any of the six subscales, essentially meaning that an officer's age or years of experience with the department has no influence on, or relationship with, the officer's professional attitudes as measured by the various subscales.

The preceding analysis has shown that the probationary performance indicators of citizen complaints and department commendations, in combination, are statistically significant predictors of professionalism as measured by each of the two professionalism indexes. For both of the professionalism indexes, citizen complaints emerges as the more powerful predictor. In combination, both variables predict approximately 11 percent of the total variances of both Niederhoffer's index and Regoli and Poole's index. The control variables of age and years of experience were found not to be significant predictors for either measure of professionalism, which tentatively suggests that an officer's age or length of time with the department has no direct influence on his or her professional attitudes. However, when Niederhoffer's Revised Index was included as a control variable in a partial analysis with Regoli and Poole's Professionalism Index and the probationary performance indicators, the relationship dropped to insignificance.

These results confirm the hypothesis that a direct relationship exists between probationary performance indicators as measured by citizen complaints and department commendations and professionalism as measured by Niederhoffer's Revised Index. This direct relationship between probationary performance and Regoli and Poole's Professionalism Index becomes insignificant when Niederhoffer's Revised Index is introduced into a first-order partial correlation analysis. Overall results are illustrated in the General Functional Elaboration Model of figure 1. Generally, L.A.P.D. officers receiving more department commendations and fewer citizen complaints during their probationary periods have a tendency to be more professional in their roles as patrol officers than those officers receiving fewer commendations and more citizen complaints. These findings hold regardless of race, gender, or prior occupation.

Relationship between Probationary Performance Indicators and Academic Status

A zero-order correlation coefficient of .1286 for department commendations and academic status indicates a statistically significant direct positive relationship between these two variables (at the .01 significance level), with department commendations explaining approximately 2 percent of the total variance of academic status. For citizen complaints, the relationship is an inverse one which results in a correlation coefficient of -.2137, amounting to 5 percent of the total variance of academic status.

For department commendations and academic status, the original relationship remains stable when the control variables of gender, rank, and prior occupation are introduced into first-order partial correlation analyses. When the control variables of age and years of experience are introduced into first-order correlation analyses, however, this correlation coefficient increases minimally, from .1286 to .1386 when age is introduced and from .1286 to .1304 when years of experience is introduced.[13] When the main variable of citizen complaints is introduced, the first-order correlation coefficient decreases to .1010, but the original relationship remains statistically significant at the .01 level. When the main variable of level of education, however, is introduced as an antecedent test variable, the original direct relationship between department commendations and academic status decreases to .0308 and is no longer statistically significant. As illustrated in figure 1, this finding suggests, according to the elaboration model, that level of education provides the explanation of the originally observed relationship between department commendations and academic status as a spurious one.

First-order partial correlation coefficients for the relationship between citizen complaints and academic status are relatively unaltered when the control variables of gender, ethnicity, age, rank, prior occupation, and years of experience are included in the analyses, the original inverse relationship remaining significant at the .01 significance level. When the main variable of department commendations is introduced into the analysis, the original relationship between citizen complaints and academic status decreases minimally from -.2137 to -.1987 but also remains statistically significant at the .01 significance level. Additionally, when level of education is introduced into the first-order analysis, the original inverse relationship between citizen complaints and academic status decreases from -.2137 to -.0912 and remains statistically significant only at the .02 significance level. At the .01 significance level of analysis, this finding also suggests, according to the elaboration model illustrated in figure 1, that level of education once again provides the explanation of the originally observed relationship between citizen complaints and academic status as a spurious or ungenuine one.

A discriminant analysis procedure was run in order to determine or verify differences among the four groups on the academic status criterion variable with respect to the simultaneous introduction of the two probationary performance predictor variables (department commendations and citizen complaints) and the control variables of age and years of experience. The purpose was to attempt to discriminate between the nonservice, in-service, preservice, and continuing groups on the academic status variable and to test the accuracy of this procedure through the development of a classification matrix.

Results of discriminant analysis for academic status as an ordinal, dependent variable produced statistical results verifying or confirming the original zero-order relationships between department commendations and academic status and between citizen complaints and academic status. The ratio level predictor variables of age and years of experience were also included in the analysis, and years of experience was found to be the major significant predictor variable, at the .05 significance level.[14] In fact, years of experience produced a Lambda of .90465, explaining approximately 9.5 percent of the total variance (percentage of explained variance = 1 - Lambda) of the academic status group centroids.

In order to understand the nature of the hypothesized relationship between the predictor and criterion variables in discriminant analysis, discriminant analysis requires that the antecedent, "causal" predictor variables be ratio level variables and the subsequent, "effect" variable be a nominal or ordinal level variable. For the present analysis, knowing the value of department commendations and citizen complaints is hypothesized as providing a relatively accurate assessment of an officer's academic status: whether an officer falls within the nonservice, in-service, preservice, or continuing group.

The variable of citizen complaints entered into the discriminant analysis as the second most significant predictor reduced the Lambda to .83894, thereby explaining approximately an additional 6.4 percent of the variance of the academic status group centroids (r^2 = .90465 - .83894). Lastly, department commendations is also a significant predictor, reducing Lambda to .81590, thereby adding approximately 2.3 percent (r^2 = .83894 - .81590) to the explained variance of the academic status group centroids.

Overall, the three variables of years of experience, citizen complaints, and department commendations explain approximately 18.2 percent of the variance of academic status. Only two significant functions were derived for prediction of the four groups making up academic status, a common outcome for this type of analysis. The extremely small eigenvalues for these two functions (.13885 for Function 1 and .07202 for Function 2), however, seem to suggest poor discriminating power for both of these functions.

An index of the predictive effectiveness for both of these discriminant functions resulted in a classification matrix. This matrix reveals that for the nonservice group, 86.5 percent of the cases were incorrectly predicted; for the in-service group, 70.9 percent of the cases were incorrectly predicted; for the preservice group, 13.1 percent of the cases were incorrectly predicted; and for the continuing group, 100 percent of cases were incorrectly predicted. Additionally, a *tau* score of 19.68 indicates that classification based on these discriminating variables resulted in approximately only 20 percent fewer errors than would be expected by random assignment.

An extremely large Box's *M* statistic of 71.27, a statistic that tests for the equality of group covariance matrices, results in a significance level of .000, which shows that group covariances are unequal. This finding violates one of the assumptions underlying discriminant analysis: that the group covariances must be equal. Because both the percentage of correct classifications is low and the equality of covariance assumption has been violated, the analysis has been unable to determine if the poor classification results have been due to the weak discriminating variables or to the violation of this assumption.[15]

The preceding analysis has shown that the hypothesized relationship between department commendations, citizen complaints, and academic status has been confirmed although these two probationary performance indicators together explain approximately 9 percent of the variance of academic status. Years of experience was also found to be a significant predictor of academic status, accounting for 11 percent of the variable by itself; however, years of experience was not found to adversely influence the relationship of probationary performance indicators (department commendations and citizen complaints) with academic status.

In the initial discussion in this section, however, it was determined that level of education was found to reduce the original zero-order correlation coefficient between department commendations and academic status to statistical insignificance; level of education also reduced the correlation coefficient between citizen complaints and academic status to statistical insignificance at the .01 significance level.

Since level of education is an ordinal-level variable, and since discriminant analysis assumes all predictor variables included in the analysis are ratio-level variables, the introduction of the variable of level of education into the discriminant analysis procedure would have violated this assumption and rendered the classification results as meaningless. This situation impairs the present discriminant analysis results from confirming or disconfirming the original relationship between probationary performance indicators (department commendations and citizen complaints) and academic status when the antecedent variable of level of education is included in the analysis. Therefore, the spurious relationship illustrated in the General Functional Elaboration Model in figure 1 is based upon the first-order partial correlation analysis discussed earlier in this section.

A relationship between probationary performance indicators and academic status of L.A.P.D. officers has been disconfirmed. An officer's student academic status at the time of the survey was found not to have been influenced by the number of department commendations or citizen complaints received while he or she was serving a probationary period. An officer's level of education prior to entry to the department was found to be the controlling factor in determining whether or not an officer continues college after entering the department, not how well an officer performed while serving a probationary period.

Relationship between Academic Status and Professionalism Indexes

Zero-order correlation coefficients between academic status and both Niederhoffer's Revised Index and Regoli and Poole's Professionalism Index reveal significant relationships at the .01 significance level. For Niederhoffer's Revised Index, the correlation coefficient is .2613, explaining approximately 7 percent of the total variance. For Regoli and Poole's index, the correlation coefficient is .1535, representing approximately 2 percent of the total variance of the index. When the control variables of gender, ethnicity, age, rank, prior occupation, and years of experience are introduced in first-order partial correlation analyses, the original relationship between academic status and each of the two professionalism indices remains stable and statistically significant. These findings support the hypothesis that a statistically significant, direct relationship exists between academic status and officer professionalism.

First-order partial correlation coefficients for the relationship between academic status and each of the two professionalism indices show a decrease in these original relationships when level of education as an antecedent test variable is introduced in the analyses. The correlation coefficient for academic status and Niederhoffer's Revised Index decreases from .2613 to .1905, but remains statistically significant at the .01 significance level. The correlation coefficient for academic status and Regoli and Poole's index decreases significantly from .1535 to .1082 and is no longer statistically significant at the .01 significance level. This latter finding suggests that the original statistically significant relationship between academic status and Regoli and Poole's Professionalism Index may in fact be a spurious one, in that antecedent variable of level of education explains this relationship as an ungenuine one.

Additionally, when citizen complaints is introduced into a first-order partial analysis as an antecedent test variable with academic status and Regoli and Poole's Professionalism Index, the correlation coefficient decreases from .1535 to .0913 and is no longer statistically significant at the .01 significance level. These findings suggest that the original relationship between academic status and Niederhoffer's Revised Index remains a statistically significant direct one; however, the original relationship between academic status and Regoli and Poole's Professionalism Index is spurious due to the introduction of level of education and citizen complaints in first-order partial correlation analyses.

When Regoli and Poole's Professionalism Index is introduced into a first-order partial analysis with academic status and Niederhoffer's Revised Index, the correlation coefficient for these two variables decreases to .2182; however, this correlation coefficient remains significant at the .01 significance level. When Niederhoffer's Revised Index is introduced into a first-order partial correlation analysis with academic status and Regoli and Poole's Professionalism Index, the original correlation between these two variables decreases from .1535 to -.0435, a correlation coefficient which is no longer statistically significant. This particular finding, which is similar to the findings in hypotheses two and three, suggests that Niederhoffer's Revised Index seems to be a more stable measure in terms of predictive validity for professional attitudes than Regoli and Poole's Professionalism Index. Elaboration analysis suggests that Niederhoffer's Revised Index as used to measure professionalism may be a more valid predictor than Regoli and Poole's index (see figure 1).

A one-way analysis of variance between academic status and Niederhoffer's Revised Index confirms the original relationship between the two variables, with an F value of 9.16 indicating that the means between the groups are significantly different (p = .000). Eta^2, examining the amount of explained total variance between the two variables, indicates that 8 percent of the variance in the professionalism scores of Niederhoffer's Revised Index is explained by academic status. The within-cell variances, however, are determined to be unequal as a result of a Bartlett-Box F value of 3.84 (p = .009). A nonparametric Kruskal-Wallis one-way ANOVA with a chi-square statistic of 16.39 (p = .000) confirms the statistically significant original relationship between academic status and Niederhoffer's Revised Index.

One-way ANOVA results for Niederhoffer's Revised Index are illustrated in figure 5, showing that the average professionalism score of 35.74 for nonservice falls below both the overall sample mean of 42.21 and the midpoint of 39, indicating extremely cynical attitudes for this group. The average score of 41.34 for the in-service group, while falling below the overall mean score of 42.21, falls above the midpoint of 39, indicating neutral or ambivalent attitudes for this group of officers. In contrast, the preservice and continuing groups, with average scores of 43.37 and 44.70, respectively, fall within the more professional range of scores. A Student-Newman-Keuls multiple range test also shows that the average score of 35.74 for the nonservice group is significantly less, or more cynical, than the average scores for the in-service, preservice, and continuing academic groups.

These findings support the view that professional attitudes are influenced by the timing of an officer's education. Additionally, whether or not an officer continues that education after appointment to the department also has some influence on an officer's professional attitudes.

Figure 5 also illustrates that nonservice officers, those who receive no advanced education either prior to or after entering the department, possess the most cynical, least professional attitudes overall. In contrast, the continuing group of officers, officers who initiate an advanced education prior to entering the department and continue that education after appointment to the department, have the most professional, least cynical attitudes of all the groups.

FIGURE 5

MEAN PROFESSIONALISM INDEX SCORES BY ACADEMIC STATUS

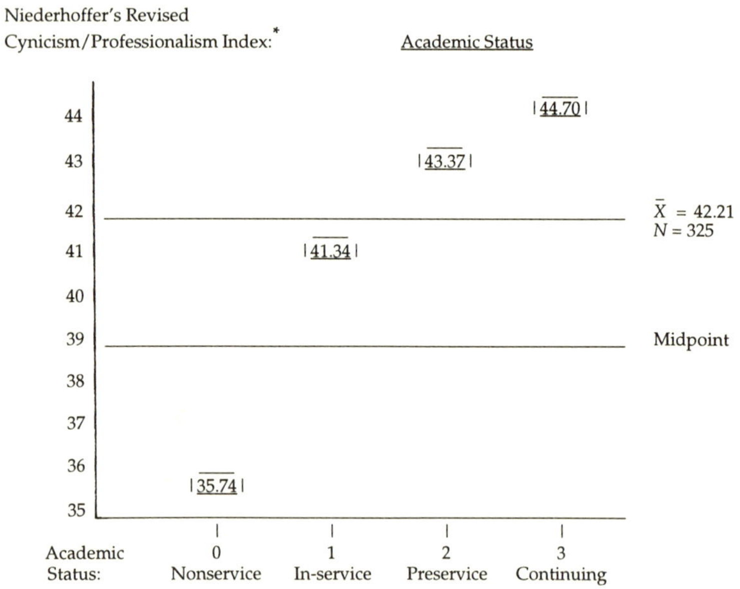

*The higher the score, the more professional the attitudes; the lower the score, the more cynical the attitudes.

Preservice officers, those who initiate their educations prior to their appointment to the department but do not continue once appointed, also possess extremely professional attitudes. The only group of officers with neutral or ambivalent attitudes is the in-service group, in which officers only begin college after appointment to the department.

A one-way analysis of variance between academic status and Regoli and Poole's Professionalism Index also confirms the original statistically significant relationship between the two, achieving an F value of 6.76 (p = .000). The total explained variance for these variables, as measured by Eta^2, amounts to approximately 5 percent. However, the Bartlett-Box F score of 8.36 (p = .000) shows that the within-cell variances are not equal for this index, and a follow-up Kruskal-Wallis H statistic of 4.47 (p = .119) for Regoli and Poole's Professionalism Index is unable to confirm the original relationship between academic status and this professionalism index.

For the individual subscales, Attitudes toward Others Effects on Police Work, Attitudes toward Ideals Concerning Police Work, and Attitudes toward Conduct Involved in Police Work, (the subscales which comprise Niederhoffer's Revised Index), all subscale group means were found to be statistically different at the .01 significance level. However, after computing both parametric and nonparametric one-way ANOVAs for the subscales making up Regoli and Poole's Professionalism Index, only the group means for Attitudes toward the Public were found to differ.

Figure 6 illustrates the subscale group mean scores by academic status for Attitudes toward Others Effects on Police Work, Attitudes toward Ideals Concerning Police Work, and Attitudes toward Conduct Involved in Police Work.

The mean scores for both nonservice and in-service groups fall below the sample mean of 13.56 for Attitudes toward Others Effects on Police Work. However, although the mean scores for preservice and continuing groups fall above the overall mean, the fact that these average scores fall below the subscale midpoint of 15 indicates that all mean scores for this subscale fall below the professional range but within the neutral range. This

FIGURE 6

MEAN PROFESSIONALISM SUBSCALE SCORES BY ACADEMIC STATUS

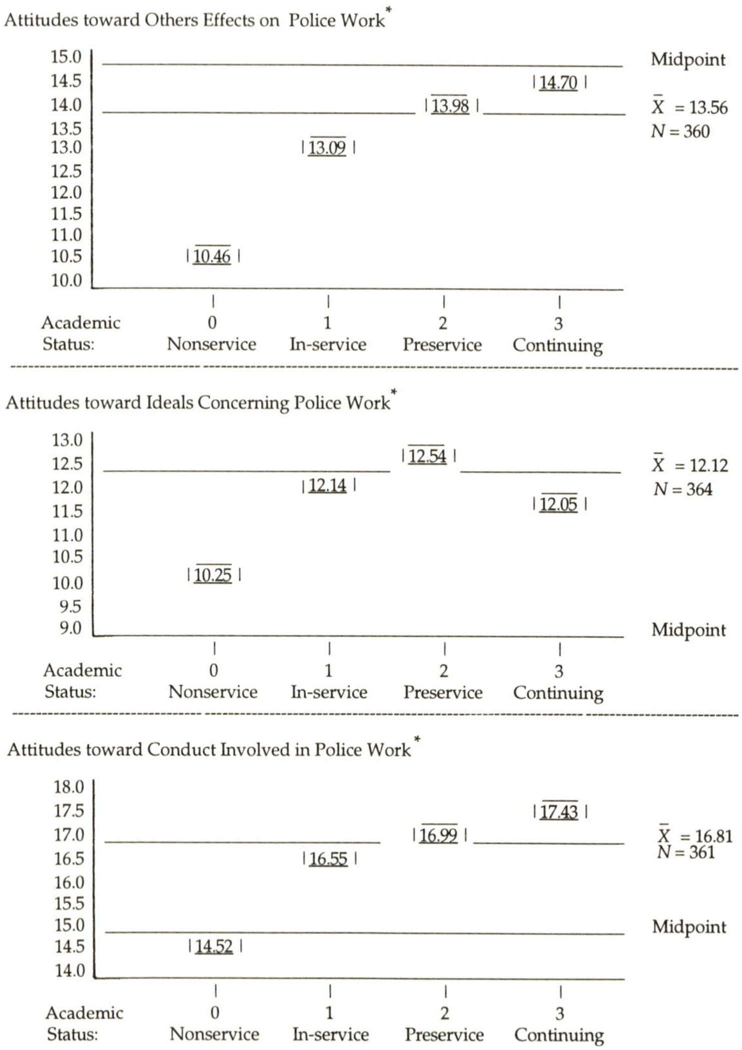

*The higher the score, the more professional the attitudes; the lower the score, the more cynical the attitudes.

finding suggests that officers, regardless of academic group membership, have neutral attitudes toward others' effects on police work.

All of the average scores on the Attitudes toward Ideals Concerning Police Work subscale fall above the midpoint range of 9, indicating more professional attitudes overall. However, average scores of 10.25 for the nonservice group and 12.05 for the continuing group fall below the overall sample mean of 12.12. This suggests that officers within both the nonservice and continuing academic groups have slightly less professional attitudes, leading toward the neutral range, in their ideals regarding police work.

For Attitudes toward Conduct Involved in Police Work, both the nonservice group, with an average score of 14.52, and the in-service group, with an average score of 16.55, fall below the overall sample mean of 16.68. However, with a midpoint of 15 representing neutral attitudes or ambivalence for this subscale, the in-service, preservice, and continuing groups fall toward the more professional range. Only the nonservice group falls within the neutral or ambivalent range of scores. This finding shows that when officers are classified according to

FIGURE 7

MEAN PROFESSIONALISM SUBSCALE SCORES BY ACADEMIC STATUS

Attitudes toward the Public*

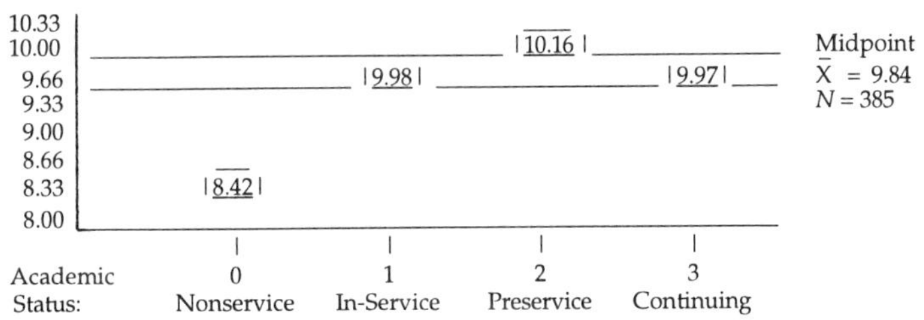

*The higher the score, the more professional the attitudes; the lower the score, the more cynical the attitudes.

academic status, average scores generally fall within the neutral to professional ranges.

For Attitudes toward the Public, the only statistically significant subscale of Regoli and Poole's Professionalism Index, figure 7 shows only the nonservice average score of 8.42 falling below the overall sample mean of 9.84 in the more cynical range. However, although the means for in-service (9.98), preservice (10.16), and continuing (9.97) fall above the overall sample mean, these scores fall closer to the neutral range since the midpoint for this subscale is 10. The relationship between academic status and Attitudes toward the Public was found to be statistically significant, with an F value of 12.95 (p = .000) and a total explained variance of approximately 9 percent ($Eta^2 = .093$).

The previous analysis and discussion have shown that a direct relationship exists between academic student status and professionalism as measured by Niederhoffer's Revised Index. Essentially, the timing of an L.A.P.D. patrol officer's career has a significant influence on his or her police professionalism. Continuing education patrol officers generally have rated the highest professionally of the four groups. In contrast, nonservice officers, those without any college education during their careers, have rated the lowest professionally, that is, achieved the highest scores for cynicism, than the other groups of officers.

Interaction between Academic Status, Professional Attitudes, and Significant Control Variables

A two-way analysis of variance, testing for any interaction effects of gender, ethnicity, rank, prior occupation, and years of experience with both academic status and Niederhoffer's Revised Index, indicates no significant interaction effects between these variables. However, analysis of the four subscales having statistically significant group mean differences (Attitudes toward Others Effects on Police Work, Attitudes toward Ideals Concerning Police Work, Attitudes toward Conduct Involved in Police Work, and Attitudes toward the Public) found that only two of the subscales were affected by statistically significant two-way interaction effects between academic status and both prior occupation and years of experience.

Prior occupation was found to have a statistically significant two-way interaction effect with academic status on Attitudes toward Ideals Concerning Police Work, achieving an *F* value of 1.87 ($p = .029$). However, an examination of the analysis of variance table shows that prior occupation does not have statistically significant main effects on Attitudes toward Ideals Concerning Police Work, having achieved an *F* value of .38 ($p = .866$).

Years of experience was also found to have a statistically significant two-way interaction effect with academic status on Attitudes toward the Public, achieving an *F* value of 3.54 ($p = .000$). However, an examination of the analysis of variance table also shows that years of experience does not have a statistically significant main effect on Attitudes toward the Public, having achieved an *F* value of 1.33 ($p = .265$).

Figure 8 illustrates the two-way interaction effects between academic status and prior occupation on Attitudes toward Ideals Concerning Police Work. All of the average scores or group means for the nonservice category of academic status fall below the overall sample mean of 12.05 for this subscale. This finding suggests that, despite the prior occupation of the L.A.P.D. patrol officer, those who had not received any college education prior to or after entering the department have less-professional attitudes regarding ideals concerning police work.

For the in-service category of academic status, average scores for the skilled trade, military, and blue-collar laborer groups fall above the overall sample mean of 12.05, whereas the professional service and the (non-college) student groups fall below the overall sample mean. This finding suggests that for officers who were employed in the military, skilled trades, or blue-collar occupations prior to entry into the department and who, after appointment to the department, began attending college, attitudes concerning ideals of police work were much more highly professional than those of professional services or student groups who initiated college education only after appointment to the department.

For the preservice category of academic status, all five occupational groups fall above the overall sample mean on the Attitudes toward Ideals Concerning Police Work subscale. This particular finding lends support to the general hypothesis; that is, officers attending college prior to their entry into policing have more professional attitudes toward the police officer role than those who do not attend college prior to appointment in the policing profession.

FIGURE 8

INTERACTION EFFECTS BETWEEN ACADEMIC STATUS AND PRIOR OCCUPATION ON ATTITUDES TOWARD IDEALS CONCERNING POLICE WORK

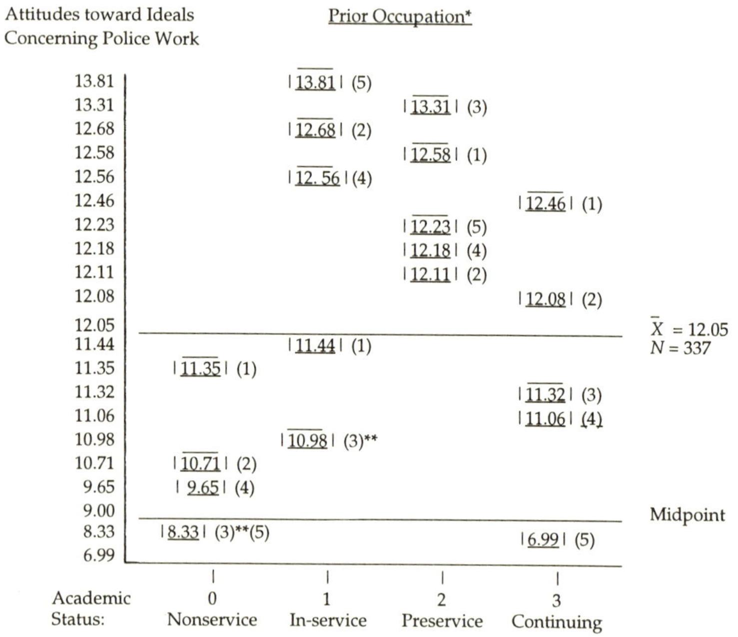

*Legend: Prior Occupation
(1) - Professionl Services
(2) - Military
(3) - Student
**Non-college
(4) - Skilled Trades
(5) - Blue-Collar Laborer

Both the professional services and military categories average scores fall above the overall sample mean on the Attitudes toward Ideals Concerning Police Work subscale for the continuing education academic status category, whereas student, skilled trade, and blue-collar laborer groups fall below the overall sample mean. With an Attitude toward Ideals Concerning Police Work subscale midpoint of 9 representing neutral attitudes or ambivalence, these results show that the average scores for the student and blue-collar laborer groups in the nonservice academic status category fall in the less professional, cynical range, whereas the other groups fall above the midpoint in the more professional range.

In the continuing academic status category, only the blue-collar laborer group falls within the cynical range, with an Attitudes toward Ideals Concerning Police Work group mean of 6.99. This average score for blue-collar laborers represents the lowest and least professional score for the entire subscale of Attitudes toward Ideals Concerning Police Work. At least for this group of officers, the stress of continuing college after appointment to the department seems to have had an extremely debilitating effect on their views of the role of contemporary police officers.

When classified by prior occupational categories, figure 9 depicts the average scores for the preservice and continuing academic status groups in the professional services category falling above the overall sample mean, and the in-service and nonservice group means falling below the overall sample mean on the Attitudes toward Ideals Concerning Police Work subscale. None of these average scores fall below the midpoint of 9, all well within the professional range of scores. The average scores for the military occupational category also fall above the midpoint in the more professional range; however, the average score for the nonservice military category falls below the overall sample mean and close to the neutral or ambivalent point. These findings suggest that for officers with a professional services and military prior occupation, those without any college prior to their entry into department score the least professional on their Attitudes toward Ideals Concerning Police Work.

For officers identifying themselves as students prior to entering law enforcement, the nonservice (or high school) academic status group falls below the midpoint on the Attitudes toward Ideals Concerning Police Work subscale, more toward the cynical range. However, both the in-service and continuing academic status groups fall below the overall sample mean close to the ambivalent point. Only the average score for the preservice academic status group falls above the overall sample mean for Attitudes toward Ideals Concerning Police Work and within the professional range.

FIGURE 9

INTERACTION EFFECTS BETWEEN PRIOR OCCUPATION AND ACADEMIC STATUS ON ATTITUDES TOWARD IDEALS CONCERNING POLICE WORK

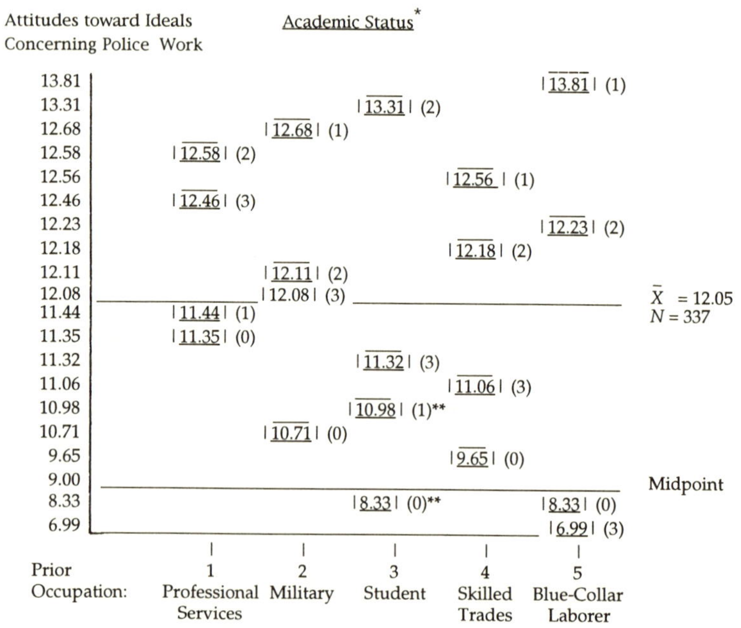

*Legend: Academic Status: (0) - Nonservice (2) - Preservice (1) - In-service (3) - Continuing

**High school graduates only who identified themselves as students

All academic status groups for the skilled trade category fall above the midpoint, with in-service and preservice academic status groups falling above the overall sample mean, and continuing and nonservice academic status groups falling below the sample mean. These findings also suggest that for students and skilled trade occupational groups, officers with no college prior to or after their appointment to the department have the least professional, most cynical attitudes regarding their ideals of police work.

Average scores on the Attitudes toward Ideals Concerning Police Work subscale for the blue-collar laborer occupational category appear to be polarized toward the two ends of the continuum. Both the in-service and preservice academic status groups average scores fall above the overall sample mean and the midpoint in the more professional range; however, the average scores for nonservice and continuing academic status groups fall below both the overall sample mean and the midpoint within the more cynical range of attitudes for Attitudes toward Ideals Concerning Police Work. The presence of contrasting scores for the blue-collar laborer groups suggest that college education and experience either before or after appointment to the department has a positive influence on professional attitudes on these officers' Attitudes toward Ideals Concerning Police Work. However, those officers with a blue-collar laborer occupational background who have not attended college, as well as those who attended prior to entry and continued after appointment to the department, possess the least professional, most cynical attitudes for this subscale of Attitudes toward Ideals Concerning Police Work.

As noted previously, years of experience was found to have a significant interaction effect with Attitudes toward the Public and academic status. Figure 10 portrays the two-way interaction effect between years of experience and academic status on Attitudes toward the Public. For this subscale, there is a minimal difference between the sample mean of 9.84 and the midpoint of 10.00. Therefore, discussion will be limited to the average scores on each of the academic status groups in relation to the overall sample mean for Attitudes toward the Public.

FIGURE 10

INTERACTION EFFECTS BETWEEN ACADEMIC STATUS AND YEARS OF EXPERIENCE ON ATTITUDES TOWARD THE PUBLIC

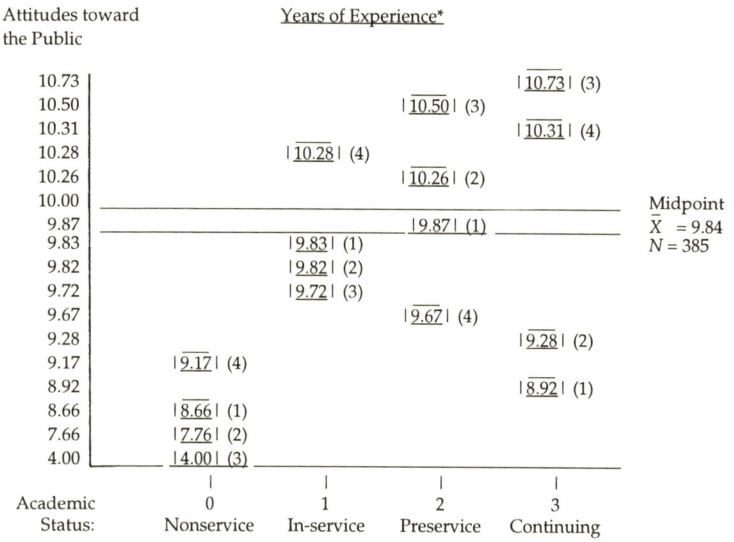

*Legend: Years of experience with L.A.P.D.:
(1) - One to Five Years
(2) - Six to Ten Years
(3) - Eleven to Fifteen Years
(4) - Over Fifteen Years

Years of experience has been broken down into four groups: one to five years, two to ten years, eleven to fifteen years, and over fifteen years groups. This breakdown compares to the groupings in Niederhoffer's original cynicism study. For the nonservice academic status category, average scores for years on the Attitudes toward the Public subscale exhibit an interesting pattern quite different from Niederhoffer's results for his original index. The over fifteen years of experience group, while falling below the overall sample mean of 9.84, received the highest average score (9.17) for this category but close to the neutral point. The next lower average score, still close to the neutral point, is the one to five year group with an average score of 8.66 on Attitudes toward the Public. Next lowest is the six to ten year group with an average score of 7.76. The lowest average score for Attitudes toward the Public, falling low in the cynicism range, is the eleven to fifteen year group, with an average score of 4.00. This finding suggests that, regardless of the number of years of experience, officers who have had no college education (either before or while working with the department) possess the least professional, most cynical attitudes toward the public.

For the in-service category on Attitudes toward the Public, the one to five years, six to ten years, and eleven to fifteen years of experience groups all fall below the overall sample mean, close to the neutral or ambivalent point. Only the over fifteen years of experience group falls above the overall sample mean, receiving an average score of 10.28 on the Attitudes toward the Public subscale. This finding suggests that the value of a college education experience only after appointment to the department, at least for the first fifteen years with the department, does not have the professionalizing effect on officers' attitudes toward the public. However, after this period of fifteen years, the college experience has a more positive effect on attitudes toward the public.

Interestingly, for the preservice academic status category, only the over fifteen years of experience group average score of 9.67 falls below the overall sample mean of 9.84 for Attitudes toward the Public, whereas the remaining one to five years, six to ten years, and eleven to fifteen years of experience groups average scores fall above the overall sample mean. For the continuing academic status group, the one to five years and the six to ten years of experience groups' average scores fall below the overall sample mean for Attitudes toward the Public and toward the more cynical range, whereas the eleven to fifteen years and over fifteen years of experience groups' average scores fall above the overall sample mean, well within the professional range.

Keeping in mind the limitations of cross-sectional survey data, these findings suggest that for officers who receive college education only prior to entering the department, this college experience has its greatest professionalizing influence on attitudes toward the public during the first fifteen years of service; after that point, the value of the college experience only prior to appointment to the department depreciates. The combination of the college experience both prior to and after appointment to the department has the least professionalizing effect for the first ten years within the department but the most professionalizing effect on attitudes toward the public after ten years with the department.

Conversely, figure 11 shows that within the one to five years of experience category, the nonservice academic status

FIGURE 11

INTERACTION EFFECTS BETWEEN YEARS OF EXPERIENCE AND ACADEMIC STATUS ON ATTITUDES TOWARD THE PUBLIC

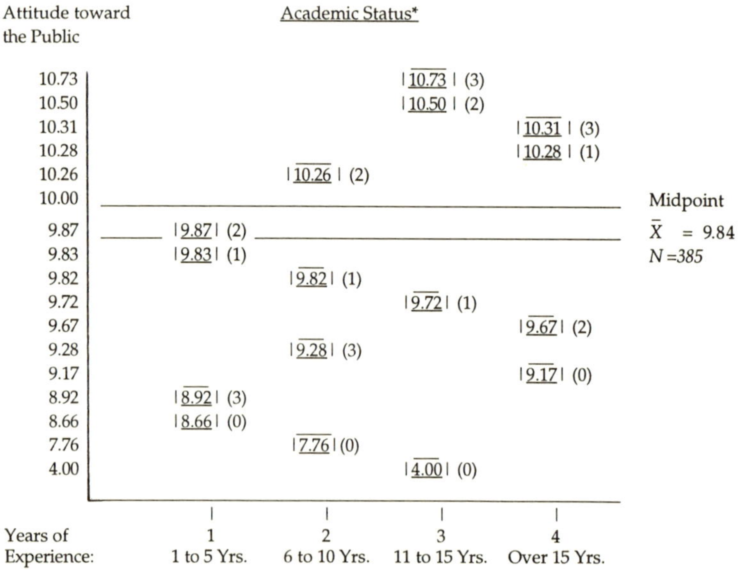

* Legend: Academic Status

(0) - Nonservice
(1) - In-service
(2) - Preservice
(3) - Continuing

group ranks the lowest or least professional, the continuing academic status group the second lowest or least professional, and the in-service academic status group just below the overall sample mean for Attitudes toward the Public. The average score of 9.87 for the preservice academic status group falls slightly above the overall sample mean but close to the neutral or ambivalent point.

For the six to ten years of experience category, once again, the average scores for nonservice, continuing, and in-service academic status groups fall below the overall sample mean, with average scores of 7.76, 9.28, and 9.82 respectively. However, the average score for the preservice academic status group falls above both the overall sample mean and midpoint with an average score of 10.26.

These results suggest that for the first five years in the department, regardless of the educational experience, all officers have less than professional attitudes toward the public. However, officers with no college experience prior to entry into the department and those with college both prior to and after entry (continuing), at least for the first five years, have the least professional, most cynical attitudes toward the public.

During the second five years with the department, the preservice academic experience has a more positive, professionalizing effect on officers, whereas officers with no college experience prior to entry into the department become less professional or more cynical toward the public.

For the eleven to fifteen years of experience category, average scores become polarized for the academic status groups. The average scores for the nonservice and in-service academic status groups on the Attitudes toward the Public subscale fall below the overall sample mean, with the nonservice academic status group average score of 4.00 falling well within the cynicism range. The average scores for preservice and continuing academic status groups fall above the overall sample mean within the professional range, with scores of 10.31 and 10.28, respectively. For the over fifteen years of experience (ready for retirement) category, both the nonservice and preservice academic status groups fall below the overall sample mean close to the neutral or ambivalent point, whereas the in-service and continuing academic status groups fall above the overall sample mean and within the more professional range of scores for Attitudes toward the Public.

These results suggest that more years of service with the department, coupled with the value of the college academic experience, have a more professionalizing effect on patrol officers. Officers without any college experience either prior to or after appointment with the department continue to become more cynical after ten years of experience, but improve slightly when nearing the retirement period. Additional academic experience during this retirement period seems to have a more positive, professionalizing effect for the officers in their attitudes toward the public.

To the extent that attitudes reflect subsequent behavior, several relevant patterns emerge from this interaction analysis. First, no matter how many the number of years of experience, nonservice groups (those without any college education) rank lowest and fall within the cynical to neutral range on Attitudes toward the Public for all categories. For the first ten years of experience, the average scores for preservice student groups give the highest, most professional scores. For the following eleven to fifteen year range, the average score for preservice students drops to second highest, just below continuing students (those with education before and after appointment). For the over fifteen years of experience range, the preservice academic status group mean falls to the second lowest average score, just above the average score for the nonservice academic status group. This trend suggests (within the limitations of a cross-sectional study) that, at least in attitudes toward the public, the impact of a preservice education, without additional follow-up education, has a leveling-off effect at fifteen years of service and depreciates thereafter.

For the one to five years, six to ten years, and ten to fifteen years of experience groups, the in-service academic status average scores (i.e., for those officers who receive schooling only after appointment) center around the neutral point, decreasing steadily over this period. However, for the over fifteen years of experience group, the overall score for Attitudes toward the Public for the in-service academic status group is higher and falls just below the continuing student academic status group. Although cross-sectional data can only approximate longitudinal data, analysis of this finding suggests that in-service officers may begin with somewhat neutral attitudes that decrease slightly, that is, become more cynical, over the years. However, when nearing retirement, postappointment education may have a reverse effect, influencing Attitudes toward the Public more positively and professionally.

For the first ten years of service, the continuing student academic status groups fall just above the nonservice academic status groups on Attitudes toward the Public, with a slight improvement in attitudes after the first five years. These less professional, more neutral attitudes generally for the continuing academic status groups may represent the anxiety associated with enhanced expectations from a preappointment college education, together with postappointment anxiety of continued schooling while adapting to the pressures of a new law enforcement career. Moreover, the following eleven to fifteen years of service category shows this continuing student academic status group achieving the highest average score on Attitudes toward the Public, above the other three academic status groups. For the over fifteen years of experience group, the average score for Attitudes toward the Public decreases slightly but remains well within the professional range of scores and higher than the other academic status groups.

The hypothesized relationships between academic status and professionalism, as measured by Niederhoffer's Revised Cynicism/Professionalism Index, has been confirmed, with academic status accounting for approximately 7 percent of the total variance of Niederhoffer's Revised Index. Gender, ethnicity, age, rank, prior occupation, and years of experience, when included in partial-correlation analyses, had no effect on this original relationship. Level of education did have some effect, which essentially assists in explaining the empirical model. An illustration and summary of these results are displayed in the General Functional Elaboration Model in figure 1.

The hypothesized relationship was not confirmed for academic status and professionalism when measured by the Regoli and Poole Professionalism Index. The original, statistically significant relationship between these two variables was disconfirmed, found to be spurious, or found to be statistically insignificant when level of education, citizen complaints, and Niederhoffer's Revised Index were included in first-order partial analyses with academic status and the Regoli and Poole Professionalism Index. Additionally, Niederhoffer's Revised Index has emerged as the more valid predictive measure of professionalism after inclusion in a first-order partial correlation analysis with academic status and Regoli and Poole's Index.

None of the control variables, when included in a two-way interaction analysis, had an effect on Niederhoffer's Revised Cynicism/Professionalism Index. However, when all of the control variables were included in two-way analyses of variance for statistically significant subscales, academic status, prior occupation, and years of experience were found to have statistically significant two-way interaction effects with both Attitudes toward Ideals Concerning Police Work and Attitudes toward the Public.

Relationship between Level of Education and Academic Status

A zero-order correlation analysis for level of education and academic status has resulted in a correlation coefficient of .6417, which is statistically significant at the .01 significance level. First-order partial correlation coefficients for gender, ethnicity, age, rank, prior occupation, and years of experience by department commendations and citizen complaints as intervening variables, indicate that the original direct relationship is unaffected by any of these variables. The General Functional Elaboration Model in figure 1 illustrates this statistically significant direct relationship between level of education and academic status.

Since both level of education and academic status are ordinal level variables, a zero-order gamma statistic was calculated for this relationship, and first-order partial gamma statistics were generated for the effects of the control variables of gender, ethnicity, age, rank, prior occupation, and years of experience. A statistically significant zero-order gamma statistic of .79776 was calculated for level of education and academic status, which confirms the direct relationship illustrated in the General Functional Elaboration Model. When the control variables of gender, ethnicity, age, rank, and prior occupation were included in first-order partial gamma analyses, the effects of these variables on the original relationship were minimal. The original direct relationship between level of education and academic status is also unaffected when department commendations and citizen complaints, as intervening test variables, are introduced in first-order partial gamma analyses.

An increased first-order gamma coefficient of .8401 was generated for the relationship between level of education and academic status when years of experience was included in the analysis. In elaboration analysis, this finding suggests that the increase in the gamma coefficient may be due to a statistically significant relationship between years of experience, as an antecedent variable, and academic status. A similar finding using discriminant analysis procedures was discussed in the previous section on hypothesis four. Nonetheless, the statistically significant original relationship between level of education and academic status is not adversely affected by the influence of years of experience as a control variable.

These results and the previous discussion have shown that not only are level of education and an officer's academic student status significantly related, but that this significant relationship affects the relationship between an officer's level of education and professionalism. Results of this final hypothesis test confirm the indirect relationship between level of education and professionalism, a relationship that is mediated by an officer's student status both before and after entering the L.A.P.D.

Summary of Findings

As stated previously in this chapter, the development of this model has served two purposes. First, in utilizing a construct validation approach linking the effects of college education with the construct of professionalism, six hypotheses were empirically tested and supported by the results. This model links higher education to early probationary performance indicators, which are linked or related to professionalism scores. This approach satisfies the construct validation method.

Second, the development of a functional elaboration model establishes support for the belief that the relationship between college education and police officer professionalism is somewhat more complex than originally conceived. Nonetheless, the relationship does exist. Considering the myriad situations and tasks officers encounter in the course of their duties, as well as their attitudes toward the performance of their complex roles, the implications of such a model could assist in clarifying the need to reexamine the minimum educational requirements for officer recruits.[16]

The empirical findings of the six hypotheses revealed expected results. Although the correlations are not high, they are seldom large in social science research. More important, as Roberg has pointed out, "discovering the directions of the relationships (or what leads to what) is at least as important as the size of the correlations" (Roberg, 1978:340). Additionally, although much of the unexplained variances may be influenced by extraneous variables not considered here, several critical control variables were included in the analysis and found not to seriously affect the primary relationships being tested.[17]

Figure 1 illustrates the results of hypothesis testing, taking into account common variability between the hypotheses. Relationships between level of education and the two professionalism indexes used here (Niederhoffer's Revised Index and Regoli and Poole's Professionalism Index) in hypothesis two were found to be significantly affected when the main intervening variable of academic status was included in the analyses. Additionally, in hypothesis four the original relationship between each of the probationary performance indicators of department commendations and citizen complaints and academic status was found to be spurious when the main antecedent variable of level of education was included in the analysis.

Testing of hypotheses one, three, five, and six confirmed the original relationships. For hypothesis one, a direct relationship was found to exist between level of education and department commendations. Additionally, an inverse relationship was found to exist between level of education and citizen complaints.

For hypothesis two, it was determined that a positive relationship exists between level of education and the two professionalism indexes. However, it was also found that the original relationship between level of education and each of the professionalism indices does not hold when the intervening variable of academic status is controlled or partialled from the analysis. According to the elaboration model, this first-order partial analysis specifies that academic status, as an intervening variable, contributed significantly to the unadjusted, statistically significant positive relationship between level of education and professionalism indexes. The relationship between level of education and professionalism is important, when interpreted in conjunction with officer academic status.

Additionally, when citizen complaints is included in a first-order partial correlation analysis with level of education and the professional indexes, the original statistically significant positive relationships in hypothesis two between level of education and professionalism scores drop to insignificance. Once again, according to the elaboration model, citizen complaints as an intervening variable specifies the original relationships between level of education and professionalism. Citizen complaints, as an intervening variable, assists in interpreting the nature of the original relationships between level of education and professionalism scores.

Through multiple regression analysis, a direct relationship between both the probationary performance indicators of department commendations and citizen complaints with Niederhoffer's Revised Index was found to exist, confirming hypothesis three. The same was found for these probationary performance indicators and Regoli and Poole's Professionalism Index. However, when the Niederhoffer professionalism variable was introduced into a partial correlation analysis, the original relationship dropped to insignificance.

For hypothesis four, it was found that a positive relationship existed between each of the probationary performance indicators (department commendations and citizen complaints) and an officer's current academic status. However, when the antecedent variable of level of education was introduced into first-order partial correlation analyses, the original relationships between both of these probationary performance indicators and academic status became insignificant. As a result of this finding, the original relationships between department commendations and citizen complaints with officer academic status are seen to be spurious; they are explained away through the introduction of the antecedent variable of level of education. Level of education, therefore, is the important factor in determining an officer's academic status. An officer's performance while on probation, as measured by the indicators of department commendations and citizen complaints, does not significantly contribute to an officer's academic status.

Solid arrows in figure 1 show the empirically confirmed relationships for four of the six hypotheses examined. The dotted vertical arrow between level of education and professionalism scores (Niederhoffer's Revised Index and Regoli and Poole's Professionalism Index) indicates that the original hypothesized relationship has been shown to be an indirect relationship rather than a direct relationship when the influence of academic status is taken into account. The dotted horizontal arrow indicates an insignificant relationship (at .01 significance level) for hypothesis four when level of education is included in the analysis.

The empirical model shows a functional relationship between education and professionalism in that (1) level of education affects probationary performance indicators which affect professionalism; and (2) level of education affects academic status which affects professionalism. Through elaboration, it has been determined that six variables did not significantly affect these relationships. However, the introduction of main variables in partial correlation analyses showed the indirectness of the relationship between education and professionalism: both probationary performance indicators and academic status interpret the manner in which level of education influences professionalism. Additionally, the introduction of level of education as an antecedent variable has explained that an originally observed relationship between the probationary performance indicators and academic status was spurious, a finding suggesting that level of education has a "causal" effect on both the probationary performance indicators and academic status.

Because educational level and academic status have been found to be important predictor variables in determining an officer's level of professionalism, a second task of determining whether college-educated patrol officers are different than their non-college-educated counterparts has been undertaken. The results of an assessment of diverse personality styles between non-college-educated and college-educated officers are discussed in the following chapter.

NOTES

1. Sherman's report essentially evaluated sixty-two previous studies of police behavior, four of those directly measuring the relationship between higher education and officer performance. Each of those four studies reported that college-educated officers tended to "behave differently" (Sherman, 1980:75).

2. Ironically, Niederhoffer found that patrol officers at the New York Police Department with two or more years of education were more cynical than his total sample. His findings would suggest that, by using his original scale, more highly educated patrol officers were less professional than less-educated officers (Niederhoffer, 1967:98–99). Regoli's original study suggested that college-level personnel were also more cynical than lower-level personnel in small police agencies (Regoli, 1976:340–45). However, Rafky's 1975 study and Wilton and Bannon's 1976 study found no relationship between cynicism and education (Rafky, 1975; Wilt and Bannon, 1976). Rudoni et al., suggest that conclusive evidence between professionalism and education is lacking (Rudoni, Baker, and Meyer, 1978).

3. Chambliss and Seidman point out that in addition to the monetary expense to the complainant, the factors of inconvenience, time, travel, reimbursement of witnesses, and employment of an attorney have historically served as deterrents to the filing of complaints. (Chambliss and Seidman, 1971:371).

4. Allegations in complaints filed against L.A.P.D. officers between 1986 and 1990 include "excessive force," improper tactics," "conduct unbecoming an officer," "neglect of duty," "dishonesty," "discourtesy," "false imprisonment," and some complaints have multiple allegations (Christopher Commission, 1991:35). Also see Shaw, "Media Failed to Examine Alleged LAPD Abuses," (Shaw, 1992d).

5. The data reported here were collected in 1990 prior to the Rodney King incident. As the *Los Angeles Times* reports in "Complaints Against L.A. Police Set Record," an unprecedented rise in citizen complaints filed against L.A.P.D. officers occurred after the release of the Christopher Commission report (Murphy, 1991).

6. These points are brought out in the discussion in chapter 2 of studies by Vogel and Adams (1983:482) as well as by Worden (1990:568).

7. Weighting factors are as follows: 1.587 for Caucasian males; .787 for African-American males; 1.282 for Latino males; .380 for "Other" males; .461 for Caucasian females; .369 for African-American females; .379 for Latino females; and .364 for "Other" females.

8. The Christopher Commission had determined that for more serious citizen complaints filed against officers between 1986–1990 (excessive force and improper tactics making up 39.2 percent of all citizen complaints), approximately 20 percent (1,802 officers) had at least one allegation filed against them (Christopher Commission, 1991:36–39). The commission did not analyze "lesser complaints" filed against officers. More or less serious complaints are not distinguished here, and there is no way of determining what proportion of the 33.8 percent of officers with at least one complaint filed against them during their probationary period fall into either category.

9. For the entire sample of L.A.P.D. officers in the prior *Blake* study, the mean officer score for responses on the item concerning newspaper coverage was highly cynical. Additionally, the mean response score for the item concerning department efficiency fell between neutral and cynical. The three other items for this subscale, attitudes toward a college degree, the public, and testifying in court ranged from neutral to professional. These first two items, then, might explain why the mean response score for this subscale falls below the mean score of 15. The present antagonistic and oftentimes hostile relationship between the press and the L.A.P.D. is described in Shaw, "Onetime Allies: Press and LAPD," and "Chief Parker Molded LAPD Image—Then Came the '60s" (Shaw, 1992b,c).

10. See appendix B for the three items that make up this subscale (V83, V84, and V85). An overview of some of the administrative

problems in the L.A.P.D. in particular (and the Los Angeles criminal justice system in general) can be found in "Justice in Distress: The Devaluation of Crime in Los Angeles," (Freed, 1990). Such problems may assist in explaining why these patrol officers apparently lacked confidence in the administration of the department prior to the Rodney King incident.

11. As Babbie explains, the elaboration model was developed in order to understand the complex relationship between variables when simultaneously introducing control variables. For an overview of the mechanics as well as the strengths and weaknesses of the elaboration model, see Babbie (1992:409–427).

12. See note 9 above.

13. As Babbie has pointed out, one of the limitations of the basic elaboration paradigm is that it does not take into account that a partial relationship may be stronger than the original (Babbie, 1992:423).

14. Since the introduction of these two variables in a first-order partial analysis increased the correlation coefficient for commendations and academic status , and, because as pointed out in note 13, this is not taken into consideration in partial analysis, these two variables were introduced with the view that they may be significant predictors in their own right. Due to an extremely high correlation between age and years experience , i.e., Pearson $r^2 = .71$, age is not a significant predictor when included in the analysis along with age years experience, as a result of multicollinearity.

15. Norusis points out that, "when sample sizes in the groups are large, the significance probability may be small even if the group covariance matrices are not too dissimilar" (Norusis, 1988:108–109). In the present analysis, an extremely high Box's *M* statistic of 71.27 and cases numbering less than 100 in three of the group categories suggests that the group covariance matrices are quite dissimilar.

16. Ironically, this is one area of reform that was not specifically addressed by the Christopher Commission in its investigations of police misconduct by officers of the L.A.P.D.

17. Gender and ethnicity are important because of affirmative action mandates; see *Blake* report (Felkenes et al., 1990, vol. 1). Also, years of experience were found to be significant in Niederhoffer's original study of *Behind the Shield* (Niederhoffer, 1967). Rank is important because as Price points out, rank differences must be taken into account when discussing police attitudes since as officers move up the ranks, "caution, skepticism, and equivocation replace certainty

about professionalism" (Price, 1977:93–94). At least for the L.A.P.D. officers on patrol examined here, rank was not found to be significant.

CHAPTER 6

Profiles of L.A.P.D. Patrol Officers

> The citizen expects police officers to have the wisdom of Solomon, the courage of David, the strength of Samson, the patience of Job, the leadership of Moses, the kindness of the Good Samaritan, the strategical training of Alexander, the faith of Daniel, the diplomacy of Lincoln, the tolerance of the Carpenter of Nazareth, and finally, an intimate knowledge of every branch of natural, biological, and social sciences. If he had all these, he *might* be a good policeman. (Vollmer, 1936:222)

Our task to this point has been to assess whether college-educated officers are better officers than non-college-educated officers and whether or not they might be the "good" police officers that Vollmer envisioned. To determine whether college-educated officers generally possess traits or characteristics different from those of non-college-educated officers, two groups of officers ("most" professional officers and "least" professional officers) were generated from the L.A.P.D. survey results (see Table 4). (See appendix A for methodology.)

Comparisons of appropriate scores and statistics indicate that officer rank, gender, ethnicity, age, and years of experience are irrelevant; that is, they were found not to be distinguishing characteristics between the two groups.

Level of education was found to be a differentiating characteristic in that the majority of patrol officers in the "least" professional group (62.7 percent) received no college education, whereas the majority of officers in the "most" professional group (68.1 percent) received at least some college education prior to entering the L.A.P.D. Academic or educational status was also a primary characteristic distinguishing between the two groups; in

TABLE 4

PROFILE OF OFFICERS ON PATROL

DESCRIPTOR *	*"MOST" PROFESSIONAL*	*"LEAST" PROFESSIONAL*
Others Effects on Police Work	Neutral - 89.8 %	Cynical - 64.8%
College Degree	Professional - 59.5%	Cyn./Neut. - 92.4%
Newspapers	Cyn./Neut. - 96.3%	Cynical - 100%
Public	Professional - 64.9%	Neutral - 55.5%
Department	Neut./Prof. - 81.2%	Cynical - 77.5%
Testifying in Court	Neut./Prof. - 82.6%	Cynical - 80.6%
Ideals concerning Police Work	Professional - 86.9%	Neutral - 64.9%
Professionalism	Professional - 91.2%	Cyn./Prof. - 78.0%
Average Police Work	Professional - 80.8%	Neutral - 83.7%
Department Summonses	Professional - 81.1%	Cynical - 53.7%
Conduct Involved in Police Work	Neutral - 70.6%	Cyn./Neut - 100%
Police Officers	Professional - 53.5%	Cynical - 82.4%
Average Detective	Neutral - 60.7%	Cynical - 89.9%
Academy Training	Neut./Prof - 89.7%	Cynical - 71.7%
Average Arrest	Professional - 97.9%	Cyn./Prof - 75.0%
**Best Arrests	Professional -71.1%	Professional - 59.8%
Attitudes toward the Public	Neutral - 91.0%	Cynical - 93.2%
Most People Locked Up	Professional - 51.1%	Cynical - 92.0%
Victims Guilty	Professional - 94.1%	Cynical - 54.1%
Respect for Officers	Cynical - 90.7%	Cynical - 95.0%
People Cooperate	Professionl - 86.3%	Cynical - 78.7%
Attitudes toward Officer Role	Professional - 77.6%	Neutral - 86.1%
Professional Calling	Professional - 87.1%	Cynical - 55.5%
Officer Dedication	Professional - 95.3%	Cynical - 55.5%
Officer Idealism	Professional - 93.0%	Cynical - 69.8%
Belief in Role	Professional - 93.8%	Neutral - 95.5%
Attitudes toward Organization	Professional - 80.0%	Cynical - 88.9%
Staff Problems	Professional - 64.0%	Cynical - 96.9%
Respect by Staff	Professional - 71.0%	Cynical - 90.7%
Too Little Authority	Professional - 82.5%	Cynical - 83.8%

*For full name and description variables, see appendix B, "Questionnaire Items Comprising Indices."

**Represents no difference between "MOST" and "LEAST" groups of officers.

the "least" professional group the majority of officers (62.7 percent) fell within either the nonservice or in-service categories, whereas the majority of officers in the "most" professional group (69.0 percent) fell within either the preservice or continuing college education categories. This finding supports Vollmer's view that education and training should be received by the officers prior to entering law enforcement rather than afterward (Vollmer, 1936:233–34).

Also, prior occupation has been determined as a distinguishing factor between the two groups of officers. For the "most" professional officers, a majority of those officers (88.1 percent) reported a prior occupation within the professional services category, whereas for the "least" professional officers, a majority (70.8 percent) reported a prior occupation within the blue-collar, laboring sector.

Student's *t*-test comparisons of mean scores for each officer group on the professional subscales and individual indicators reveal a general similarity in attitudes on one variable only, that being officers' attitudes concerning "the best arrests made." The majority of officers within the "most" professional group (71.1 percent), as well as a majority of those in the "least" professional group (59.8 percent), expressed a professional response to best arrests being made "as a result of hard work and intelligent dedication to duty." On all other items, the majority of responses for the two groups diverged. These average differences in characteristic responses are discussed in the following sections.

"Most" Professional Officers

For this group of officers (n = 91), the majority of officers had acquired at least some college education prior to entering the L.A.P.D. (68.1 percent) and had continued their education while serving on the force. Although the majority (89.8 percent) of this group expressed neutral attitudes generally (i.e., neither cynical nor professional) concerning Others Effects on Police Work, a majority (59.5 percent) indicated a professional response that a college degree as a requirement for an appointment to the

L.A.P.D. "would result in a much more efficient police department."

In contrast, a majority of officers (96.3 percent) within this group expressed either cynical or neutral attitudes toward newspapers generally, being evenly divided in their beliefs that newspapers "just report the news impartially whether or not it concerns the police" or "seem to enjoy giving an unfavorable slant to news concerning the police and prominently play up police misdeeds rather than virtues."[1]

As for this group of officers' attitudes concerning cooperation by the public, the majority of officers (64.9 percent) indicated a professional response in that they perceived the public as "eager to cooperate with police officers to help them perform their duty better." In responding to their beliefs concerning the operations of the department, the majority of responses (81.2 percent) were evenly divided between neutral and professional attitudes. The L.A.P.D. was expressed as being either "a very efficient, smoothly operating organization" or "hardly any different from other civil service organizations." The majority of this group (82.6 percent) were also evenly divided, expressing neutral and professional attitudes concerning their treatment while testifying in court. These officers expressed either the neutral view that "they are treated no differently than civilian witnesses" or the professional view that they "receive real cooperation and are treated fairly by court personnel."

A strong majority (86.9 percent) of patrol officers from this "most" professional group expressed professional attitudes on the subscale representing Ideals concerning Police Work. The majority from this group (91.2 percent) view professionalism of police work as "already here for many groups of police officers" and the average police officer as being "dedicated to high ideals of police service and would not hesitate to perform police duty even though he or she may have to work overtime" (80.8 percent), both representing professional responses. On department summonses issued by officers, the majority (81.1 percent) indicated a professional response in that such summonses were a "part of a sensible pattern in law enforcement."

For the subscale of Conduct Involved in Police Work, the majority of "most" professional officers (70.6 percent) expressed neutral views overall. On the first item of this subscale, a majority of officers (53.5 percent) expressed the professional view that police officers "understand human behavior as well as psychologists and sociologists because they get so much real life experience." The majority response (60.7 percent) concerning the average detective was neutral in that the average detective is perceived as "just about the same as the average patrol officer." Concerning academy training of recruits, the views of the majority (89.7 percent) were evenly divided between neutral and professional. These officers expressed either the professional response that academy training "does a very fine job of preparing the recruit for life in the department" or the neutral response that academy training "cannot overcome the contradictions between theory and practice." In regard to opinions on average arrests made, an overwhelming majority of these "most" professional officers (97.9 percent) believed that "the patrol officer is dedicated to perform his or her duty."

Generally, officers from this "most" professional group (91.0 percent) were neutral overall in their expressed Attitudes toward the Public subscale. The majority of this group (51.1 percent), however, expressed professional attitudes in strongly disagreeing with the statement that "most people have done something they could have been locked up for if they had been caught." Additionally, a majority (94.1 percent) were extremely professional, disagreeing with the statement that "victims are usually as guilty as criminals." In contrast, however, the majority of this group (90.7 percent) were cynical in their attitudes that the public needed to respect police officers more than they already did. Nonetheless, the majority (86.3 percent) indicated professional attitudes agreeing with the statement that "most people are willing to cooperate with the police."

This group (77.6 percent) of "most" professional officers' views on the Attitudes toward the Officer Role subscale were professional generally in that the majority of these officers expressed strong agreement on four items in this subscale: "people in this profession have a real calling for their work" (87.1 percent responded professionally); "the dedication of police officers in this profession is most gratifying" (95.3 percent responded professionally); "it is encouraging to see the high level of idealism that is maintained by police officers in this organization" (93.0 percent responded professionally); and "there are very few police officers who don't really believe in their work" (93.8 percent responded professionally).

For the overall subscale of officer Attitudes toward the Organization, the majority of responses (80.0 percent) by officers in this "most" professional group were professional, being greater than 6 on this subscale. A majority (64.0 percent) were professional in their response disagreeing with the statement that "when a problem comes up here, the people on the staff seldom agree on how it should be handled." A majority of this group (71.0 percent) also expressed professional attitudes in disagreeing with the statement that "the people in charge here never seem to respect those who do the real work." Additionally, a majority of officers (82.5 percent) indicated a professional response to the attitude that "I have too little authority to do my job the way it should be done," expressing their strong disagreement with this statement.

"Least" Professional Officers

In contrast to the previously discussed profile of the characteristics of "most" professional officers, the majority (62.7 percent) of this group of "least" professional officers ($n = 23$) had no college education prior to entering the force, and they did not further their education after their appointment to the department. Also, a majority of these officers (70.8 percent) had worked in a blue-collar laborer position prior to entering the L.A.P.D.

The majority of this group of "least" professional officers (64.8 percent) were generally cynical about Others Effects on Police Work. The majority (92.4 percent) of this group's views concerning the value of a college degree were evenly divided between the cynical or the neutral response in that they believed that a degree "would cause friction and possibly do more harm than good" or "would let into the department people who are probably ill-suited for police work." All of the officers from this group (100 percent) expressed cynical attitudes toward newspaper reporting in that newspapers "seem to enjoy giving an unfavorable slant to news concerning the police and prominently play up police misdeeds rather than virtues." The majority of this group's views (55.5 percent) toward public cooperation were cynical in that they believed the public "usually had to be forced to cooperate with police officers." Concerning their views of the department, a majority (77.5 percent) indicated a cynical response, expressing that "it is a wonder that it does one half as well as it does." Additionally, a majority (80.6 percent) of these officers also expressed cynical attitudes toward the court system in that, when testifying in court, they believed that "too often the police officers are treated as criminals when they take the witness stand."

The majority of responses (64.9 percent) for this "least" professional group of officers regarding their Ideals Concerning Police Work were neutral. In expressing their views concerning professionalism in police work, the majority of these officers (78 percent) were evenly divided between the professional view that professionalism "is already here for many groups of officers" and the cynical view that professionalism "is a dream—it will not come in the foreseeable future." Regarding this group's views toward the average police officer, a majority (83.7 percent) agreed with the neutral response that a police officer is "trying to perform eight hours of duty without getting into trouble." This group of officers expressed cynical attitudes toward the issuance of department summonses in that the majority (53.7 percent) agreed that summonses are issued by officers "because they know they must meet their quota even if it's not official."

All of the officer responses for this group of "least" professional officers concerning their Attitudes toward Conduct Involved in Police Work fell within the cynical to neutral range. A majority of officers (82.4 percent) expressed the view of their understanding of human behavior as cynical in that they agreed that officers "have a peculiar view of human behavior because of the misery and cruelty of life which they see everyday." A majority (89.9 percent) also expressed cynical attitudes toward the average detective in that they viewed the average detective as "a little arrogant and thinks he or she is a little better than a patrol officer." Additionally, the majority (71.7 percent) of this group's attitudes toward police academy training was also expressed as cynical in that they agreed that training "might as well be cut in half. The recruit has to learn all over when he or she is assigned to a division."

In contrast to the previous responses on this Conduct Involved in Police Work subscale, the majority of this group's responses (75 percent) concerning the average arrest were expressed as either cynical or professional. Police officers within this "least" professional group were divided in their beliefs that the average arrest was made because "the patrol officer is dedicated to perform his or her duty" or that "the officer could not avoid it without getting into trouble."

The majority (93.2 percent) of expressed Attitudes toward the Public for this "least" professional group were cynical. The majority of officers in this group (92.0 percent) agreed that "most people have done something they could have been locked up for if they had been caught," indicating a cynical response. A majority (54.1 percent) were also cynical about victims of crimes in that they believed that "victims are usually as guilty as criminals." As for their beliefs in people's attitude toward police officers, a strong majority (95 percent) expressed a cynical view believing that "people need to respect police officers more than they do." Additionally, a majority of these officers (78.7 percent) were cynical in their views, strongly disagreeing as to most people's willingness to cooperate with the police.

This group of officers' overall Attitudes toward the Officer Role was neutral (86.1 percent). In their expressed beliefs as to whether "people in this profession have a real calling for their work," the majority (55.5 percent) were cynical, strongly disagreeing. Additionally, the majority (55.5 percent) of officers strongly disagreed with the statement that "the dedication of police officers in this profession is most gratifying," indicating a cynical response. Concerning officer idealism in the department, once again a majority of officers (69.8 percent) were cynical in strongly disagreeing with the statement that "it is encouraging to see the high level of idealism which is maintained by police officers in this organization." However, the majority of officers

(95.5 percent) were neutral in their belief that "there are very few officers who don't really believe in their work."

Overall, cynical attitudes were expressed about the L.A.P.D. as an organization by an overwhelming majority (88.9 percent) of this "least" professional group of officers. In regard to staff problems, the majority of these officers (96.9) percent) agreed with the cynical view that "when a problem comes up here, the people on the staff seldom agree on how it should be handled." Additionally, a majority (90.7 percent) also strongly agreed with the cynical view that "the people in charge here never seem to respect those who do the real work." Finally, the majority (83.8 percent) also strongly agreed that "I feel I have too little authority to do my job the way it should be done," indicating a cynical response.

This discussion has shown that the two distinctly different groups of officers in terms of professional and nonprofessional attitudes are also different in terms of their educational achievement and academic status backgrounds. The distinctions would clearly support Vollmer's contention that more highly educated officers with education and training prior to entering policing would qualify as more "professional" police officers.

NOTES

1. Expressions of cynicism may be more indicative of reality than paranoia toward the press. In a recent series of articles on the media and the L.A.P.D., the *Los Angeles Times* reported that the police have complained of the uneven coverage by the press, sensationalistic headlines, and inaccurate and misleading stories, ignoring coverage of day-to-day dangers and problems officers encounter. The *Los Angeles Times* also reported that a city editor agreed with this criticism and stated that "I'm sure there's not a day that goes by that some cop isn't risking his or her life to save some kid . . . and I don't know that that's adequately reported. . . . Over time, that imbalance creates a 'false image of the department.'" Nonetheless, the city editor continued that he "wouldn't give up one single tough story that we've done" (Shaw, 1992d:20).

CHAPTER 7

Implications of College-Educated Officers

> The strength of any organization is measured by the character of its personnel. . . . In order that the police, universally, may fulfill the arduous responsibilities laid upon them, the public must . . . make provision for a professionally trained police personnel, fit not only in body, but also in character, education, and ideals of service. (August Vollmer, 1936:224–237)

This inquiry has provided a review of the history of law enforcement professionalization, a period in which progressive reformers have attempted to improve the efficiency of police departments as administrative agencies as well as the quality of police services through increased training and educational standards of law enforcement personnel. In attempts to upgrade the quality of police personnel, higher educational standards have slowly increased over this period, at least to that of a high school degree. However, only 6 percent of all local police departments and 18 percent of state police departments require some level of college education for new recruits (U.S. Department of Justice, 1992:5).

The overwhelming majority of research conducted over the past twenty years and reviewed in this work has shown that higher educational attainment by police officers does have some impact on their performance, values, and attitudes, primarily in a positive direction. Results of this inquiry further substantiate those findings.

An analysis of federal court rulings has shown that the federal courts have accepted the difficulties in determining "effective" performance for professional positions and have endorsed the use of a more lenient standard in determining that college education is related to professional demeanor, values, and behavior. The Fifth Circuit Court of Appeals has accepted the validity of higher educational requirements for urban police officer recruits using the more lenient, construct validation approach and has held that at least forty-five units of college education are necessary for "professional" policing.

As discussed in chapter 3, both the politics and societal acceptance of affirmative action and remedies for discrimination have been tumultuous and without social consensus. A view currently persists that the application of affirmative action mandates to the hiring of law enforcement personnel has expanded the stereotype of the "dumb cop" to the "dumb minority cop." Minority groups themselves have expressed the view that affirmative action, when applied as "preferential treatment," has stigmatized and stereotyped minorities as inferior when hired under affirmative action mandates.[1] Nevertheless, although higher educational standards may be found to be discriminatory against some minority groups (dependent upon the statistical method used to make this determination), such standards have been accepted as a bona fide occupational qualification exception for sworn police officer positions as the result of the public risk and responsibility rationale applied by the Fifth Circuit Court of Appeals.

A survey of police modes of behavior or typologies developed by prior researchers discloses that various types of policing styles fall within the professional and nonprofessional classifications developed here. These distinct classifications have shown that an apparent difference in job performance and service response exists by types, depending on whether a particular type falls within the professional or nonprofessional categories. Additionally, those types possess distinct value and attitude differences based upon whether the type is either professional or nonprofessional.

This study has developed a functional model of relationships between higher education and professionalism. The importance of this model is that it has demonstrated the complex relationship between the preservice educational level of officers and professional values. An elaboration or examination of important contributing factors to this relationship exhibited the links between officer preservice educational level, early performance indicators, subsequent educational attainment or academic status, and the professional values of patrol officers.

Generally, the model developed here, using a non-professional/professional continuum, has shown that as preservice educational level increases, professionalism increases. Not only has it been shown that college education influences the early performance and professional values of patrol officers within the L.A.P.D., but also that the continuing education and academic socialization during their tenure as sworn officers has a significant functional influence as well. Although the contribution of education has been shown to be statistically significant, the findings reported here were not as statistically strong as was originally anticipated. Higher education's main contribution, nonetheless, may lie in the fact that college education will make a potentially marginally good police officer a better police officer since, as scholars have pointed out, contemporary policing also needs the contributions of research, critical-thinking skills, and advanced learning provided by a college experience.

The present contemporary, complex, and rapidly changing American society, as Gross points out, cannot afford poorly trained or poorly educated police (Gross, 1973). Scholars have suggested, even though findings have not been conclusive, that the massive, large-scale infusion of college-educated recruits into policing would significantly affect the quality of police service (Saunders, 1970; Sherman and the National Advisory Commission on Higher Education for Police Officers, 1978). However, the concrete and long-term effects of higher education for police officers may not be evident for years to come. No doubt, an infusion of college-educated officers into law enforcement agencies introduces an element of uncertainty and a threat to the traditional "powers-that-be" within the agency.

Blumberg and Niederhoffer (1985:400) point out that college-educated officers not only will be contending for power within the police organization, but they will also be functioning as its internal critics. However, in addition, such officers will continue forging a vital connecting link between law enforcement agencies and the academic community. They also suggest that the effects of college education on police officers may not become manifest for some time, primarily due to those within the police culture who are resentful of the organizational disruptions from more highly educated officers and who are unwilling to acknowledge the importance of higher education for contemporary policing.

More than sixty years ago, Vollmer openly advocated a direct liaison between the university community and the police in order to "bring the best brains available to bear on given problems" (Woods, 1973:172). This was the connecting link that August Vollmer recognized as the main key to the professionalism of officers and the professionalization of the law enforcement organization in American society. Such a "system of institutions" not only permits "continued reflection on the ends of police work and encourage responsiveness" but it also provides the opportunity for students as future police officers (and officers as students) to continually "reexamine the contradictions between the ends he [or she] serves and the means he [or she] uses to attain them" (Brown, 1981:304).

In light of the recent controversies and scandals that have tarnished the "professional" image of the L.A.P.D.,[2] it seems reasonable to conclude that "police agencies are not perfectly free actors," (Slovak, 1986:182) and are accountable, at least to some degree, to external organizations. As Sherman has suggested in his study on scandals within law enforcement organizations, such organizations may be able to be controlled externally only by other organizations (Sherman, 1978:246). Given their present influence, prestige, and legitimacy within society, academic institutions may be that primary influential, controlling factor holding deviant police agencies accountable to society at large, the "macropolitical" arena. In addition to educating and socializing present and future law enforcement actors, academic institutions provide these semimilitary bureaucratic agencies interaction with a more humanizing environment, neutralizing what is considered to be the "natural tendency of semimilitary bureaucracies toward solution, with crippling consequences for interpersonal flexibility" (Gross, 1973:483).

This discussion has suggested that patrol officers who enter policing with some level of college education perform better in their probationary field training periods than those who do not. Additionally, those officers with some college who continue their education at some point in their law enforcement careers possess values and characteristics different from the others. In line with the Christopher Commission reasoning, these attitudes are translated into subsequent officer performance in regard to citizens, in a more positive rather than in a negative manner.

Higher education may not be a panacea for the myriad of administrative and management problems within the police organization itself. However, higher levels of education can assist a police officer on patrol to become a more "astute social observer," posing choices of action more clearly, weighing alternatives to decisions, and critically discussing and examining the recommendations and solutions of others (Lynch, 1976:65).

Although the relationship between higher education, performance, and professionalism, as discussed earlier, was not strong, statistically speaking (a problem found in most social science research), this may also be due to the fact that structural variables such as organizational size, complexity, and formalization, as well as the external working environment, affect officer attitudes to some extent. Future research should incorporate these variables into examinations of the relationships between officer performance, beliefs, and educational attainment.

Sherman has suggested that higher education may show a minimal impact on the quality of police services unless police agencies are structured in such a way as to make better use of their highly educated personnel (Sherman, 1978:166). Nonetheless, Sherman argues that it is not the individual, more highly educated officer in policing who ultimately makes the difference in the quality of police services, but the increasing levels of college-educated officers in the aggregate that will ultimately improve the overall performance of individual police departments, as well as the policing occupation as a whole (Sherman, 1978:52).

The ultimate organizational mission of law enforcement is to provide high-quality services to the citizenry in a manner consistent with democratic values. Sustained efforts to improve policing as a whole must include requiring higher levels of college education for police officers in the aggregate as one of the necessary components to law enforcement emerging as a true "profession." As August Vollmer pointed out more than a half century ago, society must require that all professionally trained police personnel be able and qualified for the police task "not only in body, but also in character, education, and ideals of service" (Vollmer, 1936:237).

American law enforcement has been perceived as the most violent in the world throughout much of the twentieth century, a perception reinforced by the Rodney King incident. Sustained efforts by community, academic, and governmental leaders to revise and increase educational standards for contemporary police officers may succeed in changing the antiquated "wild west" image and reality of twentieth-century law enforcement in America by the turn of the twenty-first century. Such an improvement, accompanied by an upgrading in present accreditation standards for police agencies, may influence not only the nature and function of policing but also reduce the incredible and increasing amount of civil liability awards resulting from the unprofessional behavior of unfit sworn officer personnel.[3]

NOTES

1. For example, see S. Monroe, "Does Affirmative Action Help or Hurt?" *Time,* May 27, 1991:22–23.

2. See series of articles in *Los Angeles Times* in 1992 by David Shaw. Also see, Independent Commission on the Los Angeles Police Department (Christopher Commission), "Report of the Independent Commission on the Los Angeles Police Department," July 9, 1991.

3. For a somewhat shocking overview of the cost of civil liability suits within law enforcement , see M. G. Neithercutt and Benjamin G.

Carmichael, "Ruminations on the Criminal Justice Breach of Trust," (1991:32–34). An upgrading of accreditation standards for law enforcement agencies accompanied by fewer liability suits by civilians for police misconduct has been "predicted" by Georgette Bennett (1987:250).

APPENDIX A

Research Methods and Design Used for Examining L.A.P.D. Officers

This work has examined the relationships between education, officer performance, and professionalism of a group of L.A.P.D. patrol officers. An L.A.P.D. questionnaire developed by a Claremont Graduate School research team for an earlier L.A.P.D. study measuring, among other factors, attitudinal and performance differences of L.A.P.D. officers (Felkenes et al., 1990, vol.2:158–59; Lasley, 1992) has been utilized here. In that original L.A.P.D. study, the research question as to whether female and minority officers were likely to be different (and therefore produce change within the organization) from the predominant group of Caucasian male officers was answered in the negative. Analysis of results using a differential random sampling method of the various subpopulations so as to assure accuracy in group comparisons,[1] found an absence of ethnic or gender differences on the various performance and attitudinal variables.[2]

Whereas the earlier L.A.P.D. study used gender and ethnic status as the primary independent variables, this work has used educational levels and academic status as the primary independent variables of interest, while including the effects of gender and ethnic status (as well as additional variables, discussed below) as control variables.

The primary question addressed here has been to determine whether an officer's educational level (the presence or absence of some level of college education) influences the probationary performance levels and subsequent professional attitudes of L.A.P.D. officers assigned to patrol. In addition, a determination is made as to whether the educational or academic status of the officer mediates or assists in interpreting the relationship between educational level, probationary performance, and professional attitudes. Using multivariate statistical results (of weighted data from a systematic random sample of officers from the L.A.P.D.[3]) an empirical model is developed from six hypotheses tested here.

Selection Methods and Techniques

Study Design

Secondary data analysis has been conducted on responses from survey questionnaires completed and returned by 950 supervisory and nonsupervisory police officers employed at the L.A.P.D. in 1990. However, the present study consists of those officer respondents who indicated that they were working on patrol at the time they completed the questionnaire.

This cross-sectional survey instrument has been used as an approximated longitudinal study, and a functional model of relationships rather than a causal one has been developed from the results.

Survey Instrument

The nonexperimental, self-report officer survey originally consisted of 104 demographic and attitudinal variables. Niederhoffer's Revised Cynicism/Professionalism Index consisted of thirteen items, and Regoli and Poole's Professionalism Index consists of eleven items or variables. See appendix B for those items used in this current study.

A description of the five major variables used in the present study includes

1. Educational level. V92—Higher education level at time of appointment to the L.A.P.D. Values range from 0, no college; 1, some college; 2, A.A. or equivalent; 3, bachelor's degree; 4, graduate work, graduate degree.

2. Academic status. Not a variable in the original survey, V300—Academic status has been calculated from the respondents' responses to V92, educational level at time of appointment and V93, educational level at time of questionnaire completion. The four categories of academic status include (a) 0, nonservice—no college education at appointment and no college subsequent to appointment; (b) 1, in-service—no college at appointment but college subsequent to appointment; (c) 2, preservice—college education at appointment but no further college subsequent to appointment; (d) 3, continuing—college attendance initiated before and continued subsequent to appointment.

3. Probationary job performance consisting of two variables. V34—Commendations—values ranging from 0 to 8; V36—Citizen complaints—values ranging from 0 to 8.

4. Cynicism Index. Originally developed by Niederhoffer (1967) and revised by Regoli and Poole (1979), consists of thirteen variables, V61 to V71 and V73 to V74, reverse coded so that values ranging from one "1" indicate a *high* level of cynicism to five "5" indicate a *low* level of cynicism on each item. (Niederhoffer's original scale ranged from one "1" representing a *low* level of cynicism or a high level of professionalism to five "5" representing a *high* level of cynicism.) Through factor analysis, Regoli and Poole had identified three subscales, which were coded in this study as V400—Attitudes toward Others Effects on Police Work, V410—Attitudes toward Ideals Concerning Police Work, and V420—Attitudes toward Conduct Involved in Police Work.

A composite, unidimensional index (V700 [Niederhoffer's Revised Cynicism/Professionalism Index]), as well as the three subscales, was utilized in the present study. The purpose of reordering the original values as well as creating the composite indexes has been to determine Niederhoffer's index and subscales' levels of statistical relationship with Regoli and Poole's index and subscales through bivariate and multiple regression analyses. Rather than attempting to replicate an inverse relationship between the subscales as in Regoli and Poole's prior study, the present study anticipated a positive correlation (a positive relationship) between the two indexes and various subscales.

5. Professionalism Index. As originally developed by Regoli and Poole, this index consisted of twelve (12) items broken down into three subscales. The present survey consists of eleven (11) items or variables because administrators at the L.A.P.D. found one question offensive. The prior *Blake* study did not analyze responses to these variables, and it was subsequently found that the V510 subscale, consisting of V79 to V82, needed to be reverse coded in order to conform to the remaining variables in this index, that is, to be positively, rather than inversely, related to the other two subscales.

The values for these Likert-type forced-choice items range from one (1)—nonprofessional attitudes to four (4)—professional attitudes. Both the unidimensional index (V800—Regoli and Poole's Professionalism Index) and Regoli and Poole's original subscales (the multidimensional index consisting of three subscales, V500—Attitudes toward the Public, V510—Attitudes toward the Officer Role, and V520—Attitudes toward the Organization) were utilized in the analysis, and statistically significant results are reported.

6. Additionally, the following control variables are included in the analysis in order to test for confounding, antecedent, or intervening influences:

V86—gender, a categorical variable coded into 1—male and 2—female;

V96—ethnicity, a categorical variable coded into 1—African American, 2—Latino, 3—Caucasian, and 4—Other;

V10—prior occupation, a categorical variable coded into five occupational groupings: 1—professional services, 2—military, 3—student, 4—skilled trades, 5—blue-collar laborer;

V11—years of experience, a ratio level variable, used as an interval variable coded into 1—1 to 5 yrs; 2—6 to 10 yrs; 3—11 to 15 yrs; and 4—over 15 yrs;

V104 —rank, an ordinal level variable recoded to 1—police officer, 2—sergeant, and 3—lieutenant;

V94—age, a ratio level variable; and,

V99—current assignment, selecting only those respondents who indicate 1—patrol, i.e., officers working patrol duty.

Theoretical Model and Hypotheses

Since data used in the present study are nonexperimental (as is most social science research) as well as cross-sectional, a cause and effect relationship between variables cannot be inferred. However, as Roberg has pointed out, a *functional* relationship can exist between levels of variables, for example, between increasing levels of education, increasing levels of performance, and increasing levels of professional attitudes, by using such a design. Roberg states that

> A functional relationship is one in which it has been demonstrated that a change in one variable is accompanied by a change in the other, but the relationship is most likely based on a number of complex interactions rather than being directly causal. (Roberg, 1978:343, n. 16)

The general functional theoretical model is one in which increasing levels of higher education lead to improved levels of probationary performance, leading to increasing levels of professional attitudes. The relationships are considered indirect, as well as direct, due to the intervention of the academic status of the officer as a significant interpretative variable. Roberg's study applied two statistical methods to test for the unadjusted relationships as well as the adjusted or controlled relationships between the main study variables (Roberg, 1978:339).

The present study also utilized these two methods. Zero-order Pearson correlation coefficients were run to test for significant unadjusted relationships between (1) higher educational level, probationary performance indicators, and professional attitudes, and (2) probationary performance indicators, academic status, and professional attitudes. Additionally, first-order partial correlation coefficients tested for the adjusted or controlled relationships for the major study variables of higher educational level, probationary performance indicators, academic status, and professional attitudes.

Figure A-1 illustrates this theoretical model.

FIGURE A-1

GENERAL THEORETICAL MODEL
FOR L.A.P.D. OFFICERS ON PATROL

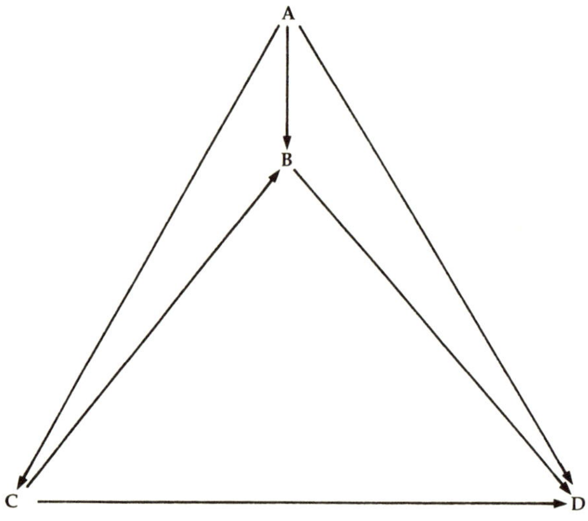

Legend:

A = Educational level at time of appointment (V92)

B = Academic status upon completion of survey (V300)

C = Probationary performance indicators (V34 and V36)

D = Professionalism scales:
Niederhoffer's Revised Cynicism Index (V700)
Regoli and Poole's Professionalism Index (V800)

The six hypotheses examined in the present study for L.A.P.D. officers on patrol are as follows:

H1: A functional relationship exists between levels of higher education and self-reported probationary performance indicators: commendations and citizen complaints, controlling for the demographic variables of gender, ethnicity, age, and prior occupation.

H2: A functional relationship exists between level of higher education and professional attitudes (as measured by Niederhoffer's Revised Cynicism/Professionalism Index and Regoli and Poole's Professionalism Index), controlling for the demographic variables of gender, ethnicity, age, rank, years of experience, and prior occupation.

H3: A functional relationship exists between self-reported probationary performance indicators and professional attitudes, controlling for the demographic variables of gender, ethnicity, age, rank, years of experience, and prior occupation.

H4: A functional relationship exists between probationary performance indicators and academic status, controlling for the demographic variables of gender, ethnicity, age, rank, years of experience, and prior occupation.

H5: A functional relationship exists between academic status and professional attitudes, controlling for the demographic variables of gender, ethnicity, age, rank, years of experience, and prior occupation.

H6: A functional relationship exists between educational level and academic status, controlling for the demographic variables of gender, ethnicity, age, rank, and prior occupation.

A comprehensive approach to understanding the nature of the relationships between two or more study variables through the controlled introduction of additional variables has been provided by Babbie (1992:409–28). As described by Babbie, an elaboration model of analysis not only takes into account the influence of demographic control variables on the main study variables, but also takes into account the position of the main study variables themselves. An elaboration model analysis assists in understanding the nature of the relationships being tested through introducing test variables as antecedent or as intervening variables in the multivariate model. Analysis of the partial relationships resulting from the introduction of the third variable indicates four possible outcomes: a replication of the original relationship; an explanation of a spurious relationship; an interpretation or clarification of the original relationship; and specification of the original relationship (specifying the conditions under which an original relationship has occurred).

In the present study, an elaboration analysis has also been utilized in order to determine not only the strength of the hypothesized relationships but also the nature of each of the hypothesized relationships when antecedent or intervening main study test and demographic variables are introduced into the analysis. The theoretical model presented in this section is clarified and developed as a functional elaboration model and is discussed in chapter 5.

Statistical Methods

Prior to hypothesis testing, descriptive statistics were generated for both V92—educational level and V300—academic status for the total sample of patrol officers, as well as being broken down by gender and ethnicity. The SPSS^x statistical commands employed included (1) Frequencies, and (2) Sort Cases and Split File by gender and ethnicity generating a bar chart with medians, modes, skewness, and kurtosis for each group. Chi-square statistics and Cramér's *V* coefficients are reported as to the existence of relationships between (1) educational level (V92) by gender (V86) and ethnicity (V96); and (2) academic status (V300) by gender (V86) and ethnicity (V96). A Crosstab analysis between academic status (V300) and ethnicity (V96) is displayed since the relationship between these two categorical variables was found to be statistically significant.

Additionally, descriptive statistics were generated for probationary performance indicators, which consist of number of commendations (V34) and number of citizen complaints

(V36). The Frequencies command procedure in $SPSS^x$ was used to generate a bar chart and the mean, standard deviation, skewness, and kurtosis for each variable. Also, the Correlation command in $SPSS^x$ was used to determine the extent to which these two probationary performance variables are related to each other at the .05 level of significance.

Third, a Frequencies command procedure was employed on the entire sample of patrol officers for (1) V700—Niederhoffer's Revised Cynicism Index (as well as the three individual subscales: V400—Attitudes toward Others Effects on Police Work, V410—Attitudes toward Ideals Concerning Police Work, and V420—Attitudes toward Conduct Involved in Police Work, subscales identified by Regoli and Poole through factor analysis); and (2) V800—Regoli and Poole's Professionalism Index (as well as three subscales identified as V500—Attitudes toward the Public, V510—Attitudes toward the Officer Role, and V520—Attitudes toward the Organization). Reported statistics include means, standard deviations, skewness, kurtosis, ranges, and minimum and maximum values for each.

Regoli and Poole had performed a principal components factor analysis with an orthogonal rotation on Niederhoffer's original twenty-item unidimensional cynicism scale. Through multiple regression analysis, they concluded that (1) three independent subscales consisting of thirteen of Niederhoffer's original questions were inversely related to their professionalism subscales; and (2) the three subscales were as reliable as Niederhoffer's original unidimensional scale. However, they failed to report the internal reliability for each of their three theoretical professional subscales or for their entire twelve-item professionalism scale.

Therefore, in order to examine the relationship of each set of the three subscales with each index, as well as the relationship between the two unidimensional indexes, both Correlation and Regression command procedures were conducted. This procedure also permitted an examination of the external validity of Neiderhoffer's Revised Cynicism Index and subscales with Regoli and Poole's Professionalism Index. Also, to determine the internal reliability and utility of the attitudinal, criterion variables either as unidimensional indexes (V700, V800) or as multidimensional indexes (V400, V410, V420; V500, V510, V520) the SPSS^x Reliability command procedure was performed and Cronbach's alpha reported.

Cronbach's alpha essentially assesses the reliability of the sum of variables for each of the indexes and subscales, the resulting coefficients being estimates of the cases' true scores. A reliability coefficient closer to 1.0 for each of the indexes and subscales represents a more reliable additive index, whereas a coefficient closer to 0 represents an unreliable index or subscale.

Kachigan has stated that a reliability coefficient close to .90 is preferred for internal reliability (Kachigan, 1986:218). Since the unidimensional indexes are shown to have reliability coefficients closer to .90 than the multidimensional subscales, they have been used in the subsequent analyses of three of the hypotheses, H2, H3, and H5. Subscale results, however, are also reported when zero-order relationships and interaction effects for the subscale variables are found to be significant at the .05 level of significance.

Reliability, Independence, and Validity

Research using survey questionnaires with carefully constructed questions eliminates unreliability in responses. As Babbie points out, such research is generally strong on reliability (Babbie, 1992:279.) Internal reliability for each of the two indexes is shown to be stronger than that of the individual subscales. A Cronbach alpha score for Niederhoffer's thirteen-item Revised Cynicism/ Professionalism Index (V700) of .7465 is higher, and therefore more reliable, than the subscales V400, V410, and V420, having alpha reliabilities of .5697, .5800, and .5021, respectively.

Regoli and Poole's combined Professionalism Index (V800) received an alpha reliability score of .7873, higher than the individual subscales of V500 and V510, having reliability scores of .5485 and .7328, respectively. However the index's reliability falls short of the internal reliability score of .7926 for V520.

A two-tail, pairwise, Pearson correlation coefficient matrix examined the relationship between the indexes as well as the independence of the subscales. All correlation coefficients were significant at $p = .000$. A correlation coefficient of .7019 for V700 and V800 indicates that these two indexes are highly and positively correlated, a finding that assists in supporting the validity of Niederhoffer's Revised Index as an index of professionalism when positively correlated with Regoli and Poole's Professionalism Index. The matrix also shows that the Niederhoffer subscales of V400, V410, and V420 are moderately correlated, .4599, .4093, and .4997, respectively. Additionally, Regoli and Poole's original subscales, V500, V510, and V520 are weakly to moderately correlated, with coefficients of .2820, .4572, and .4285, respectively.

For this study, the two sets of subscales comprising Niederhoffer's and Regoli and Poole's indexes are not mutually exclusive subdimensions for each index as Regoli and Poole had found them to be in their study. Therefore, each set of the three subscales are not independent of each other; the variances for the three subscales making up Niederhoffer's index overlap each other, and the variances for the three subscales of Regoli and Poole's Index overlap each other as well. This finding suggests that both Niederhoffer's and Regoli and Poole's indexes are unidimensional measures of professionalism, rather than multidimensional measures.

Survey research, as Babbie has also pointed out, is generally weak on validity (Babbie, 1992:279). Content validity for the professionalism items is not considered problematic here since these concerns have presumably been addressed by Niederhoffer and Regoli and Poole in the development of the original indexes. The issue of predictive validity is addressed here through multiple regression analysis for both of the indexes and the subscales. This method is used as a means of examining Niederhoffer's Revised Cynicism/Professionalism Index as a valid measurement instrument for professionalism by examining its association with Regoli and Poole's Professionalism combined index and subscales. The higher the positive relationship between the two indexes, the higher the predictive validity of Niederhoffer's instrument as a combined, additive professionalism index.

Multiple correlation analysis results show that 49 percent (adjusted $R^2 = .491$) of the variance on the Niederhoffer Revised

Cynicism/Professionalism Index (V700) can be accounted for by scores on Regoli and Poole's Professionalism Index (V800). Niederhoffer's index is also highly related to Regoli and Poole's individual subscales, predicting approximately 25 percent, 27 percent, and 39 percent of the variances of V500, V510, and V520, respectively. Conversely, scores on Regoli and Poole's combined index explain approximately 30 percent, 40 percent, and 25 percent of the subscales V400, V410, and V420, respectively. Since our variables of theoretical concern are Niederhoffer's Revised Index (V700) and the subscales making up this index as predictive instruments for the concept of professionalism, our findings suggest that the strong positive Multiple R^2's support the predictive validity of the Niederhoffer revised instrument.

The results of the previous statistical analysis show that the higher Cronbach alpha scores for both Niederhoffer's and Regoli and Poole's indexes make these composite unidimensional indexes more reliable or consistent measures of the concept of professionalism, to be used for hypothesis testing, than the individual subscales comprising each index. This finding is also supported by the absence of independence of each of the subscales as determined by correlation and multiple regression analysis. Additionally, a strong, positive adjusted R^2 between Niederhoffer's Revised Index and Regoli and Poole's Professionalism Index indicate that Niederhoffer's index can also be considered a valid predictor of professionalism, a finding that addresses the problem of predictive validity for Niederhoffer's revised thirteen-item combined index.

In the following sections on hypothesis testing, our primary interest of concern is both the existence and nature of the relationship between levels of education, probationary performance indicators, academic status, and the construct of professionalism as measured by Niederhoffer's and Regoli and Poole's unidimensional indexes. Although the individual subscales making up each of these indexes have been found not to be independent of each other, they are also considered in analyses of hypothesis testing in those events when an individual subscale can clarify the nature of an obscure relationship between the main variables and the combined professionalism index.

Hypothesis Testing

To determine the *existence* of relationships for the six hypotheses, Correlation and Part Corr procedures have been used. The unadjusted zero-order Pearson correlation coefficient is reported for each hypothesized relationship (a statistically significant relationship established at the .01 significance level). Adjusted, first-order partial correlation coefficients are also reported for each of the control variables in order to determine the stability of the hypothesized relationship between the main variables. (See tables A-1 and A-2.)

Additionally, to determine the *nature* of statistically significant relationships between the main variables (as well as that of any significant control variables) in each of the six hypotheses, both nonparametric and parametric statistical procedures have been used, depending on the nature of the criterion, predictor, and control variables. The specific statistical procedures are described below.

Hypothesis One

Analysis of variance (Means and One-way $SPSS^x$ command procedures) reports Eta^2 (similar to Pearson r^2) and significance of F-test (differences between group means) for commendations (V34) and citizen complaints (V36) (interval-level criterion variables) and level of education (V92) (an ordinal-level predictor variable). ANOVA assumes that the variances in each group are equal.

The equality of variances is determined through a Bartlett-Box F statistic, using a .05 significance level. When variances have been determined to be unequal, a Kruskal-Wallis one-way analysis of variance H statistical procedure (a nonparametric test that does not assume equal variances) is employed. The resulting chi-square statistic and probability value are also reported.

TABLE A-1

ZERO-ORDER CORRELATION COEFFICIENTS AND FIRST-ORDER PARTIAL CORRELATION COEFFICIENTS FOR <u>CONTROL</u> VARIABLES

		Un-adjusted EV[1]	Adjusted - First order Partial[2]					
H1:	V92 with V34	.1642 (.03)	.1640	.1491			.1551	
	V36	-.2268 (.05)	-.2229	-.2186			-.2092	
H2:	V92 with V700	.1834 (.03)	.1882	.1826	.1867	.1809	.1572	.1825
	V800	.1107 (.01)*	.1137*	.1025*	.1109*	.1085*	.0896*	.1111*
H3:	V34 with V700	.2012 (.04)	.2022	.2008	.2073	.2011	.1953	.2002
	V36 with V700	-.2876 (.08)	-.2949	-.2872	-.2859	-.2814	-.2772	-.2883
	V34 with V800	.1419 (.02)	.1424	.1324	.1428	.1414	.1366	.1416
	V36 with V800	-.3233 (.10)	-.3286	-.3188	-.3242	-.3192	-.3156	-.3236
H4:	V34 with V300	.1286 (.02)	.1284	.1132*	.1368	.1287	.1207*	.1304
	V36 with V300	-.2137 (.08)	-.2122	-.2054	-.2103	-.2025	-.1998	-.2133
H5:	V300 withV700	.2613 (.07)	.2648	.2611	.2597	.2477	.2444	.2619
	V800	.1535 (.02)	.1556	.1459	.1538	.1428	.1387	.1537
H6:	V92 with V300	.6417 (.41)	.6409	.6365	.6485	.6467	.6290	.6587
	(Gamma)	.79776	.8031	.7639	.7813	.8319	.7777	.8401
	By:		V86	V96	V94	V104	V10	V11
			Control Variables					

<u>Legend</u>:

Main Variables:

V92—Educational level
V34—Commendations
V36—Citizen complaints
V700—Niederhoffer's Revised Index
V800—Regoli and Poole's Professionalism Index

Control Variables:

V86—Gender
V96—Ethnicity
V94—Age
V104—Rank
V300—Academic status
V10—Prior occupation
V11—Years of experience

[1] Represents amount of explained variance.

[2] Correlation coefficients are statistically significant at the .01 significance level unless indicated otherwise.

* = less than .05 significance level

TABLE A-2

ZERO-ORDER CORRELATION COEFFICIENTS AND FIRST-ORDER PARTIAL CORRELATION COEFFICIENTS FOR MAIN STUDY VARIABLES

		Unadjusted	Adjusted - First order Partial[1]					
H1:	V92 with V34	.1642				.1362		
	V36	-.2268			-.2080			
H2:	V92 with V700	.1834		,0212 @	.1556	.1267 *		.1494
	V800	.1107 *		.0161 @	.0895 *	.0405 @	-.0258 @	
H3:	V34 with V700	.2012	.1765	.1751		.1683		.1442
	V36 with V700	-.2876	-.2570	-.2458	-.2667			-.0900*
	V34 with V800	.1419	.1262	.1246		.1014 *	.0009 @	
	V36 with V800	-.3233	-.3081	-.3010	-.3091		-.1780	
H4:	V34 with V300	.1286	.0308 @			.1010	.	
	V36 with V300	-.2137	-.0912 *		-.1987			
H5:	V300 with V700	.2613	.1905		.2424	.2136		.2182
	V800	.1535	.1082 *		.1378	.0913 *	-.0435 @	
H6:	V92 with V300	.6417			.6344	.6235		
	By:		V92	V300	V34	V36	V700	V800
			Main Study Variables					

Legend:
Main Study Variables:

V92—Educational level
V34—Commendations
V36—Citizen complaints
V700—Niederhoffer's Revised Index
V800—Regoli and Poole's Professionalism Index

[1]Correlation coefficients are statistically significant at the .01 significance level unless indicated otherwise.

* = less than .05 significance level

@ = greater than .05 significance level

TABLE A-3

STUDENT-NEWMAN-KEULS MULTIPLE RANGE TEST

V34—Commendations: by V92—Level of Education | V36—Complaints: by V92—Level of Education

Group:	Mean	N	S	A	B	G	Mean	N	S	A	B	G
None	2.64			*	*	*	.849		*	*	*	*
Some	2.94						.531	*				
A.A./Equiv.	3.46	*					.445	*				
B.A./B.S.	3.57	*					.178	*				
Grad.Wk./Degr.	3.68	*					.345	*				

*Denotes pairs of groups significantly different at .05 significance level.

Legend:

N = None
S = Some
A = A.A./Equiv.
B = B.A./B.S.
G = Grad.Wk./Degr.

Results: Group mean for no college is significantly lower than group means for A.A./Equiv., B. A. or B. S., and graduate work or graduate degree.

Results: Group mean for no college is significantly higher than group means for some college, A. A./Equiv., B.A. or B. S., and graduate work or graduate degree.

V36—Complaints:
by V10—Prior Occupation

Group:	Mean	PR	MI	ST	SK	BC
Professional Services	.432					*
Military	.749					
Student	.697					
Skilled Trade	.455					*
Blue-Collar Laborer	1.16	*			*	

Legend:

PR = Professional Services
MI = Military
ST = Student
SK = Skilled Trade
BC = Blue-Collar Laborer

*Denotes pairs of groups significantly different at .05 significance level.

Results: Group mean for blue-collar laborer is significantly higher than group mean for professional services and skilled trade.

A Student-Newman-Keuls multiple range test (similar to, but less conservative than, the Scheffe test) was run to follow-up on significant one-way ANOVA results between level of education and probationary performance indicators, so as to determine which, if any, of the groups are significantly different. In addition, two-way analysis of variance (using ANOVA command procedure in SPSS^x) was run to determine whether the control variables of gender (V86), ethnicity (V96), and prior occupation (V10) are statistically significant interacting variables at an .05 level of significance (table A-3).

The control variable, prior occupation (V10), was found to be a statistically significant interacting variable with level of education (V92) and citizen complaints (V36). Therefore, the relationship between prior occupation (V10) and level of education (V92) was determined through a Crosstab procedure in SPSS^x. Chi-square and Cramér's *V* correlation statistics as well as significance levels and group differences were reported.

In order to examine the relationship between citizen complaints (V36) and prior occupation (V10), analysis of variance (Means and One-way in SPSS^x) was run and found to be significant at the .05 significance level. However, since the

TABLE A-4

t-TESTS OF DIFFERENCES BETWEEN GROUP MEANS FOR PROBATIONARY PERFORMANCE INDICATORS

Variable	No. Cases	Mean	Standard Deviation	*F* Value	2-tail Prob.	*t* Value	Degrees of Freedom	2-tail Prob.
V34—Commendations:								
All Patrol Officers	368	3.05	2.31					
No College	137	2.64	2.26	1.04	.818	-2.58	367	.010**
At Least Some College	231	3.28	2.31					
V36—Citizen Complaints:								
All Patrol Officers	390	.57	.98					
No College	143	.85	1.25	2.40	.000	3.88*	211.95	.000**
At Least Some College	247	.41	.78					

*Using separate variance estimates due to significant differences (< .05) in within-group variances.

**Group means are significantly different (.05 level of significance).

variances of the group means were found to be unequal, a Kruskal-Wallis one-way ANOVA was also employed. Additionally, a Student-Newman-Keuls multiple range test determined the location of significant differences between group means when the one-way ANOVA results were found to be significant.

To further clarify the extent of the differences between group means for educational level (V92), (dichotomized between 0—no college and 1—at least some college) for both commendations (V34) and citizen complaints (V36), Student's *t*-tests utilizing a T-TEST command procedure in SPSS^x were run (table A-4).

Hypothesis Two

An analysis of variance (Means and One-way in SPSS^x) was performed with V700—Niederhoffer's Revised Cynicism/ Professionalism Index and V92—educational level. This analysis included the subscales of V400—Attitudes toward Others Effects on Police Work, V410—Attitudes toward Ideals Concerning Police Work, and V420—Attitudes toward Conduct Involved in Police Work, and V800—Regoli and Poole's Professionalism Index, as well as the subscales of V500—Attitudes toward the Public, V510—Attitudes toward the Officer Role, and V520—Attitudes toward the Organization, as the interval-level criterion variable. Educational level (V92) functioned as an ordinal-level, predictor variable. As in hypothesis one above, when variances were determined to be unequal, a Kruskal-Wallis nonparametric one-way ANOVA had been employed.

A Student-Newman-Keuls multiple range test was used to test for the location of significant differences between group means when the one-way ANOVA results were significant. A two-way ANOVA was run to test for statistically significant control variable interactions for gender (V86), ethnicity (V96), and prior occupation (V96), as categorical predictor variables, as well as rank (V104) and years of experience (V11), as ordinal predictor variables (table A-5).

TABLE A-5

STUDENT-NEWMAN-KEULS MULTIPLE RANGE TEST

V400—Attitudes toward Others Effects on Police Work by V92—Level of Education

Group:	Mean	N	S	A	B	G
None	12.50		*	*	*	*
Some	13.68	*				
A.A./Equiv.	14.21	*				
B.A./B.S.	14.90	*				
Grad.Wk./Degr.	15.65	*				

<u>Legend:</u>

N = No College
S = Some College
A = A.A. or Equiv.
B = B.A. or B.S.
G = Graduate Work or Graduate Degree

Results: Group mean for no college is significantly lower than group means for some college, A.A. or equiv., B.A. or B.S., and grad. work or degree.

V500—Attitudes toward the Public by V92 —Level of Education

Group:	Mean	N	S	A	B	G
None	9.53		*			
Some	10.24	*				
A.A./Equiv.	9.85					
B.A./B.S.	9.88					
Grad.Wk./Degr.	10.19					

<u>Legend:</u>

N = No College
S = Some College
A = A.A. or Equiv.
B = B.A. or B.S.
G = Graduate Work or Graduate Degree

Results: Group mean for no college is significantly lower than group means for some college.

V520—Attitudes toward the Organization by V92—Level of Education

Group:	Mean	N	S	A	B	G
None	6.81			*	*	
Some	7.20					
A.A./Equiv.	7.65	*				
B.A./B.S.	7.60	*				
Grad.Wk./Degr.	7.50					

<u>Legend:</u>

N = No College
S = Some College
A = A.A. or Equiv.
B = B.A. or B.S.
G = Graduate Work or Graduate Degree

Results: Group mean for no college is significantly lower than group means for A. A. or equivalent and B. A. or B. S.

*Denotes pairs of groups significantly different at .05 significance level.

As in hypothesis one above, the control variable of prior occupation (V10) was found to be a statistically significant interacting variable for the subscale of V500—Attitudes toward the Public. As a result, analysis of variance (Means and One-way in SPSS^x) were also run. Additionally, a Student-Newman-Keuls multiple range test to determine the location of significant differences between group means was also reported.

To further clarify the extent of the differences between group means for educational level (V92), (dichotomized between 0—no college and 1—at least some college) for Niederhoffer's Revised Cynicism/Professionalism Index (V700) (including the subscales of Others Effects on Police Work [V400], Ideals Concerning Police Work [V410], and Conduct Involved in Police Work [V420]) and Regoli and Poole's Professionalism Index (V800) (including the subscales of V400, Attitudes toward the Public [V500], Attitudes toward the Officer Role [V510], and Attitudes toward the Organization [V520]). Student's *t*-tests, utilizing a T-TEST SPSS^x command procedure, were run and results are reported in table A-6.

Hypothesis Three

Multiple regression analysis (using the REGRESSION command procedure in SPSS^x) between commendations (V34) and citizen complaints (V36) as ratio-level predictor variables and Niederhoffer's Revised Cynicism/Professionalism Index (V700) and Regoli and Poole's Professionalism Index (V800) (including all six of the individual subscales), respectively, as interval level, criterion variables was conducted. Multiple *R*, adjusted *R* square, *F* score, significance of *F*, significance of *t* and beta are reported. Interval-level control variables of age (V94) and years experience (V11) were also included in the multiple regression statistical procedure.

Hypothesis Four

Discriminant Analysis was run for academic status (V300) as a categorical, criterion variable and commendations (V34), citizen complaints (V36), years of experience (V11), and age (V94), as

TABLE A-6

t-TEST OF DIFFERENCES BETWEEN GROUP MEANS FOR PROFESSIONALISM SCORES

Variable	No. Cases	Mean	Standard Deviation	*F* Value	2-tail Prob.	*t* Value	Degrees of Freedom	2-tail Prob.
V700: Niederhoffer's Revised Cyn./Prof. Index								
All Patrol Officers	334	42.36	9.26					
No College	119	39.87	10.47	1.64	.002	-3.49*	200.19	.001**
At Least Some College	213	43.74	8.18					
V400: Others Effects on Police Work								
All Patrol Officers	369	13.61	4.27					
No College	133	12.50	4.24	1.05	.741	-3.83	365	.000**
At Least Some College	234	14.24	4.14					
V410: Ideals Concerning Police Work								
All Patrol Officers	373	12.17	2.92					
No College	137	11.71	3.19	1.36	.040	-2.22*	250.41	.027**
At Least Some College	234	12.43	2.75					
V420: Conduct Involved in Police Work								
All Patrol Officers	371	16.83	4.25					
No College	136	16.09	4.60	1.34	.055	-2.53	366	.012**
At Least Some College	233	17.24	3.98					
V800: Regoli & Poole's Professionalism Index								
All Patrol Officers	383	28.21	4.13					
No College	142	27.51	4.75	1.66	.001	-2.38*	241.29	.018**
At Least Some College	239	28.61	3.68					
V500: Attitudes toward the Public								
All Patrol Officers	395	9.86	1.66					
No College	148	9.53	1.77	1.28	.087	-3.04	391	.002**
At Least Some College	245	10.05	1.56					
V510: Attitudes toward the Officer Role								
All Patrol Officers	387	11.11	1.73					
No College	142	11.04	1.91	1.38	.030	-0.60*	259.15	.551
At Least Some College	242	11.15	1.63					
V520: Attitudes toward the Organization								
All Patrol Officers	396	7.21	1.96					
No College	148	6.81	2.23	1.61	.001	-2.91*	255.05	.004**
At Least Some College	246	7.44	1.76					

*Using separate variance estimates due to significant differences ($p < .05$) in within-group variances.

**Group means are significantly different (.05 level of significance).

ratio-level, predictor variables. (Years of experience [V11], as an ordinal predictor variable, was found by Niederhoffer as significant in determining a level of cynicism, although the relationship was a curvilinear one. It is presently believed that years of experience as a control variable is also significant but that such a relationship is not curvilinear.)

Reported statistics include (1) Wilk's lambda, significance of Lambda, significance of *F* for the individual variables; (2) eigenvalues, explained variance, canonical correlation, Wilk's lambda, chi-square statistic and significance of chi-square for the individual functions; and (3) prior probability, percentage of grouped cases correctly classified, Box's *M* and significance for the overall predictive equation. The interval-level control variables of age (V94) and years of experience (V11) have also been included in the discriminant statistical procedure.

Hypothesis Five

Analysis of variance (Means and One-way in SPSS^x) was run with academic status (V300), as the ordinal predictor variable, and V700 and V800—attitudinal indexes (and subscales), as interval-level criterion variables. When variances were determined to be unequal, a Kruskal-Wallis nonparametric ANOVA was employed.

Student-Newman-Keuls multiple range testing was used to examine the location of significant differences between group means when the one-way ANOVA results were significant (table A-7). A two-way ANOVA for statistically significant control variable interactions of gender (V86), prior occupation (V10), and ethnicity (V96), as categorical predictor variables, as well as rank (V104) and years of experience (V11), as ordinal predictor variables are reported.

Hypothesis Six

In addition to the Correlation and Part Corr command procedures in SPSS^x, the nonparametric correlation procedure (zero-order Gamma) was computed in order to determine the strength of the relationship between V92—educational level and

TABLE A-7

STUDENT-NEWMAN-KEULS MULTIPLE RANGE TEST

V700—Niederhoffer's Revised Index
by V300—Academic Status

Group	Mean	N	I	P	C
Nonservice	35.74		*	*	*
In-service	41.25	*			
Preservice	43.37	*			
Continuing	44.71	*			

Results: Group mean for nonservice is significantly lower than group means for in-service, preservice, and continuing.

V400—Others Effects on Police Work
by V300—Academic Status

Group	Mean	N	I	P	C
Nonservice	10.74		*	*	*
In-service	13.10	*			
Preservice	13.98	*			
Continuing	14.95	*			

Results: Group mean for nonservice is significantly lower than group means for in-service, preservice, and continuing.

V410—Ideals for Police Work
by V300—Academic Status

Group	Mean	N	I	P	C
Nonservice	10.25		*	*	*
In-service	12.23	*			
Preservice	12.56	*			
Continuing	11.90	*			

Results: Group mean for nonservice is significantly lower than group means for in-service, preservice, and continuing.

V420—Conduct of Police Work
by V300—Academic Status

Group	Mean	N	I	P	C
Nonservice	14.67		*	*	*
In-service	16.57	*			
Preservice	17.14	*			
Continuing	17.71	*			

Results: Group mean for nonservice is significantly lower than group means for in-service, preservice, and continuing.

V500—Attitudes toward the Public
by V300—Academic Status

Group	Mean	N	I	P	C
Nonservice	8.42		*	*	*
In-service	9.98	*			
Preservice	10.06	*			
Continuing	9.97	*			

Legend:

N = Nonservice
I = In-Service
P = Preservice
C = Continuing

Results: Group mean for nonservice is significantly lower then group means for inservice, preservice, and continuing.

*Denotes pairs of groups significantly different at .05 significance level.

V300—academic status, as ordinal-level variables. In addition, the nonparametric correlation procedure, first-order Partial Gamma was computed to assess the influence of the variables of gender (V86), ethnicity (V96), rank (V104), prior occupation (V10), and years of experience (V11) as categorical or ordinal-level control variables.[4]

Characteristics of Officers on Patrol

Using the model developed in this research, a secondary goal of this study has been to distinguish between two groups of officers on patrol: "most" professional officers and "least" professional officers.

For "most" professional officers, a Select If command procedure in SPSS^x selected all officers on patrol, officers with one or more commendations and no reported citizen complaints, officers whose mean score on Niederhoffer's Revised Cynicism/Professionalism Index was greater than the midpoint of 39, and officers whose mean score on Regoli and Poole's Professionalism Index was greater than the midpoint of 27.5. For "least" professional officers, a Select If command procedure in SPSS^x selected all officers on patrol who reported no commendations, one or more citizen complaints, received mean scores less than the midpoint of 39 on Niederhoffer's Revised Cynicism/ Professionalism Index and less than the midpoint of 27.5 on Regoli and Poole's Professionalism Index.

A comparison between the "most" professional officers and the "least" professional officers was made as to officer demographic characteristics: educational level, gender, ethnicity, rank, prior occupation, and academic status, through the Crosstab analysis procedure in SPSS^x.

Additionally, the T-TEST command procedure in SPSS^x compared the "most" and "least" professional officers in terms of age and years service with the L.A.P.D. For level of education, academic status, and prior occupation (variables that generated statistically significant Chi-square scores) percentages were also generated through the SPSS^x Frequencies command procedure. Statistically significant demographic variables are reported in tables A-8 and A-9.

TABLE A-8

t-TEST DIFFERENCES BETWEEN GROUP MEANS FOR "LEAST" AND "MOST" PROFESSIONAL OFFICERS

VARIABLE	"MOST" PROFESSIONAL		"LEAST" PROFESSIONAL	
V92—Level of Education	At Least	~ 68.15	No College	~ 62.7%
($x^2 = 9.20$; $p = .04$)	Some College			
V300—Academic Status	Preservice/	~ 69.0%	Nonservice/	~ 62.7%
($x^2 = 14.60$; $p = .002$)	Continuing		In-service	

t-TESTS

GROUPS: "LEAST"= LEAST PROFESSIONAL; "MOST" = MOST PROFESSIONAL

Variable	No. Cases	Mean	Standard Deviation	*F* Value	2-tail Prob.	*t* Value	Degrees of Freedom	2-tail Prob.
V400 "LEAST"	23	9.1233	3.162	1.07	.794	-10.49	112	.000**
"MOST"	91	16.6337	3.060					
V61 "LEAST"	23	2.3224	1.256	1.38	.392	-4.73	112	.000**
"MOST"	91	3.9004	1.475					
V66 "LEAST"	23	1.0000	.000	--	--	-2.97	112	.004**
"MOST"	91	1.6784	1.098					
V69 "LEAST"	23	2.5606	1.288	1.29	.396	-6.13	112	.000**
"MOST"	91	4.2200	1.132					
V70 " LEAST"	23	1.6516	1.326	1.22	.614	-5.18	112	.000**
"MOST	91	3.3810	1.463					
V71 "LEAST"	23	1.5888	1.307	1.24	.578	-5.62	112	.000**
"MOST"	91	3.4539	1.456					
V410 "LEAST"	23	8.2401	2.703	2.98	.000	-9.81*	26.21	.000**
"MOST"	91	13.9682	1.566					
V62 "LEAST"	23	2.9874	1.805	10.08	.000	-4.85*	23.40	.000**
"MOST"	91	4.8248	.569					
V65 "LEAST"	23	3.3258	.755	1.10	.825	-7.06	112	.000**
"MOST"	91	4.6151	.793					
V74 "LEAST"	23	1.9270	1.019	1.07	.898	-10.69	112	.000**
"MOST"	91	4.5284	1.054					
V420 "LEAST"	23	11.2380	3.053	1.03	.869	-10.25	112	.000**
"MOST"	91	18.4149	3.003					
V63 "LEAST"	23	1.3890	.898	4.51	.000	-6.98*	77.73	.000**
"MOST"	91	3.2982	1.906					
V64 "LEAST"	23	1.2012	.615	3.55	.001	-7.39*	67.40	.000**
"MOST"	91	2.5041	1.158					
V67 "LEAST"	23	1.5650	.920	2.06	.055	-7.25	112	.000**
"MOST"	91	3.6734	1.320					
V68 "LEAST"	23	3.6908	1.741	35.81	.000	-3.50*	22.58	.002**
"MOST"	91	4.9572	.291					
V73 "LEAST"	23	3.3919	2.005	1.44	.237	-1.46	112	.148
"MOST"	91	3.9820	1.671					

*Using separate variance estimates due to significant differences ($p < .05$) in within-group variance.

** Group means are significantly different (.05 level of significance).

TABLE A-9

t-TESTS

DIFFERENCES BETWEEN GROUP MEANS FOR "LEAST" AND "MOST" PROFESSIONAL OFFICERS

GROUPS: "LEAST"= LEAST PROFESSIONAL; "MOST" = MOST PROFESSIONAL

Variable	No. Cases	Mean	Standard Deviation	*F* Value	2-tail Prob.	*t* Value	Degrees of Freedom	2-tail Prob.
V500 "LEAST"	23	7.4214	1.617	1.46	.220	-9.47	112	.000**
"MOST"	91	10.5004	1.338					
V75 "LEAST"	23	1.8304	.625	1.50	.279	-4.13	112	.000**
"MOST"	91	2.5399	.765					
V76 "LEAST"	23	2.2962	.747	2.28	.007	-5.19	27.46	.000**
"MOST"	91	3.1436	.494					
V77 "LEAST"	23	1.3950	.596	1.00	1.000	-3.54	112	.001**
"MOST"	91	1.8854	.596					
V78 "LEAST"	23	1.8998	.735	2.66	.001	-6.47	26.70	.000**
"MOST	91	2.9316	.450					
V510 LEAST"	23	9.5310	1.932	3.77	.000	-6.06	25.36	.000**
"MOST"	91	12.0394	.995					
V79 "LEAST"	23	2.3831	.614	1.72	.078	-4.95	112	.000**
"MOST"	91	2.9593	.468					
V80 "LEAST"	23	2.4454	.508	2.08	.017	-5.24	27.99	.000**
"MOST"	91	3.0307	.352					
V81 "LEAST"	23	2.2402	.565	2.50	.003	-6.06	27.00	.000**
"MOST"	91	2.9866	.358					
V82 "LEAST"	23	2.4623	.595	1.71	.083	-5.31	112	.000**
"MOST"	91	3.0629	.456					
V520 LEAST"	23	4.6102	1.814	2.49	.003	-9.24	27.01	.000**
"MOST"	91	8.2591	1.149					
V83 "LEAST"	23	1.5058	.571	1.05	.932	-8.01	112	.000**
"MOST"	91	2.5910	.586					
V84 "LEAST"	23	1.3479	.657	1.66	.100	-11.06	112	.000**
"MOST"	91	2.7420	.510					
V85 "LEAST"	23	1.7565	.860	2.41	.004	-8.02	27.18	.000**
"MOST"	91	2.9261	.554					

*Using separate variance estimates due to significant differences ($p < .05$) in within-group variance.

** Group means are significantly different (.05 level of significance).

Finally, in order to determine which characteristics or traits were representative of the "most" professional officer and the "least" professional officer, T-TEST command procedures in SPSS^x were run on each of the six individual professional subscales as well as on each of the individual items comprising these subscales. The Frequencies command procedure in SPSS^x also generated percentages as to the prevalence of characteristic differences between the two groups of officers. Chapter 6 discusses the results for these statistical procedures.

NOTES

1. See *Blake*, (Felkenes et al., 1990, vol.2:60–68) for rationale of sampling and weighting.

2. For summary of results see *Blake*, (Felkenes et al., 1990, vol. 2:156–159) and Lasley (1992:165–167).

3. Supporting rationale for weighting in the present study can be found in Babbie (1992:225–227).

4. For a comprehensive review of the measurement of association for two similar level variables as well as for variables of different measurement levels, see Champion (1981:300–61).

APPENDIX B

Individual Question Items Comprising Indexes

V700—Niederhoffer's Revised Index

V400—Attitudes toward Others Effects on Police Work

V61—A college degree as a requirement for appointment to the police department:

a. would result in a much more efficient police department
b. would cause friction and possibly do more harm than good
c. would let into the department people who are probably ill-suited for police work

V66—The newspapers in general:

a. try to help police departments by giving prominent coverage to items favorable to the police
b. just report the news impartially whether or not it concerns the police
c. seem to enjoy giving an unfavorable slant to news concerning the police and prominently play up police misdeeds rather than virtues

V69—The public:

a. is eager to cooperate with police officers to help them perform their duty better
b. usually has to be forced to cooperate with police officers
c. is more apt to obstruct police work if they can than cooperate

V70—When you get to know the department from the inside you begin to feel that:

a. it is a very efficient, smoothly operating organization
b. it is hardly any different from other civil service organizations
c. it is a wonder that it does one half as well as it does

V71—Testifying in court:

a. police officers receive real cooperation and are treated fairly by court personnel
b. police witnesses are treated no differently from civilian witnesses
c. too often the police officers are treated as criminals when they take the witness stand

V410—Attitudes toward Ideals Concerning Police Work

V62—Professionalism of police work:

a. is already here for many groups of police officers
b. may come in the future
c. is a dream—it will not come in the foreseeable future

V65—The average police officer is:

a. dedicated to high ideals of police service and would not hesitate to perform police duty even though he or she may have to work overtime
b. trying to perform eight hours of duty without getting into trouble
c. just as interested in promoting private contracts as he or she is in performing police work

V74—Police department summonses are issued by police officers:

a. as a part of a sensible pattern of enforcement
b. on the basis of their ideas of right and wrong
c. because they know they must meet their quota even if it is not official

V420—Attitudes toward Conduct Involved in Police Work

V63—Police officers:

a. understand human behavior as well as psychologists and sociologists because they get so much real-life experience
b. have no more talent in understanding human behavior than any average person
c. have a peculiar view of human behavior because of the misery and cruelty of life which they see everyday

V64—The average detective:

a. has special qualifications and is superior to officers in intelligence and dedication to duty
b. is just about the same as the average patrol officer
c. is a little arrogant and thinks he or she is a little better than a patrol officer

V67—Police Academy training of recruits:

a. does a very fine job of preparing the recruit for life in the department
b. cannot overcome the contradictions between theory and practice
c. might as well be cut in half—the recruit has to learn all over when he or she is assigned to a division

V68—The average arrest is made because:

a. the patrol officer is dedicated to perform his or her duty
b. the complainant insisted on it
c. the officer could not avoid it without getting in trouble

V73—The best arrests are made:

a. as a result of hard work and intelligent dedication to duty
b. as a result of good information from an informer
c. arriving unexpectedly in a patrol area and catching a suspect by surprise

V800—Regoli and Poole's Professionalism Index

V500—Attitudes toward the Public

V75—Most people have done something they could have been locked up for if they had been caught.
[] Strongly Agree [] Agree [] Disagree [] Strongly Disagree

V76—Victims are usually as guilty as criminals.
[] Strongly Agree [] Agree [] Disagree [] Strongly Disagree

V77—People should respect police officers more than they do.
[] Strongly Agree [] Agree [] Disagree [] Strongly Disagree

V78—Most people are willing to cooperate with the police.
[] Strongly Agree [] Agree [] Disagree [] Strongly Disagree

V510—Attitudes toward the Officer Role

V79—People in this profession have a real calling for their work.
[] Strongly Agree [] Agree [] Disagree [] Strongly Disagree

V80—The dedication of police officers in this profession is most gratifying.
[] Strongly Agree [] Agree [] Disagree [] Strongly Disagree

V81—It is encouraging to see the high level of idealism which is maintained by police officers in this organization.
[] Strongly Agree [] Agree [] Disagree [] Strongly Disagree

V82—There are very few police officers who don't really believe in their work.
[] Strongly Agree [] Agree [] Disagree [] Strongly Disagree

V520—Attitudes toward the Organization

V83—When a problem comes up here, the people on the staff seldom agree on how it should be handled.

[] Strongly Agree [] Agree [] Disagree [] Strongly Disagree

V84—The people in charge here never seem to respect those who do the real work.

[] Strongly Agree [] Agree [] Disagree [] Strongly Disagree

V85—I feel I have too little authority to do my job the way it should be done.

[] Strongly Agree [] Agree [] Disagree [] Strongly Disagree

APPENDIX C

Variables Used in L.A.P.D. Study

Dependent Variables

Interval/Ratio:

Performance Variables (Probationary Experiences):

V34 No. of Self-reported Commendations (Recode/compute)
0–8

V36 No. of Self-reported Citizen Complaints (Recode/compute)
0–8

Attitudinal Variables:

V700—Cynicism/Professionalism: (Niederhoffer)
V61–V71, V73–V74—(Recode reverse 1,3,5)

V800—Professionalism: (Regoli and Poole)

V77–V82—Coded 1-4

V75–V76, V83–V85—(Recode reverse order) 1–4

Independent Variables

Nominal/Ordinal:

V92 College Education Then (Recode)—(0) None (1) Some (2) AA/2 Yrs. (3) BA/BS (4) Some Grad./Grad. degree

V300 Educational Status (Computed from V92 and V93) (0) Nonservice (1) In-service (2) Preservice (3) Continuing

Control Variables

Nominal/Ordinal:

V99 Current Assignment—Select only (1) Patrol Officer

V86 Gender—(1) Male (2) Female

V96 Race—(Recode) (1) Black (2) Hispanic (3) White (4) Other

V104 Current Rank—(1) Police Officer (2) Detective (3) Sergeant (4) Lieutenant

V11 Years Experience—(Recode to comport with Niederhoffer's groups) (1) 1 to 5 Yrs. (2) 6 to 10 Yrs. (3) 11 to 15 Yrs. (4) Over 15 Yrs.

V10 Prior Occupation—(Recode into groupings) (1) Business and Professional Services (2) Military (3) Student (4) Skilled Trades and (5) Industrial Laborer.

Interval/Ratio:

V11 Years Experience (Recode/Compute)—1–40

V94 Age

APPENDIX D

Definitions of Key Terms

The following definitions include but may not be exhaustive of key concepts discussed and utilized in the present study.

Attitude—an organization of beliefs about a specific object or situation which individually or in combination is instrumental in the attainment of one or more values. For example, an attitude or combination of attitudes toward one's job is reflected in how one values or places importance on one's role and ultimate performance.

Continuing education—completion of any number of units of college education at an accredited institution both prior to and after entry into policing. Therefore, a continuing education consists of a combination of both "pre-service" and "in-service" educations, which are defined below.

Cynical—a misanthropic or pessimistic attitude or attitudes toward one's fellow human beings.

Cynicism—a composite of cynical attitudes; a value that is manifested in a self-reflective sense of extreme distrust in the motivations of others and a preoccupation or obsession with self-gratification and self-survival at the expense of others.

Enforcer—a valued style of policing that represents a predominantly authoritarian, cynical, control-oriented, and emotionally reactive mode of behavior in role performance.

In-service education—the completion of a number of units of college education at an accredited institution only after the recruit has entered the policing role.

Level of education—attainment of formal education at an accredited institution beyond that of the high school or secondary educational level; college education divided into levels of none (no successful completion of college units), some (mean of one year), two years (equivalent to A.A. degree), four years (undergraduate degree), and graduate work/graduate degree.

Nonservice education—the absence of any formal college education both prior to and after entry into the policing role.

Organizational influence—impact of agency policies and supervisorial styles of management on the quality of service by the primary actors (police officers) toward their clientele (general public as recipients).

Organizational mission—the raison d'etre of any public administrative agency which justifies its importance and self-preservation in the overall political arena. For law enforcement agencies, this mission primarily would be the management of interpersonal relations, conflict, and violence affecting the lives of their clientele as well as the reestablishment of order or civility through the legitimate use of intrusion, coercion, or force as mandated by legislation and those regulations established by the agency to carry out the laws.

Patrol officer—officers who have identified themselves as working patrol duties; rankings of officers working patrol include police officers, detectives, sergeants, and lieutenants.

Performance—the construct of either officially recorded behavior (e.g., number of arrests) or self-reported role behaviors taking into account those attitudes and values that influence both the quantitative and qualitative aspects of such role behavior.

Policing style—a general type or method of role performance of the individual officers that includes both what officers do and how they accomplish their tasks. When measured in the aggregate, variances in operational styles may delineate distinct subcultures of policing, which can either reinforce or conflict with peer-group and/or supervisory stylistic influences. In the present research, policing style is measured as a continuum from the one extreme of the nonprofessional (cynic, enforcer type) to the opposite extreme of the professional police officer.

Preservice education—the successful completion of any number of units of college education at an accredited institution prior to a recruit's entry into the role of the police officer.

Professional—a style of and value toward policing representing a predominantly authoritative, rational, problem-oriented, and conflict-management mode of behavior when engaging in the performance of one's policing role.

Professionalism—both the role actor's value of performance as well as the organization's valuing of that individual's performance, which is manifested in an overall qualitatively superior type of service as an end product toward the organizational mission.

Professionalization—the process of improving the efficiency (management and administration) and effectiveness (substantive end product) of the public administrative agency as well as the role occupants within that agency.

Value—a composite of related attitudes consisting of knowledge, emotional affectiveness, and behavioral components that become standards guiding an individual's actions as well as one's ability to persuade and influence others. As such, values may become intervening variables between attitudes and behaviors/performance, although values are more central and stable than attitudes.

REFERENCES

Aguilera v. *Cook County Police & Corrections Merit Bd.*, 582 F. Supp. 1053 (N.D. Ill. 1984) affirmed 760 F. 2d 844 (7th Cir. 1985) cert. denied 474 U.S. 907, 106 S. Ct. 237, 88. L. Ed. 2d 238.

Albemarle Paper Co. v. *Moody*, 422 U.S. 405, 95 S. Ct. 2362, 45 L.Ed.2d 280 (1975).

American Bar Association Project on Standards for Criminal Justice. *The Urban Police Function.* New York: American Bar Association, 1972.

Anderson, Dan. "Shocked, Sad but Vindicated." *Inland Daily Bulletin*, May 10, 1992, pp. 1,5.

Angell, John E. "Toward an Alternative to the Classic Police Organizational Arrangements: A Democratic Model." *Criminology* 19 (1971):186–206.

Anson, Richard H.; Mann, J. Dale; and Sherman, Dale. "Niederhoffer's Cynicism Scale: Reliability and Beyond." *Journal of Criminal Justice* 14 (1986):295–305.

Arnold v. *Ballard*, 390 F. Supp. 723 (N.D. Ohio 1975).

Arritt v. *Grissell*, 567 F. 2d 1267 (4th Cir.1977).

Babbie, Earl. *The Practice of Social Research*, 6th ed. Belmont, CA: Wadsworth, 1992.

Bantz, Donald N. "An Examination of Section 1983 Lawsuits against State and Local Public Officials." Ph.D. dissertation, University of Southern California, 1988.

Barry, Donald M. "A Survey of Student and Agency Views on Higher Education in Criminal Justice." *Journal of Police Science and Administration* 6 (1978):345–354.

Bennett, Georgette. *Crimewarps.* New York: Anchor Books, 1987.

Bernard v. *Gulf Oil Corp.*, 841 F .2d 547 (5th Cir. 1988).

Biskupic, Joan. "Overturning Precedents." *Congressional Quarterly*, October 26, 1991a, p. 3125.

———. "Senate Passes Sweeping Measure to Overturn Court Rulings." *Congressional Quarterly*, November 2, 1991b, pp. 3200–3204.

———. "Bush Signs Anti-Job Bias Bill Amid Furor Over Preferences." *Congressional Quarterly,* November 13, 1991c, p. 3463.

Bittner, Egon. "Florence Nightingale in Pursuit of Willie Sutton: A Theory of Police." In *The Potential for Reform of Criminal Justice,* pp. 17–44. Herbert Jacob, ed. Beverly Hills, CA: Sage Publications, 1974.

Blake v. *City of Los Angeles,* 595 F. 2d 1367 (9th Cir. 1979) cert. denied 446 U.S. 928, 100 S. Ct. 1865, 64 L. Ed.2d 281.

Blumberg, Abraham S. and Niederhoffer Elaine, eds. *The Ambivalent Force: Perspectives on the Police,* 3rd ed. New York: Holt, Rinehart and Winston, 1985.

Boston Chapter, NAACP, Inc. v. *Beecher,* 371 F. Supp. 507 (D.C. Mass. 1974) affirmed 504 F. 2d 1017 (1st Cir. 1974) cert. denied 421 U.S. 910, 95 S. Ct 1561, 43 L. Ed. 2d.

Boyd v. *Ozark Air Lines, Inc.,* 568 F. 2d 50 (8th Cir. 1977).

Bridgeport Guardians, Inc. v. *Members of Bridgeport Civil Service Commission,* 354 F. Supp. 778 (D.C. Conn. 1973) affirmed in part, reversed in part on other grounds 482 F. 2d 1333 (2nd Cir. 1973).

Brooks, Laure Weber. "Police Discretionary Behavior: A Study of Style." In *Critical Issues in Policing: Contemporary Readings,* pp. 121–45. Robert G. Dunham and Geoffrey P. Alpert, eds. Prospect Heights, IL: Waveland Press, Inc., 1989.

Brown, Michael K. "A Typology of Operational Styles." In *The Ambivalent Force: Perspectives on the Police,* 3rd ed., pp. 195–207. Abraham S. Blumberg and Elaine Niederhoffer, eds. New York: Holt, Rinehart and Winston, 1985.

———. *Working the Street: Police Discretion and the Dilemmas of Reform.* New York: Russell Sage Foundation, 1981.

Brown, Stephen E. and Vogel, Ronald E. "Police Professionalism." *Journal of Crime and Justice* 6 (1983):17–37.

Burwell, William R. "Police Brutality, Authoritarianism and Locus of Control." Ph.D. dissertation, Illinois Institute of Technology, 1983.

California Commission on Peace Officer Standards and Training. "Employment Data for California Law Enforcement: 1989." California: Department of Justice, 1990.

California Government Code, Title 1, art. 2, sec. 1031(e).

California Governor's Commission on the Los Angeles Riots. *Violence in the City—An End or a Beginning?* John A. McCone, Chairman. California: State of California, 1965.

Carter, David L.; and Sapp, Allen D. "The Evolution of Higher Education in Law Enforcement: Preliminary Findings from a National Study." *Journal of Criminal Justice Education* 1 (March 1990):59–85.

Carter, David L.; Sapp, Allen D.; and Stephens, D. W. "Higher Education as a Bona Fide Occupational Qualification (BFOQ) for Police: A Blueprint." *American Journal of Police* 7 (1988):1–27.

Carter, Stephen. *Reflections of an Affirmative Action Baby*. New York: Basic Books, 1991.

Cascio, Wayne F. "Formal Education and Police Officer Performance." *Journal of Police Science and Administration* 5 (1977):89–96.

Cascio, Wayne F. and Real, Leslie J. "Educational Standards for Police Officer Personnel." *The Police Chief* 43 (August 1976):54–55.

Castro v. *Beecher*, 459 F .2d 725 (1st Cir. 1972).

Chambliss, William J. and Seidman, Robert B. *Law, Order, and Power*. Massachusetts: Addison-Wesley, 1971.

Champion, Dean J. *Basic Statistics for Social Research*. 2nd ed. New York: Macmillan, 1981.

Chavez, Linda. *Out of the Barrio*. New York: Basic Books, 1991.

Chrisner v. *Complete Auto Transit, Inc.*, 645 F. 2d 1251 (6th Cir. 1981).

Cohen, Bernard and Chaiken, Jan M. *Police Background Characteristics and Performance: Summary*. New York: The Rand Institute, 1972.

Contreras v. *City of Los Angeles*, 656 F. 2d 1267 (9th Cir. 1981) cert. denied 455 U.S. 1021, 102 S. Ct. 1719, 72 L. Ed. 2d 140.

Copley, Waldo H. "Using Education, Academy and Field Training Scores to Predict Success in a Colorado Police Department." Ph.D. dissertation, Colorado State University, 1987.

Craig v. *Los Angeles County*, 626 F. 2d 659 (9th Cir 1980) cert. denied 450 U.S. 919, 101 S. Ct. 1364, 67 L. Ed. 2d 345.

Crank, John P. "Professionalism among Police Chiefs." Ph.D. dissertation, University of Colorado at Boulder, 1987.

Crawford Fitting Co. v. *J. T. Gibbons Inc.*, 482 U.S. 437, 107 S. Ct. 2494, 96 L.Ed.2d 385 (1987).

Crockett v. *Green*, 388 F. Supp. 912, (D.C. Wisc. 1975) affirmed 534 F. Supp. 715.

Dalley, A. F. "University and Non-University Graduated Patrolmen: A Study of Police Attitudes." *Journal of Police Science and Administration* 3 (1975):458–68.

Davis v. *City of Dallas,* 483 F. Supp. 54 (N.D. Texas 1979), 487 F. Supp. 389 (N.D. Texas 1980), 777 F. 2d 205 (5th Cir. 1985), cert. denied 476 U.S. 1116, 106 S. Ct. 1972, 90 L. Ed. 2d 656 (1986).

Detroit Police Officers Ass'n v. *Young,* 446 F. Supp. 979 (D.C. Mich. 1978) reversed 608 F. 2d 671 (6th Cir. 1979), cert. denied 101 S. Ct. 3079.

Dorsey, R. Rita and Giacopassi, David J. "Assessing Gender Differences in the Levels of Cynicism Among Police Officers." *American Journal of Police* 5 (Spring 1986)1:91–112.

Dothard v. *Rawlinson,* 433 U.S. 321, 97 S. Ct. 2720, 53 L. Ed. 2d 786 (1977).

Dozier v. *Chupka,* 395 F. Supp. 836 (D.C. Ohio 1975).

Dubin, Robert. "Deviant Behavior and Social Structure: Continuities in Social Theory." *American Sociological Review* 24 (April 1959)2:147–64.

Dunham, Roger G. and Alpert, Geoffrey P., eds. *Critical Issues in Policing: Contemporary Readings.* Prospect Heights, IL: Waveland Press, 1989.

Durkheim, Emile. *The Division of Labor in Society,* tr. by George Simpson. New York: Free Press, 1965.

Eckroth v. *Flasher Public School Dist. No.39,* 583 F. 2d 415 (D.C. N.D. 1978).

Equal Employment Opportunity Commission v. *Arabian American Oil Co.,* 498 U.S. 808, 111 S. Ct. 1227, 113 L. Ed. 2d 274 (1991).

Equal Employment Opportunity Commission v. *Ball Corp.,* 661 F. 2d 531 (6th Cir. 1981).

Equal Employment Opportunity Commission v. *Chicago Miniature Lamp Works,* 622 F. Supp. 1281 (D.C. Ill. 1985).

Equal Employment Opportunity Commission v. *United Va. Bank/Seaboard National,* 555 F. 2d 403 (4th Cir. 1977).

Evans v. *City of Evanston,* 695 F. Supp. 922 (N.D. Ill. 1988).

Feldman, Kenneth and Thomas Newcomb. *The Impact of College on Students: An Analysis of Four Decades of Research.* San Francisco: Jossey-Bass, 1989.

Felkenes, George T. "Attitudes of Police Officers toward Their Professional Ethics." *Journal of Criminal Justice* 12 (1984)3:211–20.

Felkenes, George T.; Trostle, Lawrence; Lasley, James; Jones Palombo, Bernadette; and Hooper, Michael. *The Impact of* Fanchon v. City of

Los Angeles *on the Selection, Recruitment, Training, Appointment and Performance of Women and Minorities for the Los Angeles Police Department and the City of Los Angeles.* 2 vols. The Claremont Graduate School, July 1990.

Felkenes, George T. and Unsinger, Peter Charles, eds. *Diversity, Affirmative Action, and Law Enforcement.* Springfield, IL: Charles C. Thomas Publishers, 1992.

Fessler, Pamela with Biskupic, Joan and Kuntz, Phil. "Rights Bill Rises from the Ashes of Senate's Thomas Fight." *Congressional Quarterly,* October 16, 1991, pp. 3124–3126.

Finkenauer, James O. "Higher Education and Police Discretion." *Journal of Police Science and Administration* 3 (1975):450–457.

Finnegan, James C. "A Study of the Relationship Between College Education and Police Performance in Baltimore, Maryland." *Police Chief* 43 (August 1976):60–62.

Freed, David. "Justice in Distress: The Devaluation of Crime in Los Angeles." (Series) *Los Angeles Times,* December 16–22, 1990.

Geary, David P. "College-Educated Cops—Three Years Later." *Police Chief* 37 (August 1970):62–72.

———. "A Study of the Relationship of Selected Educational Factors to Police Performance." Ph.D. dissertation, Marquette University, 1979.

Gillespie v. *State of Wisconsin,* 771 F. 2d 1035, (7th Cir. 1985) cert. denied 106 S. Ct. 854.

Goldstein, Herman. *Policing a Free Society.* Cambridge, MA: Ballinger Publishing, 1977.

———. "Improving Policing: A Problem-Oriented Approach." *Crime and Delinquency* 25 (April 1979):236–58.

Gormley, William T., Jr. *Taming the Bureaucracy: Muscles, Prayers and Other Strategies.* New Jersey: Princeton University Press, 1989.

Gould, Stephen Jay. *The Mismeasure of Man.* New York: W.W. Norton, 1981.

Greene, Jack J. "Police and Community Relations: Where Have We Been and Where Are We Going?" In *Critical Issues in Policing: Contemporary Readings,* pp. 349–68. Robert G. Dunham and Geoffrey P. Alpert, eds. Prospect Heights, IL: Waveland Press, 1989.

———, ed. *Managing Police Work: Issues and Analysis.* Beverly Hills, CA: Sage Publications, 1982.

Griggs v. *Duke Power Co.*, 401 U. S. 424, 91 S. Ct. 849, 28 L. Ed. 2d 158 (1971).

Gross, Solomon. "Higher Education and Police: Is There a Need for a Closer Look?" *Journal of Police Science and Administration* 1 (December 1973):477–83.

Grove City College v. *Bell*, 465 U.S. 555, 104 S. Ct. 1211, 79 L. Ed. 2d 516 (1984).

Guffey, James E. "Police and Sheriff Department Staffing Shortages: A National Survey." A paper presented at the Annual Meeting of the Western and Pacific Association of Criminal Justice Educators, November 1991.

Guller, Irving B. "Higher Education and Policemen: Attitudinal Differences between Freshmen and Senior Police College Students." *Journal of Criminal Law, Criminology, and Police Science* 63 (September 1972):396–401.

Hahn, Harlan. "A Profile of Urban Police." *Law and Contemporary Problems* 36 (Fall 1971):449–66.

Harless v. *Duck*, 619 F. 2d 611 (6th Cir. 1976) cert. denied 449 U.S. 872, 101 S. Ct. 212, 66 L. Ed. 2d 92.

Harriss v. *Pan Am. World Airways, Inc.*, 649 F. 2d 670 (9th Cir. 1980).

Hawkins v. *Anheuser-Busch, Inc.*, 504 F. Supp. 882 (D.C. Mo. 1980).

Hodgson v. *Greyhound Lines, Inc.*, 499 F. 2d 859 (7th Cir. 1974) cert. denied sub nom. *Brennan* v. *Greyhound Lines, Inc.*, 419 U.S. 1122, 95 S. Ct. 805, 42 L. Ed. 2d 822 (1975).

Hooper, Michael K. "The Relationship of College Education to Police Officer Job Performance." Ph.D. dissertation, Claremont Graduate School, 1988.

Hoover, Larry T. *Police Educational Characteristics and Curricula.* U.S. Department of Justice, LEAA. Washington, DC.: Government Printing Office, 1975.

Ice et al. v. *Arlington County et al.*,(E.D. Va. August 1976, 4th Cir. May 16, 1977).

Independent Commission on the Los Angeles Police Department. (Christopher Commission). *Report of the Independent Commission on the Los Angeles Police Department.* July 9, 1991.

Jackson v. *Curators of University of Missouri*, 456 F. Supp. 879 (D.C. Mo. 1978).

Jackson v. *Nassau County Civil Service Commission*, 424 F. Supp. 1162 (D.C. N.Y. 1976).

Jacob, Herbert, ed. *The Potential for Reform of Criminal Justice.* Beverly Hills, CA: Sage Publications, 1974.

Jagiello, Robert E. "College Education for the Patrolman: Necessary or Irrelevant." *Journal of Criminal Law, Criminology, and Police Science* 62 (March 1971):114–21.

Johnson v. *Uncle Ben's, Inc.,* 628 F. 2d 419 (5th Cir. 1980), rehearing denied 633 F. 2d 582, vacated 451 U.S. 902, 101 S. Ct. 1967, 68 L. Ed. 2d 290.

Jones, Charles L. "A Comparison of Authoritarian Attitudes of College Educated Policemen with Non-college Educated Policemen." Ph.D. dissertation, Auburn University, 1984.

Kachigan, Sam K. *Statistical Analysis.* New York: Radius Press, 1986.

Katz, Jesse. "Other Police Forces Dismiss L.A. Study." *Los Angeles Times,* July 21, 1991, pp. J1, J7.

Kelly, Joseph A., and O'Rourke, Thomas W. "An Appraisal of the Attitudes of Police Officers toward the Concept of Police-Community Relations." *Journal of Police Science and Administration* 1 (June 1973):224–31.

Kinsey v. *First Regional Securities, Inc,* 557 F. 2d 830 (D.C. Cir. 1977).

Kirkland v. *New York State Department of Correctional Services,* 374 F. Supp. 1361 (D.C. N.Y. 1974) affirmed in part, reversed in part 520 F. 2d 420 (2nd Cir. 1975).

Klecka, William R. *Discriminant Analysis.* Beverly Hills, CA: Sage Publications, 1980.

Knowles, Lyle. "The Policeman in the Ivory Tower: A Challenge for the Professional Educator." *Police* 16 (March 1972):35–43.

Kronholm, William C. "Blue Power: The Threat of the Militant Policeman." *Journal of Criminal Law, Criminology, and Police Science* 63 (June 1972):294–99.

Landesco, John. *Organized Crime in Chicago.* Chicago, IL: University of Chicago Press, 1968.

Lasley, James. "Fulfilling the Mandates of the Law: The Consent Decrees and Compliance." In *Diversity, Affirmative Action and Law Enforcement,* pp. 137–167. George T. Felkenes and Peter Charles Unsinger, eds. Springfield, IL: Charles C. Thomas, 1992.

League of United Latin American Citizens v. *City of Santa Ana,* 410 F .Supp. 873 (C.D. Cal. 1976).

Leavitt, James S. "Criminal Justice Curriculum Development in California Community Colleges." Ph.D. dissertation, University of San Francisco, 1989.

Ledoux, John C. "The Relationship between College Education and Open-Closed Mindedness for Police Officers in Alabama." Ph.D. dissertation, Auburn University, 1980.

Lester, David. "Why Do People Become Police Officers: Study of Reasons and Their Predictions of Success." *Journal of Police Science and Administration* 11 (1983):170–74.

Lewis-Beck, Michael. *Applied Regression: An Introduction.* CA: Sage Publications, 1980.

Liberles v. *Daniel,* 477 F. Supp. 504 (D.C. Ill. 1979).

Library of Congress v. *Shaw,* 478 U.S. 310, 106 S. Ct. 2957, 92 L. Ed .2d 250 (1986).

Local Number 93, International Association of Fire Fighters v. *Cleveland,* 478 U.S. 501, 106 S. Ct. 3063, 92 L. Ed. 2d 405 (1986).

Lorance v. *AT & T Technologies,* 490 U.S. 900, 109 S. Ct. 2261, 104 L. Ed. 2d 961 (1989).

Lotz, Roy E. and Regoli, Robert M. "Police Cynicism and Professionalism." *Human Relations* 30 (1977):175–86.

Lynch, Frederick R. *Invisible Victims: White Males and the Crisis of Affirmative Action.* New York: Greenwood Press, 1989.

Lynch, Gerald W. "Criminal Justice Higher Education: Some Perspectives." *Police Chief* 43 (August 1976a):63–65.

———. "The Contribution of Higher Education to Ethical Behavior in Law Enforcement." *Journal of Criminal Justice* 4 (1976b):285–90.

McCloskey, Herbert and Schaar, John H. "Psychological Dimensions of Anomy." *American Sociological Review* 1 (February 1965):14–28.

Maddell, John D. and Washburn, Paul V. "Which College Major Is Best for the Street Cop?" *Police Chief* 45 (August 1978):40–42.

Martin, Susan Ehrlich. *Breaking & Entering: Policewomen on Patrol.* Berkeley: University of California Press, 1980.

Martin v. *Wilks,* 490 U.S. 755, 109 S. Ct. 2180, 104 L. Ed. 2d 835 (1989).

Menke, Ben A.; White, Mervin F.; and Carey, William L. "Police Professionalism: Pursuit of Excellence or Political Power?" In *Managing Police Work: Issues and Analysis,* pp. 75–106. Jack R. Greene, ed. Beverly Hills, CA: Sage Publications, 1982.

Merton, Robert K. *Social Theory and Social Structure.* New York: Free Press, 1968.

Miller, Jon and Fry, Lincoln. "Re-examining Assumptions about Education and Professionalism in Law Enforcement." 4 *Journal of Police Science and Administration* (1976):187–96.

———. "Some Evidence on the Impact of Higher Education for Law Enforcement Personnel." *Police Chief* 45 (August 1978):30–33.

Monroe, S. "Does Affirmative Action Help or Hurt?" *Time,* May 27, 1991, pp. 22–23.

Morrow v. *Dillard,* 412 F. Supp. 494 (D.C. Miss. 1976).

Muir, William Ker, Jr. *Police: Streetcorner Politicians.* Chicago, IL: University of Chicago Press, 1977.

Murphy, Dean E. "Complaints Against L.A. Police Set Record." *Los Angeles Times,* October 17, 1991, pp. B1, B8.

Murrell, David B. "The Influence of Education on Police Work Performance." Ph. D. dissertation, The Florida State University, Tallahassee, 1982.

National Advisory Commission on Criminal Justice Standards and Goals. *A National Strategy to Reduce Crime: Police.* Washington, DC: Government Printing Office, 1973.

National Commission on Law Observance and Enforcement. (Wickersham Commission). *Report on Police.* Washington, DC: Government Printing Office, 1931.

Neithercutt, M. G. and Carmichael, Benjamin G. "Ruminations on the Criminal Justice Breach of Trust." A paper presented at the Annual Meeting of the Western and Pacific Association of Criminal Justice Educators, November 1991.

Niederhoffer, Arthur. *Behind the Shield: The Police in Urban Society.* Garden City, NY: Doubleday, 1967.

———. "The Jewish Patrolman." In *The Ambivalent Force: Perspectives on the Police,* 3rd ed., pp. 113–14. Abraham S. Blumberg and Elaine Niederhoffer, eds. New York: Holt, Rinehart and Winston, 1985.

———. "Police Cynicism." In *The Ambivalent Force: Perspectives on the Police,* 3rd ed., pp. 208–210. Abraham S. Blumberg and Elaine Niederhoffer, eds. New York: Holt, Rinehart and Winston, 1985.

Norusis, Marija J. *SPSSx Introductory Statistics Guide for SPSSx Release 3.* Chicago, IL: SPSS Inc., 1988a.

———. *SPSSx Advanced Statistics Guide,* 2nd ed. Chicago, IL: SPSS, Inc. 1988b.

Officers for Justice v. *Civil Service Commission of City and County of San Francisco,* 371 F. Supp. 1328 (D.C. Ca. 1973).

Pace College v. *Commission on Human Rights of City of New York,* 339 N.E. 2d 880, 377 N.Y.S. 2d 471 38 N.Y. 2d 28 (N.Y. 1975).

Palombo, Bernadette Jones. "Affirmative Action and the Law." In *Diversity, Affirmative Action and Law Enforcement,* pp. 38–56. George T. Felkenes and Peter Charles Unsinger, eds. Springfield, IL: Charles C. Thomas, 1992.

Parker, L. Craig; Donnelly, Martin; Gerwitz, David; Marcus, Joan; and Kowalewski, Victor. "Higher Education: Its Impact on Police Attitudes." *Police Chief* 43 (July 1976):33–35.

Pascarella, Ernest T. and Terenzini, Patrick T. *How College Affects Students: Findings and Insights from Twenty Years of Research.* San Francisco, CA.: Jossey-Bass, 1991.

Patterson v. *McLean Credit Union,* 491 U.S. 164, 109 S. Ct. 2363, 105 L. Ed. 2d 132 (1989).

Payne v. *Travenol Laboratories, Inc.,* 565 F. 2d 895 (11th Cir. 1978), cert. denied 439 U.S. 835, 99 S. Ct. 118, 58 L. Ed. 2d 131.

Petersen, David M., ed. *Police Work: Strategies and Outcomes in Law Enforcement.* Beverly Hills, CA: Sage Publications, 1979.

Plummer, Keith. "Pre-Employment Factors That Determine Success in the Police Academy." Ph. D. dissertation, Claremont Graduate School, 1979.

President's Commission on Law Enforcement and Administration of Justice. *Task Force Report: The Challenge of Crime in a Free Society.* Washington, DC: Government Printing Office, 1967a.

———. *Task Force Report: The Police.* Washington, DC: Government Printing Office, 1967b.

Price, Barbara R. *Police Professionalism.* Lexington, MA: D.C. Heath, 1977.

Price Waterhouse v. *Hopkins,* 490 U.S. 228, 109 S. Ct. 1775, 104 L. Ed. 2d 268 (1989).

Pursley, Robert D. *Introduction to Criminal Justice,* 5th ed. New York: Macmillan, 1991.

Rafky, David M. "Police Cynicism Reconsidered." 13 *Criminology* (August 1975)2:68–72.

Redford, Emmette S. *Democracy in the Administrative State.* New York: Oxford University Press, 1969.

Reed, William E. "Higher Education for Police Officers: A Management Tool and a Personal Advantage." *Police Chief* 55 (November 1988)11:32, 34–35.

Regents of the University of California v. *Bakke,* 438 U.S. 265 (1978).

Regoli, Robert M. "An Empirical Assessment of Niederhoffer's Police Cynicism Scale." *Journal of Criminal Justice* 4 (Fall 1976a):232–234.

———. "The Effects of College Education on the Maintenance of Police Cynicism." *Journal of Police Science and Administration* 4 (1976b):340–45.

———. *Police in America: A Study of Cynicism.* Washington, DC: University Press of America, 1977.

Regoli, Robert M.; Crank, John P.; and Culbertson, Robert G. "Police Professionalism and Cynicism Reconsidered: An Assessment of Measurement Issues." *Justice Quarterly* 4 (1987a):257–75.

———. "Rejoinder—Police Cynicism: Theory Development and Reconstruction." *Justice Quarterly* 4 (June 1987b):281–286.

Regoli, Robert M.; Crank, John P.; Culbertson, Robert G.; and Poole, Eric D. "The Consequences of Professionalism among Police Chiefs." *Justice Quarterly* 6 (March 1989):47–67.

Regoli, Robert M. and Poole, Eric D. "Measurement of Police Cynicism: A Factor Scaling Approach." *Journal of Criminal Justice* 7 (1979):37–51.

Regoli, Robert M.; Poole, Eric D.; and Hewitt, John D. "Refining Police Cynicism Theory: An Empirical Assessment, Evaluation, and Implications." In *Police Work: Strategies and Outcomes in Law Enforcement,* pp. 59–68. David M. Petersen, ed. Beverly Hills, CA: Sage Publications, 1979.

Reynolds v. *Sheet Metal Workers Local 102* 498 F. Supp. 952 (D.C D.C. 1980).

Rice v. *City of St. Louis,* 464 F. Supp. 138 (E.D. Mo. 1978), 607 F. 2d 791 (8th Cir. 1979).

Roberg, Roy R. "An Analysis of the Relationship among Higher Education, Belief Systems and Job Performance of Patrol Officers." *Journal of Police Science and the Administration* 6 (1978):336–44.

———. "Higher Education, Belief Systems, and Police Performance." *Journal of Police Science and Administration* 8 (1980)3:335–40.

Rokeach, Milton. *The Nature of Human Values.* New York: Free Press, 1973.

Roman v. *Reynolds Metals Co.*, 368 F. Supp. 47 (D.C. Tex. 1973).

Rudoni, Dorothy; Baker, Ralph; and Meyer, Fred A., Jr. "Police Professionalism: Emerging Trends." *Policy Studies Journal* 7 (1978):454–60.

Sanderson, B.E. "Police Officers: The Relationship of College Education to Job Performance." *Police Chief* 44 (August 1977):82–83.

Saunders, Charles B., Jr. *Upgrading the American Police.* Washington, DC Brookings Institution, 1970.

Scott v. *City of Anniston Alabama*, 597 F. 2d 897, (11th Cir. 1979) cert. denied 446 U.S. 917, 100 S. Ct. 1850, 64 L. Ed. 2d 271.

Shaw, David. "The Media & the LAPD: From Coziness to Conflict." *Los Angeles Times*, May 24 to May 28, 1992a.

———. "Onetime Allies: Press and LAPD." *Los Angeles Times*, May 24, 1992b, pp. 1, 32–33.

———. "Chief Parker Molded LAPD Image—Then Came the '60s." *Los Angeles Times*, May 25, 1992c, pp. 1, 26–27.

———. "Media Failed to Examine Alleged LAPD Abuses." *Los Angeles Times*, May 26, 1992d, pp. 1, 20–21.

———. "Story of King Beating Put L.A. Media in Spotlight." *Los Angeles Times*, May 27, 1992e, pp. 1, 14–16.

———. "Gates Hammered by Media Over LAPD Riot Response." *Los Angeles Times*, May 28, 1992f, pp. 1, 20–21.

Sherman, Lawrence W. "Causes of Police Behavior: The Current State of Quantitative Research." *Journal of Research in Crime and Delinquency* 17 (1980):69–95.

———. *Scandal and Reform: Controlling Police Corruption.* Los Angeles, CA: University of California Press, 1978.

———. "Effects of Police Reform on Political Culture: Three Case Studies." In *Police Work: Strategies and Outcomes in Law Enforcement*, pp. 37–58. David M. Petersen, ed. Beverly Hills, CA: Sage Publications, 1979.

Sherman, Lawrence W. and Blumberg, Mark. "Higher Education and Police Use of Deadly Force." *Journal of Criminal Justice* 9 (1981):317–31.

Sherman, Lawrence W. and National Advisory Commission on Higher Education for Police Officers. *The Quality of Police Education.* Washington, DC: Jossey-Bass, 1978.

Shernock, Stanley K. "The Effects of College Education on Professional Attitudes among Police." *Journal of Criminal Justice Education* 3 (Spring 1992)1:71–92.

Skolnick, Jerome H. *Justice Without Trial: Law Enforcement in a Democratic Society.* New York: John Wiley, 1966.

Skolnick, Jerome H. and Bayley, David H. *The New Blue Line: Police Innovation in Six American Cities.* New York: Free Press, 1986.

Slovak, Jeffrey S. *Styles of Urban Policing: Organization, Environment, and Police Styles in Selected American Cities.* New York: New York University Press, 1986.

Smith, Alexander B.; Locke, Bernard; and Fenster, Abe. "Authoritarianism in Policemen Who Are College Graduates and Non-College Police." *Journal of Criminal Law, Criminology, and Police Science* 61 (1970)6:312–15.

Smith, Alexander, B.; Locke, Bernard; and Walker, William F. "Authoritarianism in College and Non-College Oriented Police." *Journal of Criminal Law, Criminology and Police Science* 58 (1967)1:129–33.

Smith, Dennis C. "Dangers of Police Professionalism: An Empirical Analysis." *Journal of Criminal Justice* 6 (1978):199–216.

Smith, Dennis C. and Ostrom, Elinor. "The Effects of Training and Education on Police Attitudes and Performance: A Preliminary Analysis." In *The Potential for Reform in Criminal Justice,* Herbert Jacob, ed., pp. 45–81. Beverly Hills, CA: Sage Publications, 1974.

Smith, Page. *Killing the Spirit: Higher Education in America.* New York: Viking Penguin, 1990.

Snizek, William E. "Hall's Professionalism Scale: An Empirical Reassessment." *American Sociological Review* 37 (1972):109–12.

Snipes, Jeffrey B. and Mastrofski, Stephen D. "An Empirical Test of Muir's Typology of Police Officers." *American Academy of Criminal Justice* 14 (Spring 1990) 2:268–296.

Sontag v. *Bronstein,* 306 N.E. 2d 405, 33 N.Y. 2d 197, 351 N.Y.S .2d 389 (N.Y. 1973).

Spurlock v. *United Airlines, Inc.,* 475 F. 2d 216 (10th Cir. 1972).

State of California, Commission on Peace Officer Standards and Training, California Code of Regulations, Title II: Peace Officer Standards and Training, art. 1, sec. 1002.

Staufenberger, Richard A. "The Professionalization of Police: Efforts and Obstacles." *Public Administration Review* 37 (Nov./Dec. 1977)6:678–85.

Steele, Shelby. *The Content of Our Character.* New York: St. Martin's Press, 1990.

Steinman, Michael. "Managing and Evaluating Police Behavior." *Journal of Police Science and Administration* 14 (1986):185–92.

Stephenson, D. Grier, Jr.; Bresler, Robert J.; Friedrich, Robert J.; and Karlesky, Joseph J. *American Government,* 2d ed. New York: Harper Collins, 1992.

Sykes, Gary W. "The Functional Nature of Police Reform." In *Critical Issues in Policing: Contemporary Readings,* pp. 286–297. Robert G. Dunham and Geoffrey P. Alpert, eds. Prospect Heights, IL: Waveland Press, 1989.

Tafoya, William L. "The Virtuosos of Policing." *American Academy of Criminal Justice* (Spring 1990)2:205–227.

Tannehill, Ronald and Janeksela, Galan M. "Role and Task Analysis—An Effective Tool for Manpower Development and Curriculum Development in Law Enforcement Education." *Journal of Police Science and Administration* 12 (March 1984)1:19–26.

"The LAPD: How Good Is It? A Special Report," *Los Angeles Times,* December 18, 1977, sec. 8, p. 1.

Thomas v. *City of Evanston,* 610 F. Supp. 422 (D.C. Ill. 1985).

Thompson v. *McDonnell Douglas Corp.,* 416 F. Supp. 972 (D.C. Mo. 1976) affirmed 552 F. 2d 220 (8th Cir. 1978).

Thompson v. *Mississippi State Personnel Bd.,* 674 F. Supp. 198 (N.D. Miss. 1987).

Toch, Hans. "Cops and Blacks: Warring Minorities." In *The Police,* Gerald Leinwand, ed. New York: Simon & Schuster, 1972, pp. 195–205.

Townsend v. *Nassau County Medical Center,* 558 F. 2d 117 (2nd Cir. 1977), cert. denied 434 U.S. 1015, 98 S. Ct. 732, 54 L. Ed. 759 (1978).

Trojanowicz, Robert C. and Nicholson, Thomas G. "A Comparison of Behavioral Styles of College Graduate Police Officers v. Non-College-Going Police Officers." *Police Chief* 43 (August 1976):56–59.

Uniform Guidelines on Employee Selection Procedures 29 CFR Part 1607 (1978).

United States v. *City of Buffalo,* 457 F. Supp. 612 (W.D. N.Y. 1978), affirmed 633 F. 2d 643 (2nd Cir. 1980).

United States v. *City of Chicago,* 385 F. Supp. 543 (D.C. Ill. 1974), 573 F. 2d 416 (7th Cir. 1978).

United States v. *City of Los Angeles,* 595 F. 2d 1386 (1979).

United States v. *City of St. Louis,* 410 F. Supp. 948 (D.C. Mo. 1976).

U.S. Department of Justice, Bureau of Justice Statistics. *National Update,* vol. 1., no. 4, April 1992.

U.S. Department of Justice, Community Relations Service. "Principles of Good Policing: Avoiding Violence Between Citizens." In *Critical Issues in Policing: Contemporary Readings,* pp. 164–204. Robert G. Dunham and Geoffrey P. Alpert, eds. Prospect Heights, IL: Waveland Press, 1989.

United States. Kerner Commission. *Report of the National Advisory Commission on Civil Disorders.* Washington, DC: Government Printing Office, 1968.

Usury v. *Tamiami Trail Tours, Inc.,* 531 F. 2d 224 (5th Cir. 1976).

Urchida, Craig D. "The Development of American Police: An Historical Overview." In *Critical Issues in Policing: Contemporary Readings,* pp. 14–30. Robert G. Dunham and Geoffrey P. Alpert, eds. Prospect Heights, IL: Waveland Press, 1989.

Van Maanen, John. "Working the Street: A Developmental View of Police Behavior." In *The Potential for Reform of Criminal Justice,* pp. 83–129. Hebert Jacob, ed. Beverly Hills, CA: Sage Publications, 1974.

Vogel, Ronald and Adams, Reed. "Police Professionalism—A Longitudinal Cohort Study." *Journal of Police Science and Administration* 11 (December 1983)4:474–84.

Vollmer, August. *The Police and Modern Society.* Berkeley: University of California Press, 1936.

Vulcan Society of Westchester County, Inc. v. *Fire Department of City of White Plains,* 505 F. Supp. 955 (D.C. N.Y. 1971).

Vuyanvich v. *Republic National Bank of Dallas,* 505 F. Supp. 224 (N.D. Tex. 1980).

Waintroob, Andrea R. "The Developing Law of Equal Employment Opportunity at the White Collar and Professional Level." *William and Mary Law Review* 21 (1979):45–67.

Walker, Samuel. *A Critical History of Police Reform: The Emergence of Professionalism.* Massachusetts: Lexington Books, 1977.

———. "The Origins of the American Police–Community Relations Movement: The 1940s." In *Criminal Justice History: An International Annual,* pp. 225–246. Henry Cohen, ed. New York: John Jay Press, 1980.

———. "Employment of Black and Hispanic Police Officers." *Review of Applied Urban Research* (October 1983):1–6.

———. "Employment of Hispanic and Black Police Officers 1983–1988: A Follow-Up Study." *Badge 911: The National Publication of the Latino Peace Officers Association* (March, 1990):6–9.

Walker v. *Jefferson County Home,* 726 F. 2d 1554 (11th Cir. 1984).

Walls v. *Mississippi State Department of Public Welfare,* 730 F. 2d 306 (5th Cir. 1984).

Ward, Richard H.; Webb, Vincent J.; and the Joint Commission on Criminology and Criminal Justice Education and Standards. *Quest for Quality.* New York: University Publications, 1984.

Wards Cove Packaging Co. v. *Atonio,* 490 U.S. 642, 109 S. Ct. 2115, 104 L. Ed. 2d 733 (1989).

Washington v. *Davis,* 426 U.S. 229, 96 S. Ct. 2040, 48 L. Ed. 2d 597 (1976).

Watson v. *Fort Worth Bank and Trust,* 487 U.S. 977, 108 S. Ct. 2777, 101 L. Ed. 2d 827 (1988).

Weiner, N. L. "The Educated Policemen." *Journal of Police Science and Administration* 4 (1976):450–57.

Weirman, Charles L. "Variances of Ability Measurement Scores Obtained by College and Non-College Educated Troopers." *Police Chief* 45 (August 1978):34–36.

Western Addition Community Organization v. *Alioto,* 369 F. Supp. 77 (D.C. Cal. 1973) affirmed 514 F. 2d 542 (9th Cir. 1975) cert. denied 423 U.S. 1014, 96 S. Ct. 446, 46 L. Ed. 2d 385.

White v. *Vathally,* 732 F. 2d 1037 (1st Cir.1984).

Wilson, James Q. *Varieties of Police Behavior: The Management of Law and Order in Eight Communities.* Massachusetts: Harvard University Press, 1968.

Wilt, G. Marie and Bannon, James D. "Cynicism or Realism: A Critique of Niederhoffer's Research Into Police Attitudes." *Journal of Police Science and Administration* 4 (1976):38–45.

Woods, Joseph G. "The Progressives and the Police: Urban Reform and the Professionalization of the Los Angeles Police." Ph.D. dissertation, University of California, Los Angeles, 1973.

Worden, Robert E. "A Badge and a Baccalaureate: Policies, Hypotheses, and Further Evidence." *Justice Quarterly* 7 (September 1990)3:565–92.

Wycoff, Mary Ann and Susmilch, Charles E. "The Relevance of College Education for Policing: Continuing the Dialogue." In *Police Work: Strategies and Outcomes in Law Enforcement*, pp. 17–36. David M. Petersen, ed. Beverly Hills, CA: Sage Publications, 1979.

Zelig, Mark. "College Education and Police Performance—A Critique of Roberg." *Journal of Police Science and Administration* 8 (1980)1:98–100.